THE SHAKESPEARE FOLIOS

General Editor: Nick de Somogyi
Typographical Consultant: Simon Trussler

Macbeth
The Tragedie of Macbeth

NICK DE SOMOGYI

Nick de Somogyi was educated at Dulwich College, and at Pembroke College, Cambridge (where he gained his doctorate), and now works in London as a freelance writer and researcher, and as a genealogist at the College of Arms. His publications include *Shakespeare's Theatre of War* (1998), *Jokermen and Thieves: Bob Dylan and the Ballad Tradition* (1986), and, as editor, *The Little Book of War Poems* (1999). He is the founding editor of the Globe Quartos series, and has also lectured on Shakespearean drama for the Museum of London, the Rose Theatre Trust, and Shakespeare's Globe. His media work includes contributions to the Open University, BBC Radio 4, and Carlton Television.

SIMON TRUSSLER

Simon Trussler is co-editor of *New Theatre Quarterly* and author or editor of numerous books on drama and theatre, including *Shakespearean Concepts* (1989) and the award-winning *Cambridge Illustrated History of British Theatre* (1993). Formerly Reader in Drama in the University of London, he is now Senior Research Fellow at Rose Bruford College.

This edition of the plays of William Shakespeare has a simple aim: to present to modern readers the full text of the 1623 First Folio in as accessible a form as possible, and without altering or editing it, either in substance or in detail.

Each play has therefore been carefully reproduced with all the idiosyncrasies (in spelling, punctuation, and layout) of the First Folio – but in modern type. Instead of the cramped, double-column typography of the early seventeenth century, our reproductions provide freshly legible and accessible texts that preserve their original quirks. We offer readers the opportunity to draw their own conclusions about the form, validity, and significance of the First Folio's every line.

The 'rules' underpinning our transcription from ancient to modern are spelled out in the Series Introduction, but our watchword has been to maintain the absolute integrity of the First Folio – even when it seems to make no sense at all. For there is no doubt that it does contain mistakes, occasioned by the slips and inattentions that inevitably accompanied the process of publication.

For this reason, we have also prepared a modernized version of the Folio text, which appears on every facing page of our editions. This provides a line-by-line parallel script in which spelling and punctuation are standardized, and which adopts the familiar conventions of printed plays – italicized stage-directions, capitalized character names, and so on.

In addition, whenever the Folio text seems indefensible, this modern edition offers an alternative reading taken from another edition of the play (often a Quarto published during Shakespeare's lifetime). These occasions – and others, where the Folio presents a significant problem – are explained in the Textual Notes at the end of each of our volumes. These Textual Notes (it should be remarked) do not provide a glossary for difficult words and phrases: they are solely concerned with clarifying the particular difficulties posed by the First Folio text. Their function is simply to ask, 'Does the Folio mean what it says? And, if not, what might it have meant to say?'

As our individual Introductions explain, each of Shakespeare's plays found its own distinctive way into the 1623 First Folio. We have therefore occasionally supplemented our parallel editions with an Appendix, detailing (for example) additional material included in earlier Quarto editions of a play but omitted from its Folio version.

Finally, and simply, our aim is to afford our readers access to the earliest definitive edition of Shakespeare's plays, and so reveal the First Folio in all its problematic glory.

Nick Hern
Nick de Somogyi
Simon Trussler

Macbeth

The Tragedie of Macbeth

WILLIAM SHAKESPEARE

*The First Folio of 1623
and a parallel modern edition*

edited by
NICK DE SOMOGYI

London
NICK HERN BOOKS
www.nickhernbooks.co.uk

The Shakespeare Folios

This edition of *Macbeth / The Tragedie of Macbeth*
first published in Great Britain in 2003 as a paperback original
by Nick Hern Books Limited, 14 Larden Road, London W3 7ST

Cover Design: Ned Hoste
Cover Photography: Graham Price

A CIP catalogue record for this book
is available from the British Library

ISBN 1 85459 677 2

Typeset by Country Setting, Kingsdown, Kent CT14 8ES

Printed in Great Britain by CLE Press, St Ives, Cambs PE27 3LE

Acknowledgements

It is a cause for regret that John Heminge and William Condell did not include a full Acknowledgements page in the prefatory material to their First Folio of Shakespeare's works. True, they included fulsome praise for their aristocratic patrons, the brothers William and Philip Herbert, and appended a list of 26 'Names of the Principal Actors in all these Plays'; but there is no namecheck for those who procured the 'True Original Copies' from which their collection was printed; nor for all the many publishers, scribes, typesetters, editors, and proof-readers who lent a hand in its production.

As editor of the Shakespeare Folios series, my principal debts are to Nick Hern, whose vision and patience have steered the project to fruition; and to Simon Trussler, whose inspiring expertise in both 17th- and 21st-century technologies has lent 'to airy nothing | A local habitation and a name'. The detail and colour of our series have depended upon the kindness and dedication of its many assistant contributors. I should therefore like to record my thanks to Ned Hoste and Graham Price for their cover design; and to the Governors of Dulwich College for their kind permission to reproduce images from Philip Henslowe's manuscript diary, and from the copy of the First Folio, held in its library. Dr Jan Piggott, the Archivist at Dulwich College, has been characteristically generous with both his time and mind; as has Thomas Woodcock, Norroy and Ulster King of Arms, whose assistance in securing access to the manuscript archive of the College of Arms is greatly appreciated. Ann Cooke's contribution to the series has been invaluable, both for her scrupulous attention to detail, and for her expert advice in establishing a systematic editorial policy. Jackie Bodley, Caroline Downing, and Jane Maud have each provided a fresh and alert set of eyes, illuminating much that was dark.

Heminge and Condell, Shakespeare's first editors, concluded the dedication of their volume with the hope that whatever 'delight' their edition contained would reflect upon their patrons, while acknowledging full responsibility for all its 'faults'. Both the sentiment and substance of this courtesy is true of the Shakespeare Folios, a series dedicated to all anonymous contributors.

NICK DE SOMOGYI

Contents

Series Introduction

The First Folio of 1623: 'True Original Copies'

When the time came for Shakespeare to emulate his own Richard II, and 'choose executors, and talk of wills' (3.2), he chose to remember just three of his theatrical colleagues from London. He drafted his own will in the Winter of 1615–16, after retiring to Stratford, where he died the following April. In it he bequeathed 26 shillings and eightpence to each of 'my fellows John Heminge, Richard Burbage and Henry Condell . . . to buy them rings.' All three were actors, senior members of the King's Men, as Shakespeare himself had lately been. It was Burbage who had first given voice to Richard II's 'talk of graves, of worms, and epitaphs,' twenty-odd years before, and who had premièred the roles of Richard III, Brutus (in *Julius Caesar*), King Lear, 'young Hamlet . . . the grievèd Moor [Othello, that is], and more beside.' Those parts 'That lived in him,' as an Elegy on Burbage lamented in 1619, 'have now for ever died.'[1]

Well, not quite 'for ever'. For soon after Heminge and Condell inherited the mantle of Burbage's leadership of the King's Men, they performed for Shakespeare what they called a further 'office to the dead . . . only to keep the memory of so worthy a friend and fellow alive' – and one far more substantial than wearing a mourning ring, or even composing an elegy. Taking upon themselves the role of literary executors, they struck a complicated deal with a consortium of London publishers; squared the tangled demands of primitive copyright; and, after years of work, at last 'collected and published' *Mr. William Shakespeares Comedies, Histories, & Tragedies* in a lavish 900-page volume, now known as the First Folio. ('Folio' refers to the large format of its page, as we might describe a 'coffee-table book'; second, third, and fourth editions of the Folio collection were published in 1632, 1663–4, and 1685.) Heminge and Condell's book was published ('in the best Crown paper, far better than most Bibles', as one Puritan critic sniffed)[2] towards the end of 1623, in a run of around a thousand copies, 'by Isaac Jaggard, and Ed. Blount', Isaac's father William having supervised the printing process.[3] Readers could buy an unbound copy – in paperback, as it were – for about fifteen shillings; but a hardbacked copy bound in calfskin sold for a pound: the monthly salary of a Jacobean schoolteacher.[4]

It is clear that Heminge and Condell thought of their book in terms of a Last Will and Testament. Their dedicatory epistle to their aristocratic patrons – William Herbert, Earl of Pembroke and his brother Philip – wittily appoints them 'guardians' to plays that are now Shakespeare's 'orphans', 'outliving him, and he not having the fate, common with some, to be executor to his own writings.' Perhaps they were thinking of Ben Jonson, who had set a precedent in 1616 by compiling his own collected *Workes* into a Folio edition, and who now contributed two prefatory poems to Shakespeare's: one, 'To the Reader' (printed opposite Shakespeare's famous portrait), which diverts our attention from the actor's appearance to the playwright's legacy ('look | Not on his picture, but his book'); and the other his honest and affectionate lines 'To the memory of my beloved, The Author Mr William Shakespeare: And what he hath left us'.

Something of the same sense of bequest playfully haunts Heminge and Condell's preface, 'To the Great Variety of Readers', in the legalese with which they set out their stall:

> It had been a thing, we confess, worthy to have been wished that the author himself had lived to have set forth and overseen his own writings. But since it hath been ordained otherwise, and he by death departed from that right, we pray you do not envy his friends the office of their care and pain, to have collected and published them; and so to have published them, as where (before) you were abused with diverse stolen and surreptitious copies, maimed and deformed by the frauds and stealths of injurious impostors that exposed them: even those are now offered to your view, cured and perfect of their limbs; and all the rest, absolute in their numbers, as he conceived them.

Of the 36 plays included in the First Folio, around half had never been printed before. These range across Shakespeare's working life, including early and late Histories (*1 Henry VI*, *Henry VIII*), early and mature Comedies (*Two Gentlemen of Verona*, *Twelfth Night*, *Measure for Measure*), and middle and late Tragedies (*Julius Caesar*, *Antony and Cleopatra*), as well as most of his so-called 'Romances' (*The Tempest*, *The Winter's Tale*, *Cymbeline*) – though the Folio editors' threeway division fails to distinguish this last category. It is these previously unpublished plays, some of them over thirty years old, which Heminge and Condell claimed to be presenting 'as he conceived them'.

The remaining plays represent some of the most popular successes of Shakespeare's dramatic career. These had already been published, between 1594 (*Titus Andronicus*, *2 Henry VI*) and 1622 (*Othello*), in the slim paperback editions known, from the four-way folding of their printed sheets, as Quartos, which sold for about sixpence. Often, more than one such edition was produced: there had been six Quartos, for example, of *Richard III* by the time the Folio was published in 1623. These successive editions were usually little more than reissues, typeset from their immediate Quarto predecessor. Sometimes these plays had been pirated (we might say 'bootlegged') in opportunistic Quarto versions whose mangled texts at best approximate the scripts Shakespeare's company had successfully performed. 'To be, or not to be,' says Hamlet in the First Quarto of his play (1603), 'ay, there's the point. | To die, to sleep: is that all? Ay, all.'[5] The first Quartos of *Romeo and Juliet* (1597), *Henry V* (1600), and *The Merry Wives of Windsor* (1602) contain similar abridgements and abbreviations. It is these flawed editions (long known as 'bad Quartos') which Heminge and Condell describe as 'diverse stolen and surreptitious copies, maimed and deformed by the frauds and stealths of injurious impostors,' and which their Folio has restored, so they claim, to their proper health, 'cured and perfect of their limbs'. The status of these 'bad Quartos' is currently the subject of much reappraisal by a new generation of critics objecting to the moral overtones of the term: plays were inherently collaborative enterprises, it is argued, so any discrepancies from the Folio's 'authorized' texts recorded in the 'bad Quartos' do not necessarily render them 'inferior', 'corrupt', or 'debased'; they are merely differently abled. Heminge and Condell's preface is the starting-point for this debate.[6]

Not all of the Quartos, however, were quite as 'maimed and deformed' as they claimed. For the pirated texts of *Romeo and Juliet* and *Hamlet*, for example, were swiftly superseded into print by apparently authoritative versions – the so-called 'good Quartos'. Other plays, including *Much Ado About Nothing* and *The Merchant of Venice*, were simply reprinted from their ('good') Quartos in the Folio text.[7] But even when such authoritative editions were used in preparing the Folio, they were often supplemented by 'new' (previously unpublished) material, procured, evidently with some care, by Heminge and Condell.

These authentically Shakespearean 'additions' range from a previously unknown prologue (*Troilus and Cressida*) or extra speech (*2 Henry IV*), via passages of supplementary dialogue (*Hamlet*), to entire scenes (*Titus Andronicus*). The Folio texts of *Othello* and *King Lear*, furthermore, effectively present, by a series of sometimes minute but often substantial differences from their Quarto editions, entirely distinct – but equally authorial – versions of the same play. It is now generally accepted, in other words, that the Folio versions of these, and certain other plays, are the product of a systematic set of second thoughts by Shakespeare himself; that they represent the equivalent of Pope's re-aimed and revised *New Dunciad* (1742); Coleridge's reworded and poignantly glossed 'Rime of the Ancient Mariner' (1817); or the subtly reworked ending Dickens provided for *Great Expectations* (1868).[8]

Ben Jonson, after all, likened poets to blacksmiths in his lines 'To the memory of my beloved': each 'must sweat . . . and strike the second heat | Upon the Muse's anvil . . . For a good poet's made, as well as born. | And such wert thou.' This is not to say, of course, that the First Folio can exactly be likened, for example, to the Macmillan 'Wessex Edition' of Thomas Hardy's novels (1912), the 1850 edition of Wordsworth's *Prelude*, or even the Folio *Workes of Benjamin Jonson* (1616), all of which the authors themselves prepared, revising and annotating as they went. Shakespeare inconveniently 'departed from that right' by dying, as Heminge and Condell remind us. But their 1623 Folio, assiduously and laboriously compiled,[9] and 'Published,' as its title-page promises, 'according to the True Original Copies', presents seventeen previously unpublished plays; the full text of five plays previously available only in abbreviated 'bad' Quartos; and the handsome reprints of fourteen others, variously supplemented with new material.

The exact nature of these 'True Original Copies' – the material procured by Heminge and Condell from which their Folio was typeset – remains an enormously complicated matter, and one subject to a baffling variety of contending theories. It is important to stress, however, that by no means all the Folio plays were printed from Shakespeare's 'quill-inscribed' manuscripts (the so-called 'foul papers' of his working drafts); nor yet from the polished 'fair copy' he may have prepared.[10] Some, for example, were apparently set from transcripts *of* those manuscripts, prepared by a professional scribe; others from the so-called 'prompt-book' or 'theatre copy' – the transcript prepared from Shakespeare's draft as a guide to its original performance; still others from professional transcripts *of* those transcripts. Finally, while some Folio plays were straightforward reprints of good Quartos, others apparently made use of annotated, pasted, and interleaved copies of those Quartos.

The problem is rendered thornier still by the fact that to speak of 'the' Folio text is potentially misleading. As the outstanding research of Charlton Hinman demonstrates, the volume was (rudimentarily) proof-read in two-page sections while they were being printed; these corrections were then incorporated on the galleys; but the uncorrected pages that had meanwhile come off the press were nevertheless subsequently included in finished copies of the book.[11] Because of this arbitrary mixture of corrected and uncorrected pages, it is thought that no copy of *Mr. William Shakespeares Comedies, Histories, & Tragedies* is minutely identical to another; and there-fore that no single copy represents 'the' ideal Folio text. Hinman's facsimile edition of *The First Folio of Shakespeare* (1968, 2nd edition 1996) magnifi-cently supplied this want, providing a composite sequence of its most legible pages, in their most fully corrected state, compiled and reproduced from about thirty surviving copies. (Around 250 copies of the 1623 volume are thought to be extant worldwide.) Our Shakespeare Folios series, however, is based upon a single surviving edition rather than what Hinman himself called the 'theoretical entity' of his reconstructed volume (xxii).

Our copy-text is that of the facsimile edition prepared by Helge Kökeritz (1954) from a single copy, formerly owned by the nineteenth-century collector Henry Huth (1815–78), and subsequently presented by Alexander Smith Cochran to the Elizabethan Club at Yale University. Kökeritz's facsimile, however, has occasionally – and then very obviously – been 'touched up', presumably where the 1623 original is illegible.[12] Such impositions have been checked and, where necessary, corrected, against Hinman's facsimile, the critical apparatus of modern editions, and the (im-perfect) copy of the 1623 Folio held at the library of Dulwich College.[13]

Fuller accounts of the paperchase of 'textual transmission' particular to each Folio play (from page to stage, manuscript to transcript, Quarto to Folio) can be found in the individual introductions to each of our editions, and in the diagrams that preface them. It will be clear from this brief sum-mary, however, that we must take care to recognize that none of these texts exactly reproduces the 'original', authorial scripts that Shakespeare wrote – even supposing that any of them ever achieved this definitive form: do an author's revised second thoughts still count as 'original'? Is the mere script of a play (of all things) ever 'definitive'? 'Look how the father's face | Lives in his issue,' reads Jonson's memorial poem; the fact is, though, that the plays' family trees are far more complicated than that, and include whole collateral branches of orphaned cousins twice-removed. 'All men make faults,' as Shakespeare's own Sonnet 35 reminds us, and the line resounds through the multiple chains of copyists, annotators, actors, editors, type-setters ('compositors'), and proof-readers that stretch out behind the Folio texts of his plays – not to mention the equally complex pedigrees of the Quarto texts used in creating them.

Heminge and Condell's advertisement of the credentials for their book ('according to the True Original Copies'), then, must be treated with a pinch of salt. (How, after all, can *anything* be at once a copy and an original?) Yet their First Folio substantially contains what they call the literary 're-mains of your servant Shakespeare': a canon of plays collected by the men who had acted in most of them; in a form which they took pains to estab-lish as the most authoritative versions available; and by which they chose to remember them, and him, to posterity. These are the texts which our series of Shakespeare Folios reproduces, that they may, as Othello says there, 'a round unvarnish'd tale deliver' (1.3). His words provide the opportunity to explain both what our parallel play-texts are, and, equally importantly, what they are not.

Facsimile or Restoration? Reproducing the Folio

Each volume of our Shakespeare Folios comprises a parallel edition. The right-hand page of each spread reproduces the text of the 1623 First Folio; the facing page presents that text in a modernized form. The editorial policy governing this running 'translation' is detailed in the next section. It remains here to explain the procedures we have adopted in restoring the Folio text to modern readers.

As with the cleaning of an old painting, the chief aim in reproducing the Folio has been delicately to strip away the accumulated varnish, candle-soot, and overpainting of the centuries, in order to restore to the piece the vigour and clarity of its original colours, while remaining true to the precise nuances of its graphic form. Our texts therefore scrupulously reproduce in modern type the exact spelling, punctuation, and layout of a single edition of the 1623 First Folio, dissolving the patina of age that any mere facsimile would necessarily present. It is the distinctive typographic appearance of those seventeenth-century pages, invisible to their first readers, which lends them an inescapably 'antique' look to modern eyes, like the atmospheric (but entirely accidental) gloom of an Old Master.

Nothing looks older, or more misleadingly 'quaint' than old technology. It is therefore the aim of our reprocessed Folio texts to maintain the fertile impact of their original verbal form, while removing all purely incidental or superficial distractions. We have therefore replaced with its modern form the Folio's potentially misleading use of the 'long *s*' ('Where the bee ſucks, there ſuck I', *The Tempest*, 5.1), a typographic remnant current only in the German use of 'ß' to represent a double-*s*. For the same reason, while meticulously retaining the spelling, punctuation, lineation, use of capital letters and italic font of its model, our Folio texts have systematically applied this fidelity according to modern typographic procedures, as follows.

Readers wishing to avoid the minutiae of this process may care to turn to p. xvii

As the facsimile page reproduced below (p. 198) demonstrates, the 1623 Folio (known for convenience as 'F') is printed in double columns, with the first word of the following page, the so-called 'catch-word', appearing at the bottom right of each page's right-hand column. (This was a printer's safeguard to ensure that the pages followed on correctly.) A series of so-called 'signatures' ('C2' or 'bb3', for example), which refer to the alphabetical sequencing of the printed sheets into their assembled form, also intermittently appears beneath the right-hand column of F's right-hand ('recto') pages. The text is also paginated at the top left and right of each double-spread, with the relevant title running across the uppermost border of each page.[14] Since each of our Folio pages occupies slightly less than half of each of the 1623 columns, we have silently removed these technical marks, while imposing a border around each page in simulation of those surrounding the original columns. The width of those 1623 columns is sometimes too narrow to accommodate the final word, or part-word, of a verse line, and the original compositors set the overspill wherever it would fit:

> *Ham.* Very like, very like : ſtaid it long?   (dred.
> *Hor.* While one with moderate hast might tell a hun-

For the same reason, they sometimes crammed a particularly lengthy line flush to its speech-prefix:

> *B.Cant.*God and his Angels guard your ſacred Throne,

Our Folio texts seek to avoid these unsightly and accidental interruptions and conflations. We have therefore throughout applied a standard space between speech-prefixes and their corresponding text; and have wherever possible set overspilled lines in full, while registering the procedure, in the case of divided words, with a vertical stroke. We therefore set these lines from *Hamlet* (1.2) and *Henry V* (1.2) as follows:

> *Ham.* Very like, very like: staid it long?
> *Hor.* While one with moderate hast might tell a hun|dred.

> *B. Cant.* God and his Angels guard your sacred Throne,

When our own Folio pages cannot accommodate a full verse-line, we reproduce the position and form of the original overspill. The lineation and word-breaks of all prose passages are exactly retained from F.

Shakespeare, in common with most of his fellow dramatists, seems to have used punctuation sparingly; and it is more likely the original compositors who are responsible for F's (to modern eyes sometimes eccentric, sometimes misleading) scattering of commas, colons, and brackets.[15] Nevertheless, as G. Blakemore Evans reminds us, these were 'men who had a contemporary feeling for the spoken relation of words and the rhythm and emphasis of Elizabethan English.'[16] We therefore reproduce exactly the Folio's original 'pointing', though our fidelity to F has once again been enhanced and clarified by modern procedures: all punctuation marks have been set flush to their preceding words, and automatically followed by a single space (as in this sentence).

By the same token, while F sometimes uses italic punctuation marks within normal 'upright' passages, and *vice versa*, our texts automatically deploy italic punctuation within italic passages, and upright punctuation elsewhere. F uses italics not only to designate speech-prefixes and stage-directions, to distinguish the on-stage recital of songs, letters, sonnets, bills, and so on, but also in setting most proper names, foreign languages, and exotic terms: 'When he himselfe might his *Quietus* make | With a bare Bodkin? . . . Soft you now, | The faire *Ophelia*?'). We reproduce all these decisions, even on those rare occasions when the original compositors mixed italic and upright type within a single word or speech-prefix. We have, however, ignored all instances of what might appear to our eyes as 'bold' type: this is a nineteenth-century typographic form, and merely an accidental irregularity of ink or type in the 1623 volume.

Having 'cleaned' the 1623 Folio's typography in this way, it seemed immediately apparent that the scale of other potential obstacles to its direct understanding was dramatically reduced. The Jacobean custom of printing 'i' for 'j', and 'u' for 'v', and *vice versa* (so that Othello promises to 'deliuer' an 'vn-varnish'd Tale'), seemed of a piece with the fresh, fluid, and often illuminating spellings used throughout the collection. (The idiosyncracies of its spelling, however, may equally reflect the habits of the Folio's compositors as Shakespeare's own.) We have likewise retained its use of superior letters and contracted abbreviations – 'Which in th'eleuēth yere of ȳ last Kings reign' (*Henry V*, 1.1) – as part of the same high fidelity towards it, while acknowledging that F's deployment of these abbreviations, and its sometimes irregular lineation, are often the result of the particular process by which its pages were printed.[17] The slight oddity of such occasions, especially when shorn of their Jacobean type, soon evaporates from the forefront of a reader's mind. And, in any case, each of our Folio pages is accompanied by its facing text: a parallel edition which provides a fully modernized and theatrically coherent 'running commentary' on the original.

'So all my best is dressing old words new.' The aspiration of Shakespeare's Sonnet 76 is one shared by our Folio reproductions, in the crisp typography of their renewed form. The process of clarification they embody may perhaps be likened to a digitally remastered CD of a 78 r.p.m. analogue recording: we have sought to remove the distracting hiss and clicks of its early mediation, while enhancing the volume, tone, and range of the original recording. The parallel scripts that appear on their facing pages re-record that material in a more immediately accessible form, as the following section details.

Edition or Imposition? Modernizing the Folio

The modern edition that accompanies the text of our Folio reproductions seeks to install a finer filter still between the 1623 text and its modern readers, by refining out the grosser elements of the First Folio's impurities. It therefore modernizes all spelling; introduces the principles of a systematic punctuation; and inserts, where strictly necessary, a number of stage-directions ('SDs'). The SDs we impose are dictated either by the needs of stage-practice – where characters enter but do not exit from a scene, for example – or by reference to the descriptions offered in the text itself.[18] It indicates, by a system of aligned indentations ('staircases') those occasions where a verse-line is divided between two or more speakers.[19] It prints as

regular verse those lines which the F compositors either set as successive
half-lines, to fill out their page, or as prose, to save them space (see below,
note 17). It introduces into verse-lines an indication of the stress required
in pronouncing the final *–ed* of verbs (though elided *–ued* and *–ied* endings
are not so shown):

> Why thy **canoniz'd** bones, **hearsèd** in death,
>
> *(Hamlet*, 1.5, pp. 38–9)

> But **died** thy sister of her love, my boy?
>
> *(Twelfth Night*, 2.4, pp. 62–3)

And it highlights, by a system of end-notes, a series of occasions of
particular textual interest and complexity. These Textual Notes range from
the simple attribution of those generally accepted emendations which
significantly re-interpret F's readings – or those of the Quarto ('Q') where
such texts exist; via the signalling of arguably more valid readings, where F
nonetheless makes good sense; and the noting of substantial passages that
are unique either to F or Q; to lengthier appraisals of more stubbornly
intractable textual problems.

Each of Shakespeare's plays brings with it a discrete set of textual
problems, and our procedures in dealing with them are explained at length
in our individual introductions, together with a full account of that play's
textual pedigree. Broadly speaking, however, the editorial policy of our
facing editions has been as far as possible to maintain the integrity of the
Folio texts they modernize – the most authoritative versions Heminge and
Condell were able to provide.

All additional material – the editorial apparatus we have imposed – is set
within square brackets, unless otherwise stated in the particular introduction. So, where the Folio text reads:

> *Enter the King, Humfrey, Bedford, Clarence,*
> *Warwick, Westmerland, and Exeter.*

our modern edition reads:

[1.2]
> *Enter the* KING, GLOUCESTER, BEDFORD, *Clarence,* WARWICK,
> WESTMORLAND, *and* EXETER [*and attendants*]
>
> *(Henry V*, 1.2, pp. 10–11)

As in this example from *Henry V*, we introduce act- and scene-numbers
when F omits them; modernize and retain, where possible, the exact
wording of F's SDs; and capitalize the form of the character's name used
in its speech-prefixes ('SPs'). Where necessary, we supplement those SDs,
in this example with the attendants later instructed to fetch in the French
ambassador. The names of mute characters – those, like Clarence here,
who nowhere speak in the play, but whose presence is nevertheless
signalled – are not capitalized. The choice of SP is sometimes complicated
by F's occasionally expressive variations, as the Duke of Gloucester's
appearance here as '*Humfrey*'. Later in the same play, Fluellen is suddenly
designated '*Welch*' when he converses with Captains MacMorris ('*Irish*')
and Jamy ('*Scot*') (3.2, pp. 72–3); and in *Romeo and Juliet*, Lady Capulet is
variously referred to as '*Wife*', '*Lady of the house*' and '*Mother*', according to
the function she performs. Our modern texts render all such SPs and SDs
consistent (he is '*Fluellen*' throughout, she '*Lady Capulet*', and Prince
Humphrey '*Gloucester*'), in order to provide an immediate gloss for the
benefit of a momentarily confused reader of the Folio. Sometimes, however, our process of clarification has had to deal more substantially than
with matters of spelling, punctuation, or stage-business.

Some of these necessary intercessions are more straightforward than
others; as when, for example, in F *Hamlet*, Laertes bafflingly vows to
behave towards his dead father's friends 'like the kinde Life-rend'ring
Polititian,' providing them 'Repast . . . with my blood' (4.5, pp. 172–3).
Cross-reference to that play's 1604 Second Quarto ('Q2') reveals the
mistake – and a mistake it certainly is, apparently by a careless compositor
of the Folio page. For in that text it is the 'kind life-rendring Pelican' – the
bird popularly thought to feed its young with blood pecked from its own
breast – to which Laertes compares himself. On occasions like these, our
Folio page retains 'Polititian', as part of its scrupulous fidelity to the 1623
text; but our parallel edition imports and modernizes the Q2 reading: 'And,
like the kind life-rend'ring pelican, | Repast them with my blood.'

On the other side of the critical field are those occasions, in plays which
have survived in both Quarto and Folio forms, which present a straight
choice between two equally legible alternatives. Thus, while Old Hamlet's
corpse has been 'quietly interr'd' in Q2, in F it has been 'quietly enurn'd'
(1.4, pp. 38–9). It is the constant policy of our parallel editions to allow the
1623 First Folio to speak for itself whenever it speaks sense. In this case,
therefore, our Folio text crisply resets the original line, and our edition
merely modernizes its spelling (according to the version given in the *Oxford*

English Dictionary), signalling the required stress as described above, to read 'Wherein we saw thee quietly inurn'd.'

Sometimes, however, such a choice turns out to be less straightforward than it seems. Perhaps the most famous of these textual problems – or 'cruxes', as they are known – occurs in *Othello*. In his final speech, its hero presents himself as 'one, whose hand . . . threw a Pearle away | Richer then all his Tribe' (5.2) – but in doing so, is he 'like the base *Indian*' (Q, 1622) or 'the base Iudean' (F, 1623)? The problem is intricate with the various textual entanglements we have discussed, not least since both readings make more than good sense.

In Q, the Moor abjectly compares himself to a native of the newly colonized Indies, proverbially indifferent to the priceless natural resources around him, carelessly discarding Desdemona's love and life; 'her bed is *India*,' exclaims Shakespeare's Troilus of his Cressida, 'there she lies, a Pearle' (1.1). In F, on the other hand, Othello likens himself to Judas Iscariot, the disciple from Judaea ('Iudean'), who betrayed Jesus with a kiss (as Othello did Desdemona: 'I kist thee, ere I kill'd thee'); killed himself (as Othello is shortly to do); and squandered his chances of salvation – the 'one pearl of great price' of St Matthew's Gospel (14, 46). The word 'Tribe' allows both biblical and ethnic contexts.

The problem is that whichever reading is correct, the other is most probably an error for it, since the letters 'i' and 'j' were used interchangeably, and the letters 'n' and 'u' were easily confused, whether when read from manuscript, or handled as a piece of letter-type. In such keenly contested cases as these, we reproduce Othello's words exactly from the Folio ('Like the base Iudean'), and amplify that voice in our modernized version ('Like the base Judaean'), while signalling the difficulty in a Textual Note.

In many of the plays contained in the Folio, of course, there is no other text with which to compare a doubtful reading; or if there is, like the abbreviated 'bad' Quarto of *Henry V* (1600), it is of limited use. Mistress Quickly's account of Falstaff's death in that play is justly famous: 'I knew there was but one way: for his nose was as sharp as a pen, and 'a babbled of green fields' (2.3, pp. 50–51). The trouble is that the lines did not appear in this form until Lewis Theobald devised them for his edition of the *Works* in 1733. In the Folio, they read as follows: 'I knew there was but one way: for his Nose was as sharpe as a Pen, and a Table of greene fields.' As the relevant note in our edition of the play details, critical interpretation of these last six words (which have no exact equivalent in the Quarto) has ranged from the probable – 'he talked ['Table' misread from 'talkd'] of green fields [the 'green pastures' of Psalm 23]' – to the bizarre – '[his face was] a table [the spitting image] of [Sir Richard] Grenville's [the captain of the ship *Revenge*, killed in 1591]'. Theobald's 'babbled', with its subtle play between the trill of a stream narrowing through pasture, and the fluent gibberish of a dying man, has itself snaked its way into the standard reading. For all its enduring brilliance, however, Shakespeare himself may never have written it. 'To alter,' as Dr Johnson, one of his greatest editors, commented, 'is more easy than to explain.'[20]

Puzzles like these are generally tucked away in the small print, copious notes, and appendices of Shakespearean editions. Our own facing texts provide the standard reading for passages that make doubtful sense, like this one; but our hope remains that by affording plain access to the Folio originals, their occasional difficulties may be aired as simply as possible. It is not the aim of our series, however, to provide a full 'critical apparatus' for the plays. Glossaries, commentaries, lists of variant readings, accounts of stage histories and of the vast critical and editorial tradition – all these remain the invaluable function of the great modern editions (the Oxford, the Cambridge, the Arden, the Riverside) to which our series is indebted. Each of our volumes merely supplements its parallel text with the notes mentioned above, and with an introduction which explains the nature of the Folio text we reproduce, and details some of the effects uniquely achieved by the contours of its original appearance.

The chimera of a true Shakespearean 'original' seems to have gone up in the smoke of a great fire that swept through Warwick in 1694 – according to a report by a 'Stroling Player' in 1729. '*Two* large *Chests* full of this GREAT MAN's *loose Papers* and *Manuscripts*,' he bemoaned, 'were carelessly scatter'd and thrown about, as Garret Lumber and Litter . . . till they were all consum'd in the general Fire and Destruction of that Town'.[21] Shakespeare's King John (5.7) seems to have been prophetic:

> I am a scribled forme drawne with a pen
> Vpon a Parchment, and against this fire
> Do I shrinke vp.

The sole exception to this gloomy likelihood are three or four manuscript pages, now in the British Library, that form part of *Sir Thomas More*, a play by Anthony Munday, Thomas Dekker, and others, which was conceived

around 1593, later much revised, but probably never performed, and
certainly never published in their lifetime. It is now generally accepted that
the so-called 'Hand D' of these pages is William Shakespeare's.[22] They
remain the sum-total of his theatrical manuscripts – two hundred lines or
so, from a body of work totalling around a hundred and twenty thousand.

It is true that Heminge and Condell's Shakespeare Folio, unlike Jonson's,
omits all his narrative verse and sonnets, but these have survived from
their original editions; so, thankfully, have *Edward III* and *The Two Noble
Kinsmen*, the collaborative plays with which Shakespeare topped and tailed
his career; the absence of a First Folio text of *Pericles* is more grievous, for
the Quarto of that play – one of the author's greatest popular successes –
is a poor shadow indeed; two further plays have fared still worse: *Love's
Labour's Won* (1597) and *Cardenio* (1613) remain mere ghosts. But the
labour of love, and monumental act of remembrance, that is *Mr. William
Shakespeares Comedies, Histories, & Tragedies* (1623) remains the nearest thing
we have to the contents of those '*Two* large *Chests*' last heard of in 1729.

The parallel texts which our series of Shakespeare Folios presents have
a simple aim: to provide readers, actors, students, teachers, and directors
with an uncomplicated and accessible purchase on the canonical form by
which Shakespeare's colleagues first commended his 'printed worth' to
posterity. In the absence of a 'definitive' version of any of Shakespeare's
plays, the modern scripts we have edited from the Folio can only ever be
provisional. But our readers are actively invited to test their findings against
our own meticulously recreated 'true original copies'. So, with Heminge
and Condell, we ask you to 'Reade him, therefore; and againe, and againe';
and with Shakespeare's own Armado we exclaim, 'Deuise Wit, write Pen,
for I am for whole volumes in folio.'[23]

Notes

1. 'An Elegie on the death of the famous actor Rich: Burbage' (1619), E.K. Chambers, *The Elizabethan Stage*, 4 vols (Oxford, 1923), 2, 309.
2. William Prynne, *Histrio-Mastix* (1633), Preface 'To the Christian Reader'.
3. See W.W. Greg, *The Shakespeare First Folio: Its Bibliographical and Textual History* (Oxford, 1955); Charlton Hinman's Introduction to *The Norton Facsimile: The First Folio of Shakespeare* (Hamlyn, 1968); and Peter Blayney's Introduction to its second edition (1996).
4. Edward Alleyn, the actor who later founded Dulwich College, noted the payment of £3 to 'Mr Younge, my chapline and schoole-master, for his quarters wages' on 24 March 1618, in his Diary and Account-Book (Dulwich College MSS, IX). The same document notes that Alleyn dined with John Heminge ('Mr Hemings') on 4 June 1622, possibly in connection with the compilation of the First Folio.
5. *The First Quarto of Hamlet*, ed. Kathleen O. Irace (Cambridge, 1998), Scene 7.
6. The debate has recently issued into two useful series of Quarto-based editions: Graham Holderness and Bryan Loughrey's old-spelling 'Shakespearean Originals: First Editions' (Harvester, 1992–3); and the modern-spelling 'Early Quartos' volumes of The New Cambridge Shakespeare (1994–2000).
7. It is probably for copyright reasons that the names of two other publishers, John Smethwick and William Aspley, were acknowledged on its final page: 'Smethwick and Aspley both owned the copyrights of plays already published in quarto, and were presumably named because they (unlike half a dozen more cautious copyright owners) chose to join the venture as proportional shareholders rather than to sell or lease their rights to the principals' (Peter Blayney, Introduction to the Second Edition of *The Norton Facsimile*, 1996, p. xxviii).
8. See Maynard Mack, *Alexander Pope: A Life* (Yale, 1985), pp. 774–96; Richard Holmes, *Coleridge: Darker Reflections* (Flamingo, 1999), pp. 418–20; and *Great Expectations*, ed. Angus Calder (Penguin, 1965), pp. 494–6. Among other notable revisers may be counted Tennyson ('The Charge of the Light Brigade', 1854 and 1855); Brecht (*Leben des Galilei*, 1938, 1943, and 1944–7); and Evelyn Waugh (*Brideshead Revisited*, 1945 and 1959: 'here re-issued with many small additions and some substantial cuts'). For an enthralling summary, see John Kerrigan, 'Shakespeare as Reviser', in *English Drama to 1710*, ed. Christopher Ricks (Oxford, 1987).
9. 'Shakespeare, at length thy pious fellows give | The world thy works,' reads Leonard Digges's dedicatory poem in the Folio (my italics). 'Half of the plays were still in manuscript, many of them old and annotated prompt-copies, and if each editor prepared for the press an average of two a year, it was as much

as could be expected' (F.E. Halliday, *Shakespeare in his Age*, 1956, reprinted 1971, p. 347). Halliday counts Burbage as a third editor.

10. 'A Shakespeare play first assumed material form as the author's bundle of manuscript sheets. The company of players required a manuscript fair copy of the play . . . Into the fair copy were entered playhouse changes' (Brian Gibbons, Preface to The New Cambridge Shakespeare: The Early Quartos, 1994–2000).

11. *The Norton Facsimile* (1968), pp. xv–xxii.

12. Kökeritz's 'facsimile' of *Hamlet* (5.2), for example, reads 'They are not neere my Conference' (p. 769), which falsely emends the true reading, 'neere my Conscience'.

13. The editor and publisher gratefully acknowledge the Master and Governors of Dulwich College for their permission to reproduce details from Henslowe's Diary and the 1623 First Folio on the cover of this volume; and Dr Jan Piggott, Keeper of Archives, for his generously invaluable assistance with this series.

14. The lengthy titles of *The Tragedie of Othello | the Moore of Venice* and *The Tragedie of | Anthony and Cleopatra* are set across the upper borders of the full double-spread, divided as shown here.

15. That the Folio's punctuation can be misleading is illustrated by Horatio's description of the ghost in *Hamlet*, who

> with solemn march
> Goes slow and stately by them. Thrice he walk'd
> By their oppress'd and fear-surprisèd eyes.
>
> (1.2, pp. 24–5)

In the Folio, the second line reads, 'Goes slow and stately: By them thrice he walkt,' which sits rather awkwardly with the subsequent repetition of 'by'. The compositor who set the line in the play's Second Quarto (1604) seems to have understood the syntax rather better: 'Goes slowe and stately by them; thrice he walkt . . .'

16. G. Blakemore Evans, 'Shakespeare's Text: Approaches and Problems', in *A New Companion to Shakespeare Studies*, ed. Kenneth Muir and S. Schoenbaum (Cambridge, 1971), pp. 222–38 (p. 234).

17. In order to distribute the work more efficiently, the Folio printers would estimate the amount of space required for each play, then mark up the manuscript or Quarto copy-text they were using. The process is known as 'casting off copy'. If the calculations went awry, the compositors would have to artificially fill out or compress their material in setting it. 'Much of the verse that appears as prose in the Folio probably reflects a need to save space, and prose was sometimes printed as verse in order to waste space' (*The Norton Facsimile* (1968), p. xvii).

18. In *Hamlet*, for example, the Folio notes that the Prince '*Killes Polonius*', but the Queen later elaborates the sequence of events: 'Behind the arras hearing something stir, | He whips his rapier out, and . . . kills | The unseen good old man' (4.1, pp. 154–5). Our modern script therefore introduces the direction '[POLONIUS *withdraws behind the arras*]', and later supplements F as follows: '[*He runs his sword through the arras and*] *kills* POLONIUS' (pp. 140–43). We have also sometimes incorporated the evidence of contemporary stage-practice provided by a play's Quarto edition(s).

19. Sometimes F presents three successive half-lines, as in the first scene of *Henry V* (pp. 5–7), when its clergymen debate the King's recent Budget:

> *Bish. Ely.* This would drinke deepe.
> *Bish. Cant.* 'Twould drinke the Cup and all,
> *Bish. Ely.* But what preuention?

In common with most editions, our modern text treats Canterbury's words as a swift riposte, and therefore part of the same verse-line as Ely's first comment. Such an arrangement lays a weighted pause (or 'caesura') after Ely's question, before the full pentameter of Canterbury's reply:

> *Ely*　　　　　This would drink deep.
> *Canterbury*　　　　　　　　　　　　　'Twould drink the cup and all.
> *Ely*　　　　　But what prevention?
> *Canterbury*　　The King is full of grace and fair regard.

But the lines might equally be arranged as follows, lending the subtle sense of urgency to Ely:

> *Ely*　　　　　This would drink deep.
> *Canterbury*　　'Twould drink the cup and all.
> *Ely*　　　　　　　　　　　　　　　　But what prevention?
> *Canterbury*　　The King is full of grace and fair regard.

Since our parallel edition sets the generally adopted nuance opposite its Folio original, our readers can test, or challenge, that consensus.

20. Quoted in Leslie Hotson, 'Falstaff's Death and Greenfield's', *Times Literary Supplement* (6 April, 1956), p. 212.

21. *An Answer to Mr. Pope's Preface to Shakespear* (1729), quoted in S. Schoenbaum, *William Shakespeare: A Compact Documentary Life* (Oxford, 1977), pp. 305–6.

22. British Library, Harleian MS. 7368. Opinion is divided as to the extent of Shakespeare's contribution. For a full account, see *Sir Thomas More: A Play by Anthony Munday and others, revised by Henry Chettle, Thomas Dekker, Thomas Heywood and William Shakespeare*, ed. Vittorio Gabrieli and Giorgio Melchiori (Manchester, 1990), 1–53.

23. *Love's Labour's Lost*, 1.2. This is the only occurrence of the word 'folio' in the whole of Shakespeare's works.

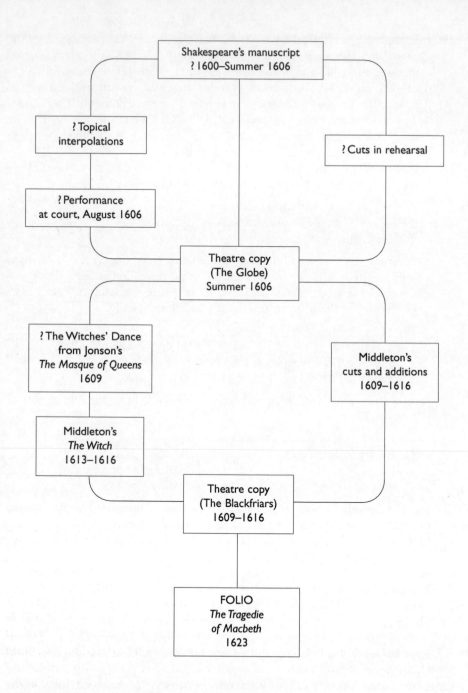

Macbeth: a likely Genealogy of the Text

Introduction

'Wrought with things forgotten': the Dates of *Macbeth*

On the face of it, 'The Mystery of *Macbeth*' (as one scholar called it in 1928) should be no such thing.[1] The play survives in a single version – the 1623 Folio text – which, it is generally agreed, closely derives from a so-called 'prompt-book' or 'theatre copy', the authoritative script that would have been prepared from Shakespeare's working papers, and marked up with the consistent speech-prefixes and specific stage-directions necessary for its smooth performance. By the same token, the date of 'the Scottish Play' appears relatively straightforward. King James VI of Scotland acceded to the English throne in March 1603, whereupon Shakespeare's company, the Lord Chamberlain's Men, were promoted to the status of the King's Men. *Othello* and *Measure for Measure*, both of which were performed before King James in late 1604, include elements calculated to appeal to his known interests.[2] *Macbeth* capitalizes still further on those interests: not only did King James believe himself descended from the historical Banquo, but his own 1597 treatise on witchcraft, *Demonologie*, was reprinted in London in 1603, and in the following year he strengthened the laws against conjuration.[3] Add to this the long-standing theory that the Porter's reference to 'an equivocator . . . who committed treason' (2.3, pp. 48–9) in fact alludes to the trial and subsequent execution, in May 1606, of Father Henry Garnet for his part in the 1605 Gunpowder Plot, and everything falls into place: Shakespeare must have finished writing *Macbeth* around the Summer of 1606, with *King Lear* (1605) under his belt, and *Antony and Cleopatra* (1607) a gleam in his mind's eye.[4]

This traditional dating is still, more or less, the best that scholarship can do; the problem is that the play Shakespeare finished work on that Summer was different – possibly hugely different – from the version subsequently printed in Heminge and Condell's Folio collection. The apparent simplicity of *Macbeth*'s unique textual status, therefore, suddenly poses its profoundest riddle. For while editors of *Hamlet*, say, or *Othello* must negotiate the priority of those plays' variously distinct Quarto and

Folio texts,[5] editors of *Macbeth* face the greater task of constructing the play's history from a single surviving version that was published nearly twenty years after its supposed première – 'supposed' because, as Nicholas Brooke laconically comments, 'There is no evidence to contradict 1606, but there is also very little to support it.'[6] So it is that John Dover Wilson's 1947 edition includes its discussion of the play's date and text under the heading 'The three *Macbeths*', while Brooke's (1990) divides his account between 'The Original Play' and 'The Revised Version'.[7] But three versions of *Hamlet* are indeed extant, and an original *Othello* does seem to have been systematically revised. The single Folio text of *Macbeth* demands altogether more arduous skills of deduction; like Sherlock Holmes's 'curious case of the dog in the night-time', discussion of the play's early stage-life must be argued from what isn't there.[8]

Entirely better documented is Giuseppe Verdi's operatic treatment of *Macbeth*, a work he premièred in 1847, then systematically revised nearly twenty years later.[9] The textual history of Shakespeare's *Macbeth* includes a similarly belated revival, though the extent to which the author himself contributed to, or was even aware of, that subsequent adaptation is unknown. The dates of *Macbeth* extend across 25 years of evidence and four centuries of conjecture.

The paperchase begins with its publication, in late 1623, as the thirty-first play and seventh tragedy of *Mr. William Shakespeares Comedies, Histories, & Tragedies* – the First Folio – where it occupies pp. 131–51 (sig. ll6r–nn4r).[10] Shortly before publication, that book was entered, on 8 November 1623, in the Stationers' Register, and the play of 'Mackbeth' included among sixteen plays 'not formerly entred to other men' – those plays, in other words, which were being published there for the first time.[11] Quite why it was never printed in an individual Quarto edition, given its mixture of the sensational and the topical (and its sustained popularity with audiences ever since), is hard to understand. Had it been, much of the following discussion might have stood on a surer footing.

As things stand, however, critical attention must focus upon two short stage-directions included in that Folio text: '*Sing within. Come away, come away, &c.*' (3.5, pp. 92–3) and '*Musicke and a Song. Blacke Spirits, &c.*' (4.1, pp. 100–101; see also our facsimile page below, p. 198). None of the many other songs in Heminge and Condell's volume are abbreviated so severely ('*&c.*'), and it seems clear that these references were intended, not for the book's readership, but for members of the play's cast (the actors playing Hecate and her Witches), to whom the lyrics of the songs were presumably familiar. Happily, that familiarity endured, such that when William Davenant came to adapt *Macbeth* for the Restoration stage in the 1660s, he was able to include a full text of the missing songs.[12] Davenant took enormous liberties with the Folio play,[13] but there is reason to believe that his versions of 'Come away' and 'Black spirits' were in fact authentic restorations to the Folio text. This is the good news; the bad news is that Shakespeare didn't write them.

We know this because of a ninety-page manuscript copy, in Oxford's Bodleian Library, of a play called *The Witch*, which is described on the title-page as having been 'long since acted by His Majesty's servants [i.e. the King's Men] at the Blackfriars'.[14] The play, a lurid and racy melodrama, features a coven of witches, led by Hecate, whose charms and potions lubricate the sexual intrigues of its plot. Crucially, it also includes two sequences with obvious links to *Macbeth*: a 'Song' performed by Hecate and spirits 'in the air', beginning 'Come away, come away, | Hecate, Hecate, come away!' (3.3); and 'A charm-song about a vessel', beginning 'Black spirits and white, red spirits and grey', during which Hecate and her coven toss suitably grisly ingredients into the cauldron they stir (5.2). The lines (around sixty in all) evidently comprise the material to which those two '&c.'-marks in the Folio text of *Macbeth* refer. (The fact that they reappeared almost verbatim in the 1674 Quarto of Davenant's adaptation makes it a certainty.) But who wrote *The Witch*? And what on earth are parts of it doing in *Macbeth*?

The first of these questions is easier to answer than the second. The Bodleian manuscript includes a brief epistle by the dramatist Thomas Middleton acknowledging authorship of 'this ignorantly ill-fated labour of mine'.[15] The attribution has never been challenged – though neither the epistle nor the play itself is in Middleton's handwriting. It has been demonstrated, in fact, that this handsome presentation copy was the handiwork of the professional copyist (or 'scrivener') Ralph Crane.[16] And here the chronology of *Macbeth* gets enormously complicated since, maddeningly, Crane's transcript of *The Witch* is undated.

It must have been prepared at some point between 1618 (the date of Crane's earliest known association with the King's Men) and 1627 (when Middleton died). It follows that Middleton must have written *The Witch* in advance of this transcript – substantially in advance, since his epistle refers to the 'long . . . obscurity' in which his play has lain and the fact that it was '*long since* acted by His Majesty's servants at the Blackfriars'. This latter detail is also important: the company secured the lease on the indoor theatre across the river at Blackfriars (part of a converted monastery) in August 1608, and began performing there late the following year. *The Witch* – along with the songs with which we are concerned – must therefore have been performed there some time between late 1609 and (allowing enough time for the play's 'long . . . obscurity') *c.*1620. Middleton's own, rather guarded description of his play as 'ignorantly ill-fated' strongly implies that it had flopped, and experts in the field, working from the internal evidence of Middleton's stylistic development, have tentatively narrowed the parameters of the play's short-lived première to *c.*1613–16 – though such estimates remain just that: informed guesses.[17]

What is certain is that at some point between 1609 and 1618, Thomas Middleton's *The Witch* was briefly produced by the King's Men – Shakespeare's company – at the Blackfriars theatre; that play (subsequently transcribed for a private connoisseur between 1618 and 1627) contained material that was also included in performances of Shakespeare's *Macbeth* by the time of its publication in the 1623 Folio. Since *Macbeth* otherwise seems to belong to the Summer of 1606 (see above, p. xxvii), the obvious implication is that Middleton's songs were subsequently transplanted onto Shakespeare's play for a later revival. The alternative – that Middleton nabbed the songs from *Macbeth* – is extremely unlikely, since they 'are given in their full form in Middleton's play and are integral to the staging of their respective scenes, whereas they seem to be unwarranted intrusions, if not positive violations of tone and mood, in the Shakespeare text'.[18] As we shall see in the following section, those two brief stage-directions in the Folio text of *Macbeth* offer a loose thread that threatens to unravel the garment of the entire play. The first critic to pick at that thread was Isaac Reed, who published an edition of *The Witch* (its first) in 1778. It is worth summarizing the general consensus that has since evolved as to when and why Middleton's songs were stitched into Shakespeare's play in the first place.

The clue is in Middleton's reference to the Blackfriars theatre, and the consequent expansion of the King's Men's repertoire from 1609. For as well as providing a convenient Winter sanctuary for the company from their Summer headquarters at the open-air Globe, the indoor playhouse also presented the opportunity for a wider range of theatrical 'effects'. Influenced by the vogue for so-called 'masques' at James's court (ostentatiously elaborate blends of music, poetry, choreography, and design), the Blackfriars, with its artificial lighting, intimate atmosphere, subtle acoustics, and handy stage-machinery, promoted the spectacle of illusion over the merciless daylight of the Globe.[19] Shakespeare's *Cymbeline* (1610), where *'Jupiter descends in thunder and lightning, sitting upon an eagle'* (4.4), and *The Tempest* (1611), with its various calls for thunder, soft music, strange vanishings, and graceful dances, seem to have been composed with these new resources in mind.[20] And so, too, by the author's own admission, was Middleton's *The Witch*, whose songs and dances, disembodied voices 'in the air', and *coups de théâtre* ('a spirit like a cat descends') found their way into *Macbeth*.[21]

It is easy to see why the supernatural apparatus and largely nocturnal setting of Shakespeare's otherwise slightly old-fashioned play must have seemed to offer useful raw material for a revival at the new Blackfriars venue. Ben Jonson had demonstrated the spectacular potential of the theme of witchcraft in his *Masque of Queens*, which was produced at court before King James in February 1609, in an elaborate production by Inigo Jones.[22] Some critics, indeed, have linked the 'Antimasque of Witches' in that piece, 'full of preposterous change and gesticulation',[23] with two suspiciously similar stage-directions in Middleton's *The Witch* (*'Here they dance The Witches' Dance and exeunt'*, 5.2) and the Folio *Macbeth* (*'The Witches Dance, and vanish'*, 4.1, pp. 106–7). One theory holds that the same dance troupe (under the enjoyably named choreographer Jerome Herne) performed the same set-piece, in the same extravagant costumes, in all three productions. It is true that the Jacobethan dramatists were nothing if not thrifty, recycling and revamping their old material as regularly as their latterday university commentators.[24] But to accept, as John Dover Wilson did, that the three productions – Jonson's masque, Middleton's play, the revived *Macbeth* – indeed swiftly succeeded one another in the years 1609–11,[25] throws up more questions than it answers. How can such a date, for example, be made to square with the general view that Middleton wrote *The Witch* in around 1613–16?.[26] And if Middleton did revive *Macbeth* in around 1610, where on earth was Shakespeare when his play was being (as most agree) so 'tastelessly tinkered' about with?[27]

Whatever the truth, it seems that the very least we can say is that *Macbeth* existed in at least two substantially different forms, which might conveniently be called the Globe version (premièred there by 1606) and the Blackfriars version (revised for a revival there at some point between 1609 and 1616, and subsequently printed in the 1623 Folio).

Unfortunately, even this distinction demands qualification, since the earliest known record of the play's existence is a detailed eye-witness account, dated 20 April 1611,[28] of its performance not at the Blackfriars but at the Globe. The author of this account, Dr Simon Forman, a physician

and astrologer (the professions were not unrelated), approximately describes and even quotes the play we know, but provides few clues as to
which of our hypothetical versions – Shakespeare's 'Globe' original or
Middleton's 'Blackfriars' adaptation – he saw there. (Both venues continued to be used, and productions transferred in much the same way as
they do today.) Worse still, Forman seems to have conflated his memories
of the performance with his own reading of Shakespeare's source
(Holinshed's *Chronicles*), recounting 'how Macbeth and Banquo, two
noblemen of Scotland, riding through a wood, there stood before them
three women, fairies or nymphs, and saluted Macbeth, saying three times
unto him: "Hail Macbeth, King of Codon [i.e. Cawdor], for thou shalt be
a king, but beget no kings," etc.' (see 1.3, pp. 12–13).[29] The actors playing
Macbeth and Banquo are extremely unlikely to have entered the stage of
the Globe on horseback, let alone 'riding through a wood'; but that is how
they are depicted, as scholars have long noticed, in a woodcut illustration
in Holinshed's *Chronicles*, the text of which also describes the three witches
as 'nymphs or fairies'.[30] Forman's informed imagination, then, seems to
have pieced out the actors' imperfections with his thoughts,[31] and the
evidence of his testimony is accordingly tainted.

Tainted or not, it is a great pity that Forman didn't start to compile his
'Book of Plays and Notes Thereof' a decade or two earlier. Had he done,
much light might have been shed upon the precise chronology of Shakespeare's plays, including *Macbeth*'s place within it. It is eye-witness documents like these, after all, that provide the only solid evidence for the dates
of two other Folio-only plays, *Julius Caesar* and *Twelfth Night*, performed in
September 1599 and February 1602 respectively.[32] In their absence, the
date of Shakespeare's 'original' *Macbeth* turns out, on close inspection, to be
as difficult to establish as that of its subsequently 'revised' revival.

As we have seen, the play is traditionally thought to have been premièred at the Globe in the Summer of 1606, in the wake of the previous
November's Gunpowder Plot. The Porter's drunken references to 'an
equivocator' may well have sounded echoes to the capital trial of the Jesuit
conspirator Father Garnet that March (when he 'fell into a large discourse
of defending equivocations, with many weak and frivolous distinctions')[33]
– not least since 'Farmer' was one of the aliases Garnet had used ('Here's a
farmer . . .', 2.3, pp. 48–9).[34] And even if such a specific reference was not
intended, the general theme of regicidal treachery that pervades the play,
extending even to the innocent prattle of Macduff's little son ('What is a
"traitor"?', 4.2, pp. 110–11), must surely have seemed timely reflections on

the magnitude of Guy Fawkes's foiled attempt. And then there is the mysterious case of 'the master o'th' *Tiger*': 'Weary se'nnights [= weeks], nine times nine,' chants the First Witch, 'Shall he dwindle, peak, and pine' (1.3, pp. 10–11). As E.A. Loomis diligently researched, a ship called *The Tiger* put into Milford Haven on 27 June 1606, after a calamitous odyssey to the Far East that had begun over eighteen months before, on 5 December 1604. To be precise, the arduous and eventful journey had lasted 567 days,[35] which is – astonishingly – the total of the Witch's sum (seven times nine times nine). Allowing for news of the epic trip to have reached London, then, the lines can scarcely have been written before, say, late July – always assuming, of course, that a specific allusion to this particular *Tiger* was intended.

This, however, need not be the case, no more than with any of these alleged topicalities, which might just as well be considered coincidences or simple generalities. The regicidal plot and structure of *Macbeth*, after all, more or less duplicates that of *Richard III* (1594);[36] 'equivocation' was a buzzword as early as 1601, long before Father Garnet appeared on the scene, when Hamlet used it to describe the riddling quibbles of the Grave-digger (himself a dramatic ancestor of *Macbeth*'s Porter);[37] and naming a ship *The Tiger* seems to have been the maritime equivalent of calling a dog 'Rover', Shakespeare himself using the same name in *Twelfth Night*, nearly three years before Loomis's particular *Tiger* set sail.[38] Besides, even if these various passages indeed comprise specific allusions to events between November 1605 and June 1606, who is to say that they were not themselves additions to Shakespeare's 'original' play, as extraneous in their way as Middleton's all-singing, all-dancing witches?

Enter 'The three *Macbeths*', and the theory that the single Folio text of the play we have in fact bears the imprint of at least two earlier productions, previous to Middleton's adaptation at the Blackfriars in 1609–16. The play's calculated flattery of King James – its 'show' of kings (4.1, pp. 104–5), references to the practice of 'touching' (4.3, pp. 124–5), and so on – has been linked to the documented performance at court of three (unnamed) plays by Shakespeare's company before the King in early August 1606, during the state-visit of his brother-in-law, Christian IV of Denmark. According to this view, Shakespeare added the more blatant of these topical sequences, 'for the entertainment of the royal audience, to an already existing text', while at the same time editing down that existing text to fit within the restricted auspices of its command performance.[39] The theory goes some way to explain both the brevity of the Folio text and the disproportionate *longueurs* within it. It has been noticed, for example, that Lady Macduff's banter with her little son about traitors and hanging (4.2, pp. 110–13) is conducted in prose, while the surrounding scene is in verse: 'the likelihood of an insertion is increased,' comments Dover Wilson.[40]

An 'insertion' into what? Perhaps into the 'original' play, replies Wilson, which was perhaps performed by the company of 'English comedians' whose presence in Edinburgh is recorded as early as 1599; perhaps King James VI of Scotland had seen a production of this 'ur-*Macbeth*' some years before he became King James I of England; and perhaps Shakespeare himself was part of its cast.[41] The theory has not found favour, but the principles upon which it was built are unignorable. English playwrights did not have to wait for a Scottish king to succeed Elizabeth before dramatizing episodes from their neighbours' history. Philip Henslowe commissioned plays for his Rose theatre about Robert II and 'Malcolm, King of Scots' in 1599 and 1602; and the story of Macbeth seems to have been old hat at least by 1600, when the celebrated comedian Will Kemp (a former member of Shakespeare's company and perhaps the first ever Falstaff) satirized the vogue by describing his encounter with 'a penny-poet, whose first making was the miserable stolen story of Macdoel, or Macdobeth, or Macsomewhat, for I am sure a Mac it was'.[42]

'But enough of guessing,' as Dover Wilson cries (p. xlii). The fact remains that there is no evidence of the play's performance at either of King James's courts; no evidence of its performance at the Globe until 1611; and no conclusive evidence of the extent to which its (probable) Blackfriars revival tampered with Shakespeare's original design. Generations of textual scholars have come to echo the play's hero, as he hallucinates the bloody dagger he is to use – and have reached much the same conclusion: 'Come, let me clutch thee! | I have thee not, and yet I see thee still' (2.1, pp. 40–41). The play that remains before our eyes, the unique text of *Macbeth* reproduced in the following pages, certainly dates from 1623, partially dates from 1609–16, probably mostly dates from 1605–6, but may conceivably date in part from 1599.

Such a tentative, involved, and distended chronology is true of most dramatic works, as they pass from author's study to rehearsal space, first-night stage to back-room revision, publishing house to repertory revival. Something like it underlies the three texts of *Hamlet*, the two scores of Verdi's *Macbeth*, and – an extreme case, admittedly – the fully *five* 'basic' versions of that composer's *Don Carlos*.[43] Shakespeare's *Macbeth* may well have passed through a similar process; the problem, we repeat, is that the

Folio text of the play is the only version to have survived. The following section is designed to explore whether this surviving text can properly be described as 'Shakespeare's *Macbeth*' at all.

'A book where men may read strange matters': the Texts of *Macbeth*

Macbeth is the shortest play but two in Heminge and Condell's Folio collection, and its shortest tragedy.[44] If the Folio texts of *Macbeth* and *Hamlet* were to be performed simultaneously in adjacent theatres, one audience would be going home while another was still absorbed in the latter's 'closet-scene' (3.4). This fact has not, however, prevented generations of scholars from pruning *Macbeth* still further. We have already sketched some of the implications of the Folio's abbreviated references to the songs 'Come away' and 'Black spirits', and of its terse stage-direction '*The Witches Dance, and vanish*': but Middleton's songs and Jonson's dance are not the only elements of Shakespeare's play to have been considered spurious since its first publication in 1623. In fact, if all these scholars were to be believed, audiences of a performance of Shakespeare's contribution to *Macbeth* would be able to nip next door in time to catch *Hamlet*'s 'play-within-the-play' (3.2). The full list of these allegedly 'dubious' passages makes for dispiriting reading. Once again, the problem starts with those singing witches.

At the time of writing, critics remain agreed that Middleton's contribution to the Folio text extended beyond the two songs he recycled from *The Witch*. In particular, the entire presence of Hecate herself has long been thought superfluous since, as one recent authority summarizes the matter, her lines 'have little or no effect on the plot and are different in style to the surrounding dialogue'.[45] It is now considered almost certain, in other words, that the whole of 3.5 (pp. 90–93), Hecate's five-line speech to '*the other three witches*' [sic] before the second song (4.1, pp. 100–101), and the eight-line speech beginning 'Ay, sir, all this is so' (4.1, pp. 106–7), which precedes the witches' dance,[46] are all components of Middleton's later revival of Shakespeare's play. It is indeed hard to disagree with E.K. Chambers's distaste for their 'alien' tone: 'One can hardly imagine the awful beings, who meet Macbeth and Banquo on the blasted heath, singing little songs and dancing "like elves and fairies" [4.1, pp. 100–101]'.[47]

Charles Lamb had traced the essential differences between Shakespeare's and Middleton's witches as early as 1808:

Hecate in Middleton has a son, a low buffoon: the hags of Shakespear have neither child of their own, nor seem to be descended from any parent. They are foul anomalies, of whom we know not where they are sprung, nor whether they have beginning or ending.[48]

That description well defines the eerie force of those indefinably disturbing 'imperfect speakers', the bearded women who 'look not like th'inhabitants o'th'earth | And yet are on't', and who perform 'A deed without a name'.[49] Subsequent critics, however, sought to treat them as 'foul anomalies' in a quite different sense: as unwarranted impositions onto Shakespeare's 'original' play.

Having identified Middleton's hand in parts of *Macbeth*, in other words, suspicion fell (*pace* Lamb) on the play's remaining 'witch-scenes', where his fingerprints were duly detected. Editors from W.G. Clark and W.A. Wright (1863–6) to Henry Cuningham (in his 1912 Arden edition) therefore variously considered as spurious the whole of 1.1 (pp. 3–4)[50] and the opening section of 1.3 (the lines preceding Macbeth and Banquo's entrance, pp. 8–11). The Victorian scholar F.G. Fleay – the presiding spirit of 'textual disintegration' – further considered that the 'apparition'-speeches in 4.1, had been 'worked over' by Middleton.[51] That now-discredited view was sustained, on the grounds of the scenes' 'dramatic badness' and their 'vulgar and malodorous machinery', as late as 1931 in J.M. Robertson's extremist tract, *Literary Detection*.[52] And meanwhile, once the critical scissors were out, it proved difficult not to wield them elsewhere.

Out went 5.2 (the Scottish lords' account of their alliance with the English against Macbeth, pp. 136–9); out went the last four lines of 5.5 ('singularly weak', according to Clark and Wright);[53] and out went the play's final section (from Malcolm's victorious entrance, 5.7, pp. 154–9), which demonstrate, so it was claimed, 'evident traces of another hand'.[54] Middleton's authorship of the 'Bleeding Captain' scene (1.2) has also long been suspected: nineteenth-century editors found the Captain's 'bombastic phraseology' suspiciously un-Shakespearean,[55] though later scholars attributed its archaic style to the play's 'original' late-Elizabethan composition (see above, p. xxxiv);[56] a subsequent consensus reasonably holds that Shakespeare specifically designed this loftier rhetoric as part of the play's extraordinary range of literary style. Recent opinion, however, has once more placed Middleton in the frame, along with his responsibility for Macbeth's closing soliloquy in 4.1.[57]

And then there is the Porter, the 'infernal janitor'[58] whose drunkenly obscene stand-up routine (2.3, pp. 48–51) caused such dismay among Shakespeare's greatest critics. Alexander Pope, for one, 'degraded' the sequence 'to the bottom of the page' in his 1723–5 edition, along with many other 'suspected passages' in the canon 'which are excessively bad'.[59] (These demoted passages include Macbeth's lines on 'Sleep that knits up the ravell'd sleeve of care', his fear that 'this my hand will rather | The multitudinous seas incarnadine', and Macduff's appalled reaction to the death of 'all my pretty chickens and their dam | In one fell swoop').[60] A century later, Samuel Taylor Coleridge likewise considered the Porter's lines 'disgusting' – though his admiration for the phrase 'the primrose way to th'everlasting bonfire' (2.3, pp. 48–9) led him to speculate that, while the passage as a whole was 'written for the mob by some other hand', Shakespeare himself had supplied those words 'with the remaining ink of a pen otherwise employed'.[61] This kind of literary cherry-picking, and the 'pick-'n-mix' *Macbeth* it produced, continued to define the play's shifting identity. So while the Porter's rôle was restored to the stage in the 1850s,[62] Kenneth Muir's Arden edition still felt the need to defend the scene's brilliant authenticity as recently as the 1980s.[63]

'Now, the next part *you're* not going to like . . .' The textual history of *Macbeth* at times resembles the shrinking contract negotiated between Groucho and Chico Marx in *A Night at the Opera* (1935): 'Now what have we got left?' 'Well, I've got about a foot and a half.'[64] Thus, further inches came off the 'original' script of *Macbeth* according to the theory, outlined above, not that they were the work of 'another hand', but that Shakespeare later added them himself, for that hypothetical royal command perform-ance in August 1606. So while Shakespeare may himself have penned the Porter's speech (2.3, pp. 48–51), the supernatural 'show of eight kings' (4.1, 104–5), Lady Macduff's prose banter with her precocious son (4.2, pp. 110–13), Malcolm's lines on the 'sweet milk of concord' and 'universal peace', and on the 'healing benediction' of royal touching (4.3, 120–25), all of these passages (so the theory went) should properly be regarded as superfluous additions to his original design.[65] At the same time, however, as dashing off these choice pieces of additional flattery 'for the enter-tainment of the royal audience' – or so the theory went – Shakespeare also had to condense his original script to fit the political limitations of its revival (James's guest, King Christian of Denmark, apparently having little understanding of English).[66]

John Dover Wilson's view that 'the 1606 text was in fact an abridgement of a longer play' (p. xxxiii), and that this abridgement was further hacked about by Middleton a few years later, was designed to explain the abnormal brevity of the 1623 Folio text, which previous critics had variously assigned to Shakespeare's 'unusual dramatic technique' and the censorship of its 'awkward political implications'.[67] It is certainly true that *Macbeth*'s 'multiplicity of very brief scenes' finds an equally unusual parallel in *Antony and Cleopatra* (1607);[68] but true, too, that, in the Winter of 1604, Shakespeare's company had performed another Scottish play, about another regicidal conspiracy, and that this play had been immediately suppressed.[69] *The Tragedy of Gowrie* now exists only in name; *The Tragedy of Macbeth* has fared somewhat better – but the political sensitivities surrounding both plays may explain why no Quarto edition of *Macbeth* was ever printed, and why the Folio *Macbeth* leaves so many problems in its wake. For whatever reason, the play we have displays an extraordinary series of 'narrative discontinuities (or irregularities, or illogicalities)',[70] which generations of scholars have variously struggled to explain.

Why, for example, does Malcolm immediately demote the 'bleeding Captain' to the rank of Sergeant in 1.2 (pp. 3–5)? Why does Macbeth describe the Thane of Cawdor as 'a prosperous gentleman' (1.3, pp. 12–13) when he himself has taken a leading part in the victorious battle against 'that most disloyal traitor' (1.2, pp. 6–7)? Why does Lady Macbeth refer to her husband's having broached the subject of Duncan's murder with her when no such conversation has taken place (1.7, pp. 34–5)? Why does Lady Macbeth speak of breast-feeding her children (1.7, pp. 34–5) when, as Macduff later tells us, Macbeth 'has no children'? (4.3, pp. 128–9)? Why does she resolve to murder Duncan herself ('Leave all the rest to me', 1.5, pp. 28–9), and then in fact leave the task to her husband (2.2, pp. 42–5)? Does Lady Macbeth really faint when the murder is discovered (2.3, pp. 56–7), or is it 'a pre-arranged ruse' to divert attention from her husband's faltering testimony? Why does Banquo say nothing about the Witches' prophecy in the aftermath of Duncan's assassination and Macbeth's succession to the throne, especially since he suspects that 'Thou [Macbeth] play'dst most foully for it' (3.1, pp. 64–5)? Why is Banquo killed by 'three Murderers' in 3.3 (pp. 78–9) rather than the two whom we have seen Macbeth commission (3.1, pp. 68–73)? Why is it that Lennox speaks in the same breath of Macduff's flight to England and his reception there, and then prays for an angel to precede his arrival (3.6, pp. 96–7)? Why, having made such a prayer, does Lennox next appear as an apparently loyal servant to Macbeth himself (4.1, pp. 106–7)? And why does Macduff desert his wife in the first place (4.2, pp. 108–9)? What has precipitated Lady Macbeth's sudden descent into deranged somnambulism (5.1, pp. 130–35)? How exactly did she die (5.5, pp. 146–7)?[71]

Analysis of the plot of *Macbeth* soon comes to sound like the murder inquiry its unique Folio text never dramatizes. The many literary detectives to have since re-opened the case divide, broadly speaking, into two camps: those who treat these 'foul anomalies' as evidence of the play's textual abridgement; and those who defend them either as instances of its subtle power, or else simply as dramatic irrelevances.

Dame Edith Evans stood squarely in the former camp. She is said to have explained her reluctance to give the world her Lady Macbeth by claiming that the play provides insufficient motivation for the character's psychological collapse between the Banquet scene (3.4, pp. 80–91) and the Sleepwalking scene (5.1, pp. 130–35): 'there's a page missing'.[72] Scholars have provided much expert testimony in support of this view, supplying a veritable sheaf of hypothetical material: a missing scene between 1.3 and 1.4, in which Macbeth 'called at Inverness on his way to Forres, told his wife of the Weird Sisters', and confessed that 'thoughts of murder had crossed his mind';[73] another scene, before the murder, featuring 'a further dialogue between husband and wife, preceded perhaps by a scene in which, going to the bedroom, knife in hand, she cannot bring herself to the action';[74] and further scenes and episodes in which Banquo fully explains his otherwise suspicious behaviour (he was 'working with Macduff on behalf of Malcolm'),[75] where the identity of the Third Murderer is revealed, and where Macduff 'debated with his wife the policy of going and had her approval' such that Lady Macduff's outburst to Ross ('His flight was madness', 4.2, pp. 108–9) can be understood as a means 'to divert suspicion from herself'.[76] If such material did indeed once belong to an uncut *Macbeth*, of course, there is very little to be done about it: whoever was responsible – Shakespeare himself, Middleton, the state censor, all or none of the above – destroyed most of the evidence. It is one thing to restore the odd dropped-out line,[77] quite another to reconstruct whole Shakespearean scenes. The best that judicious directors can do, in fact, is to subject the play to still further cuts and rearrangements – reorganizing, for example, the sequence in which Middleton's Witch-scenes are played, to minimize the oddity of Lennox's description of Macduff's flight (3.6, pp. 96–7).[78] In the case of *Macbeth*, 'The mystery of the missing manuscript' endures.

That phrase is Ezra Pound's. It belongs to the preface he supplied to the facsimile edition of *The Waste Land* (1971), which reproduced Eliot's earliest drafts of the poem, scribbled over with Pound's own, highly influential annotations.[79] 'I am thankful that the lost leaves have been unearthed,' commented Pound, fifty years on. No such 'lost leaves' survive of *Macbeth* – but then again, if Eliot's 'original drafts' formed the basis of a definitive edition, *The Waste Land* would be called *He Do The Police in Different Voices*, and its first line would read, not 'April is the cruellest month', but 'First we had a couple of feelers down at Tom's place'.[80] The Folio text of *Macbeth*, in other words, may actually be, narrative anomalies and all, far superior to its earlier drafts; may be, in truth, the masterpiece that its status as 'one of Shakespeare's most frequently performed plays' implies.[81] There is no evidence, after all, to say that Shakespeare did not actively collaborate with Middleton – as Eliot did with Pound – on the play's subsequent Blackfriars revival, as one recent editor suggests;[82] nor that Heminge and Condell did not mean what they said when they described their collection of Shakespeare's plays as 'absolute in their numbers, as he conceived them' (see above, p. x). If so, it is surely possible to argue that *Macbeth*'s loose narrative threads, that have exercised the wits of so many scholars, in fact comprise its enduring texture.

It is generally the play's readers, as opposed to its audiences, who fret over the 'discontinuities (or irregularities, or illogicalities)' of its plot – readers such as the American 'crime-fiction expert' in James Thurber's wry short story 'The Macbeth Murder Mystery' (1942), who treats an old Penguin edition of the play as a detective story ('You can imagine how mad I was when I found it was Shakespeare').[83] The conclusions she comes to ('In the first place, I don't think for a moment that he killed the King . . . There wasn't any ghost . . . Macbeth was *shielding somebody!*') shrewdly guys the sorts of dense, analytic textual scholarship that had (to take just one example) fingered various members of the cast for the rôle of Third Murderer.[84] Thurber's parody draws attention to a persistent overlap between Shakespearean textual criticism (of *Hamlet* and *Macbeth* in particular) and detective fiction,[85] from the 'empirical . . . scientific' methods of the Victorian 'disintegrators' ('You know my methods. Apply them'),[86] via 'The Mystery of *Macbeth*' (1928) and *Literary Detection* (1931), to the 'solution', 'proof', and 'verdict' of John Dover Wilson's edition (1947).[87] The language of 1930s whodunnit and 1940s *film noir* somehow now cleaves to the discussion of *Macbeth* – appropriately so when we consider the broad sweep of its plot, with its murderers, suspects, motives, doctors, and fall-guys.[88]

It is of course inconceivable that Shakespeare plotted *Macbeth* with such a scrupulous and readerly audience in mind; extremely unlikely, too, that whatever plot he originally devised survived entirely unscathed into the play's Folio text. By the same token, it is feasible to assume that a proportion, at least, of the play's anomalies simply derive from the workings of his theatrical imagination. Were Shakespeare to be interrogated about Lady Macbeth's children, Banquo's complicity, or the identity of the Third Murderer, he would most likely shrug his shoulders, astonished at the question. The famous story is told that, during the filming of Raymond Chandler's *The Big Sleep* in 1946, the scriptwriters came across 'an apparently insoluble turn of plot' – there were more bodies than murderers. The director, Howard Hawks, sent a telegram to Chandler himself. Who killed the chauffeur? 'NO IDEA,' replied the author.[89] Shakespeare might well have cabled much the same reply – 'The play's the thing',[90] after all. And if some of *Macbeth*'s loose ends were 'so inconspicuous' as to have 'passed unnoticed' for over two hundred years,[91] they are perhaps best left alone to work their quietly unsettling force.

'An awful lot of layers! More and more! | Come on! When do I reach the inner core?' Readers of the last few pages of this Introduction may be forgiven for finding some fellow feeling with Ibsen's Peer Gynt, peeling the onion of his own life in search of its essence: 'Damned if I do! However far I go | It's only peel – smaller and smaller'.[92] The 'inner core' of Shakespeare's *Macbeth* indeed seems to recede and diminish before our eyes, like its own trolls, 'melted | As breath into the wind' (1.3, pp. 12–13). Already the shortest tragedy, not only has it been stripped of many of its characters (Hecate, the Witches, the Bleeding Captain, the Porter), scenes (1.1, 1.2, 1.3, 3.5, 4.1, 5.2), and 'excessively bad' lines (see above, p. xxxvii), but almost everything that *was* Shakespeare's he seems either to have cobbled together and interpolated, in a regrettable moment of royalist grovelling ('the King's Evil', the 'show of eight kings'),[93] or else stood by, complicitly or otherwise, as it accumulated on the cutting-room floor, at the zealous hands of state censorship, theatrical expedience, or constrained revision. All of which is not to mention the final layer of peel – the often bungled transmission of 'Shakespeare's play' from manuscript prompt-book to printed text.

We have said (above, p. xxvii) that the 1623 Folio text of *Macbeth* was typeset more or less directly from the theatrical transcript, or 'prompt-book', that would have guided its production. Unfortunately, this authoritative manuscript seems to have been prepared relatively late in the play's life – hence the endless fields of speculation we have mapped surrounding it. Some early Shakespeare texts – the Second Quarto edition of *Hamlet*, for example, or the Folio (and one and only) text of *All's Well That Ends Well* – have been shown to derive from the author's working papers, the so-called 'foul papers' he would have submitted to the company in advance of rehearsals, and which would have been tweaked, cut, and revised in that process. The Folio text of *Macbeth* stands at the opposite extreme, as the end-product of a lengthy sequence of theatrical modification and adjustment, apparently including the insertion into it of a set of 'working sheets' from Middleton's revision, covering the scenes 3.5 to 4.1.[94] In addition, however, that hand-me-down version passed through a further set of hands in the 1620s, when the play was prepared for the press.

It used to be thought that the sporadically irregular metre and accumulation of half-lines in the Folio play's verse provided further evidence of its abridgement, the scars, as it were, of a wholesale series of cuts. Minute and laborious scholarship has since determined, however, that a great many of these oddities are the responsibility of one of the typesetters (or 'compositors') who worked on it. Two separate craftsmen, known to specialists as 'A' and 'B', have been identified from the tics and mannerisms of their work as having a hand in the Folio text of *Macbeth*.[95] They seem to have divided the play roughly in half between them, 'A's' stint covering 1.1–3.3, and 'B's' the remainder.[96] But while 'B' was often 'cavalier' with the words he set, and sometimes 'set up prose as though it were verse', 'A' had a 'regrettable tendency to rearrange normal blank verse into a succession of irregular lines'.[97] Neither man, in other words, was ideally qualified to preserve the intricacies of Shakespearean blank verse. With pages from the same theatrical manuscript before them, 'B' played safe by reproducing it, as best he could, line by line (even if that meant using capitals to transform good prose into bad verse), while 'A' preferred to set his Folio columns as neatly and economically as possible (even if that meant disrupting the verse-lines of his copy, assembling them into a traffic jam of accumulated overspills).[98] At the same time, recent scholarship has increasingly trusted to the Folio's arrangement of the play's lines, and resisted the remorselessly pentametric form into which editors since Rowe have squeezed it, in favour of a defter, more limber flexibility.[99] The science is necessarily inexact, but our parallel text of the play has been designed to generate discussion and experiment among its readers and players, and to highlight the constant negotiation they must make between authorial intention, compositorial negligence, and editorial imposition. Those distinctions are sometimes very difficult to verify, not least because there is no way of double-checking the Folio's lineation (or, indeed, its text) against any earlier Quarto edition.

In the Folio text of *Hamlet*, Polonius bafflingly opines that 'Your bait of falshood, takes this Cape of truth' (2.1), but it is actually the 'carp' of truth that Polonius is angling for, as cross-reference to the play's Second Quarto reveals (incidentally confirming that Compositor 'B' was not alone in his 'cavalier' habits with words). If the Folio version of this line were the only one to have survived, it is likely that an enterprising scholar would have deduced the proper word, but equally likely that another would have contested that reading – and this is the problem with *Macbeth*. Consider, for example, Banquo's description of 'This Guest of Summer, | The Temple-haunting Barlet', who proves, 'By his loued Mansonry', that the air is sweet around the Macbeths' castle (1.6, pp. 28–9). It is clear from what follows that Banquo is speaking of a bird ('No jutty . . . but this bird | Hath made his pendant bed'); just as there is no fish called a 'cape', however, there is no bird called a 'barlet'. Combining a knowledge of ornithology and palaeography, the editor Nicholas Rowe ostensibly solved the problem in 1709: not 'Barlet' but 'Martlet', the bird we know as the swallow or house martin, each of which is a 'Summer visitor', still commonly found 'nesting in old buildings'; the letters 'B' and 'M' were surprisingly similar in Jacobean handwriting, and the compositor might simply have omitted the 't' in the same way that his colleague omitted the 'r' of Polonius's 'carp'.[100] Rowe's 'martlet' is the standard reading – though later scholars have argued that 'marlet' might be the rare and obsolete form Shakespeare used, and even that 'the word "barlet" . . . will yet turn up'.[101] By the same token, although most modern editors retain Lewis Theobald's correction of F's meaningless 'Mansonry' to 'mansionry' (1733), there is nothing to say that Alexander Pope's version, 'masonry' (1728), is not what Shakespeare originally wrote (see our Textual Note 13 below). Not only, in other words, has critical doubt been cast upon the date, authorship, status, integrity, sequence, and lineation of whole swathes of the *Macbeth*, but the play we think we know from modern editions in fact contains hundreds of readings like these that are necessarily hypothetical. Getting on for half of the extracts from the play included in the *Oxford Dictionary of Quotations* have, at one time or another, either been regarded as spurious ('At one fell swoop') or else substantially deviate from the original Folio text ('The temple-haunting martlet').

Faced with such an array of anomalies and uncertainties, it is perhaps worth remembering John Dover Wilson's observation 'that the literary critics who are most sweeping in their condemnation of the text are often loudest in their praise of the play'.[102] So while this Introduction has sought to emphasize to its readers the constant possibility (or even likelihood) that our parallel texts stand at some distance from the play Shakespeare wrote, on the other hand, might it not be the case that these multitudinous problems, whether by design or accident, in fact contribute to the eerie endurance of the play's dark energy? The uncertainties we have detailed (of its date and authorship, its plot and text) make company, after all, with the apparitions and illusions of its dramatic technique,[103] the dense and tortuous compression of its poetic method,[104] the contradictions, antitheses, and equivocation inherent to its 'general style',[105] and even the generic status it continues to enjoy as one of the Folio's tragedies.[106]

This sense of disorientation comes close, in my view, to defining the play's 'inner core'. I vividly remember being enthralled, one evening, by a radio version of *Macbeth*, while struggling through both a Summer flu and the distortions, crackles, and whines of BBC Radio 4's long-wave reception on an elderly valve 'wireless'. A few years later, I bought the same production on cassette, but was then frustrated to discover that the clean, crisp, FM stereo of this re-issue simply couldn't reproduce the weird acoustics and flu-befuddled twilight of my original listening. Stripped of the weird murmur of its LW transmission, and in the clear light of day, the production suddenly seemed predictable and histrionic.[107] It was the interference that had somehow realized and released the play's atmosphere. The same is true, I want to suggest, of the textual accidents, anomalies, discrepancies, and confusions we have so laboriously traced through *The Tragedie of Macbeth* – rather in the same way, perhaps, as that latterday 'horror', *The Blair Witch Project* (1999), achieves its 'creeping dread and festering anxiety' from the artless and amateur footage it contrives.[108]

The parallel edition of *Macbeth* that follows seeks to combine the long-wave atmospherics of its unaltered Folio text with the frequency-modulated, hi-fi clarity of a modern script. Neither version is definitive, of course; but our hope remains that together they may negotiate the play's comprehensively achieved 'double sense'.[109] 'Fair is foul, and foul is fair'; 'Is this a dagger that I see before me?'. Now you see it, now you don't; don't look now.

Notes

1. W. J. Lawrence, *Shakespeare's Workshop* (Basil Blackwell, 1928), p. 24.

2. On *Othello* and King James's poem on the 1571 Battle of Lepanto, see Emrys Jones, '*Othello*, *Lepanto*, and the Cyprus Wars', *Shakespeare Survey* 21 (1968), 47–52; for an extreme account of *Measure for Measure*'s Jacobean topicality, see David L. Stevenson, 'The Role of James I in Shakespeare's *Measure for Measure*', *English Literary History* 26 (1959), 188–208. The plays were performed at court on, respectively, 1 November and 26 December 1604 (see *Jacobean and Caroline Revels Accounts, 1603–42*, ed. W.R. Streitberger, Malone Society (Oxford, 1986), p. 8.)

3. See *Macbeth*, ed. A.R. Braunmuller (Cambridge, 1997), pp. 2–3; and *Three Jacobean Witchcraft Plays*, ed. Peter Corbin and Douglas Sedge (Revels, 1986), pp. 2–3. This introduction, and our parallel texts themselves, are particularly indebted to two recent editions of *Macbeth*, namely those edited by Nicholas Brooke (Oxford, 1990) and A.R. Braunmuller (Cambridge, 1997). Kenneth Muir's Arden edition (1951, 9th edition, 1962) remains useful.

4. On Father Garnet, see *Macbeth*, ed. Muir, pp. xv–xix; on *Antony and Cleopatra* in relation to *Macbeth*, see *Macbeth*, ed. Braunmuller, p. 7.

5. *Hamlet* appeared in a First Quarto in 1603 (an inferior 'bootleg' of an early performance script), a Second Quarto in 1604–5 (printed from the author's working papers), and in the 1623 Folio (a version accommodating some of the topical additions of its original performances). The First Quarto and First Folio texts of *Othello* (first performed 1602–4) appeared in 1622 and 1623 respectively. Each set of texts presents a plethora of variants.

6. *Macbeth*, ed. Brooke, p. 59.

7. *Macbeth*, ed. John Dover Wilson (Cambridge, 1947), p. xxii; *Macbeth*, ed. Brooke, pp. 59 and 64.

8. Arthur Conan Doyle, 'Silver Blaze' (1892), *The Memoirs of Sherlock Holmes*, ed. Christopher Roden (Oxford, 1993), p. 23.

9. See Julian Budden, *The Operas of Verdi*, revised ed., 3 vols (Clarendon Press, 1992), 1, 267–80.

10. Technically speaking, the First Folio is a 'folio in sixes', by which three sheets of paper, folded once (< < <), were folded and sewn into a single three-sheet, six-page, twelve-sided 'quire' (or 'signature') identified by a letter of the alphabet (e.g. 'C1'), the two sides of which are known as the 'recto' (on the right-hand page of a single page-spread: 'C1r') and the 'verso' (on the

reverse of that page: 'C1v'). The 1623 Folio being a long book, when the letters of the alphabet were exhausted, successive quires used such variants as double-letters and lower-case letters – though each of the Folio's three sections begins a new system. Its Comedies therefore occupy pp. 1–303 (A1r–Cc2r); its Histories pp. 1–232 (a1r–x4v); and the Tragedies pp. 1–399 (aa1r–bbb6r). The late inclusion of *Troilus and Cressida* complicated matters, however; and the pagination of the Tragedies was further thrown by misprinting p. 157 as '257', and so on, for the rest of the book.

11. W.W. Greg, *The Shakespeare First Folio: Its Bibliographical and Textual History* (Oxford, 1955), p. 59.

12. For a full discussion, see *Macbeth*, ed. Brooke, pp. 54–5 and 225–32.

13. 'The devil damn thee black, thou cream-fac'd loon! | Where got'st thou that goose-look?' (5.3, pp. 138–9) becomes 'Now friend, what means thy change of countenance?' (see *Macbeth*, ed. Brooke, pp. 38–9).

14. *Three Jacobean Witchcraft Plays*, ed. Corbin and Sedge, pp. 13–14. Subsequent act- and scene-numbers are to this edition.

15. *Three Jacobean Witchcraft Plays*, ed. Corbin and Sedge, p. 86.

16. The pioneering studies are those of F.P. Wilson, 'Ralph Crane, Scrivener to the King's Players', *The Library* 7 (1927), 194–215; W.W. Greg, 'Some Notes on Crane's Manuscript of *The Witch*', *The Library* 22 (1942), 208–19; and T.H. Howard-Hill, *Ralph Crane and Some Shakespeare First Folio Comedies* (Virginia, 1972). By coincidence (probably), Crane's association with the King's Men also included a series of commissions to prepare at least five transcripts of Shakespeare's plays from which the First Folio typesetters could work.

17. *Three Jacobean Witchcraft Plays*, ed. Corbin and Sedge, p. 14; *The Selected Plays of Thomas Middleton*, ed. David L. Frost (Cambridge, 1978), p. xv; see also notes 26 and 27 below.

18. *Three Jacobean Witchcraft Plays*, ed. Corbin and Sedge, p. 13.

19. See, for example, Samuel Schoenbaum, *William Shakespeare: A Compact Documentary Life* (Oxford, 1977), pp. 264–7.

20. See Schoenbaum, *William Shakespeare*, p. 265, and *The Tempest*, ed. Virginia Mason Vaughan and Alden T. Vaughan (Arden, 1999), pp. 6–9. Of course, the King's Men continued to perform at the Globe, and Shakespeare continued to write with an eye on both venues. Theatrical companies like his had not forgotten their roots, and remained expert in tailoring their productions to new surroundings – for one-off performances at court, for example, or in the country houses and inns of their many provincial tours.

21. *The Witch*, 3.3.

22. *The Witch*, ed. Corbin and Sedge, pp. 3–4.

23. *The Works of Ben Jonson*, ed. C. Herford and P. and E. Simpson, 11 vols (Oxford, 1925–52), 7, 301.

24. The best evidence for this practice is the accounts book (or 'Diary') kept by the theatrical entrepreneur and manager of the Rose, Philip Henslowe, who paid Ben Jonson to write 'additions in *Jeronimo* [probably Kyd's *Spanish Tragedy*]' in September 1601; William Bird and Samuel Rowley for 'their additions in [Marlowe's] *Dr Faustus*' in November 1602; and Thomas Middleton himself to provide a new 'prologue & a epilogue' for a revival of Robert Greene's *Friar Bacon and Friar Bungay* 'at court' that December (*Henslowe's Diary*, ed. R.A. Foakes and R.T. Rickert (Cambridge, 1961), pp. 182, 206, and 207).

25. *Macbeth*, ed. Dover Wilson, pp. xxvii–xviii.

26. Nicholas Brooke argues (in his 1990 edition) that Middleton, fresh from jazzing up *Macbeth* with some original 'Hecate'-songs, may have later developed these ideas into a full-scale play (pp. 65–6).

27. Lawrence, *Shakespeare's Workshop*, p. 25. According to its present website, the forthcoming Oxford edition of Middleton's *Works* negotiates the problem by dating *The Witch* to mid-1616, and his adaptation of *Macbeth* to the Autumn of 1616 – by which dates Shakespeare was dead.

28. Forman actually dated his account Saturday, 20 April 1610, but the thinking is that, since the year used to begin on 25 March, he bungled the year, as we still tend to do when writing cheques in January. (The 20th of April was a Saturday in 1611, but not in 1610.)

29. For a full (modernized) text of Forman's account see *Macbeth*, ed. Brooke, pp. 235–6); for the original spelling, see E.K. Chambers, *William Shakespeare: A Study of Facts and Problems*, 2 vols (Oxford, 1930), 2, 337–8. The Forman manuscript was once suspected of being a forgery, but is now generally accepted as genuine.

30. Shakespeare is unlikely to have seen the woodcut (reproduced at the beginning of Dover Wilson's 1947 edition) since it was left out of the second edition of Holinshed's *Chronicles* he used.

31. As Shakespeare's Chorus to *Henry V* (1.0) requests.

32. The Swiss tourist Thomas Platter recorded visiting 'the straw-thatched house' (the Globe) for a performance of *Julius Caesar* on 21 September 1599; the law-student John Manningham noted in his diary that *Twelfth Night* was performed 'at our feast' in the Middle Temple on 2 February 1602. See *Henry V*, ed. David Daniell (Arden, 1998) and Schoenbaum, *William Shakespeare*, p. 213.

33. The description is from a letter by John Chamberlain dated 5 April 1606, quoted in *Macbeth*, ed. Muir, p. xvi.

34. See *Macbeth*, ed. Braunmuller, p. 5.

35. E.A. Loomis, 'The Master of the *Tiger*', *Shakespeare Quarterly* 7 (1956), 457. The calculation only works, however, if the days upon which the ship set sail and docked in harbour are deducted.

36. For a useful discussion of the similarities between the plays, see *Richard III*, ed. Janis Lull (Cambridge, 1999), pp. 16–19.

37. 'How absolute the knave is! We must speak by the card, or equivocation will undo us' (5.1).

38. 'And this is he that did the *Tiger* board, | When your young nephew Titus lost his leg' (5.1).

39. *Macbeth*, ed. Dover Wilson, pp. xxx–xxxi. See also Leeds Barroll, *Politics, Plague, and Shakespeare's Theater: The Stuart Years* (Cornell University Press, 1995), pp. 147–50. Barroll concludes that the topicalities of 'equivocation' and the flattery of King James are incompatible factors in dating the play (p. 150).

40. *Macbeth*, ed. Dover Wilson, p. xxxi.

41. The central evidence for the theory is that the English troupe was led by Lawrence Fletcher (described as 'comedian to his Majesty'), whose name later appeared in the list of actors formally named in James's patent, dated 17 May 1603, as the King's Men. Indeed, Fletcher heads that list, preceding Shakespeare, Burbage, Augustine Phillips, Heminge, and Condell – though he does not feature among 'The Names of the Principall Actors in all these Playes' printed at the outset of the 1623 Folio. He died in 1608. (See Schoenbaum, *William Shakepeare*, pp. 250–51.)

42. *Henslowe's Diary*, pp. 124 and 199–200; *Kemp's Nine Days Wonder, Performed in a Dance from London to Norwich* (1600), ed. Susan Yaxley (Larks Press, 1997), p. 26.

43. Namely: '(1) the original full-length conception of 1866 preceding the cuts made before the first performance; (2) *Don Carlos* as published in 1867 with five acts and ballet; (3) the Naples version of 1872, identical with (2) except for the alterations in the Posa–Philip and final Carlos–Elisabeth duets; (4) the new four-act version without ballet of 1884; and (5) the Modena amalgam of 1886, published by Ricordi as "new edition in five acts without ballet" ' (Julian Budden, *The Operas of Verdi*, 3, 38–9). The Folio *Macbeth* might be described in these terms as 'the 1616 revival with songs and dance, published in five acts'.

44. Only *The Comedy of Errors* and *The Tempest* are shorter. Of the tragedies, *Titus Andronicus*, *Julius Caesar*, and *Timon of Athens* are marginally longer. The Quarto versions of *Richard III* and *Hamlet* are Shakespeare's longest plays.

45. *The Oxford Companion to Shakespeare*, p. 271.

46. The Folio assigns the speech ('Ay, sir, all this is so') to the First Witch rather than Hecate, though, as Nicholas Brooke points out, it is in Hecate's 'distinctive tone', and – if she indeed remains on stage (see our Textual Note 46 below) – 'once she is there, she becomes in a sense First Witch' and her speech 'probably displaced an original one' (*Macbeth*, ed. Brooke, p. 176).

47. *The Tragedy of Macbeth*, ed. E.K. Chambers (The Warwick Shakespeare, Blackie & Son, 1893), p. 180.

48. Charles Lamb, *Specimens of Early Dramatic Poetry*, quoted by William Hazlitt in his 1817 *Characters of Shakespear's Plays* (Hazlitt, *The Round Table and Characters of Shakespear's Plays* (J.M. Dent & Sons, 1969), p. 194).

49. 1.3 (pp. 12–13), 1.3 (pp. 10–11), 4.1 (pp. 100–101).

50. The director Tyrone Guthrie controversially cut the first scene from his 1934 production of the play (*Macbeth*, ed. Braunmuller, p. 32).

51. *Macbeth*, ed. Chambers, p. 180.

52. J.M. Robertson, *Literary Detection* (George Allen & Unwin, 1931), p. 84.

53. Sceptically quoted in *Macbeth*, ed. Dover Wilson, p. 185.

54. Sceptically quoted in *Macbeth*, ed. Muir, p. xxiii.

55. *Macbeth*, ed. Chambers, p. 184.

56. The theory was advanced by George Saintsbury, endorsed by H.J. Grierson, and modified by John Dover Wilson in his 1947 edition.

57. See *Macbeth*, ed. Brooke, p. 58. The forthcoming and long-awaited Oxford edition of *The Collected Works of Thomas Middleton* promises to shed light on this matter.

58. *Macbeth*, ed. Chambers, p. 183.

59. *The Works of Shakespear. Collated and corrected by the former editions*, ed. Alexander Pope, 6 vols (London, 1723–5), 5, 541; his procedures are explained at 1, xxii: these 'suspected passages', he comments there, 'seem Interpolations by being so inserted that one can intirely omit them without any chasm, or deficience in the context'.

60. 2.2 (pp. 44–5), 2.2 (pp. 46–7), and 4.3 (pp. 128–9); see *The Works of Shakespear*, ed. Pope, Vol. 5, pp. 540, 541 ('no, this my hand will rather | Make the green one red'), and 583.

61. Samuel Taylor Coleridge, '*Macbeth*' (1818), in *Lectures and Notes on Shakespeare*, ed. T. Ashe (George Bell and Sons, 1907), pp. 368 and 377 ('Of the rest not one syllable has the ever-present being of Shakspere').

62. By Samuel Phelps's revivals at Sadler's Wells between 1844 and 1865 (*Macbeth*, ed. Brooke, p. 46).

63. Muir's Arden edition was first published in 1951, but its last edition (1984) is still available. The brilliant consonance of the Porter's lines principally concerns the adaptation it makes from the traditions of the medieval miracle plays (where various devils attend the gates of Hell-mouth: see *Macbeth*, ed. Brooke, pp. 79–81), but Muir's account (pp. xxiii–xxix) of the 'multitudinous antitheses' of its jokes, so characteristic of the play's larger concerns, remains essential reading.

64. *A Night at the Opera* (1935), written by George S. Kaufman and Morrie Ryskind.

65. *Macbeth*, ed. Dover Wilson, pp. xxviii–xxxiii.

66. *Macbeth*, ed. Dover Wilson, p. xxx, n.2.

67. W.W. Greg, *The Editorial Problem in Shakespeare* (Oxford, 1942), p. 147.

68. Greg, *The Editorial Problem*, p. 147; Greg, *The Shakespeare First Folio*, p. 390.
69. See *Macbeth*, ed. Braunmuller, pp. 2–4 and 9.
70. *Macbeth*, ed. Braunmuller, p. 88.
71. On these various problems and more, see, for example, A.C. Bradley, *Shakespearean Tragedy: Lectures on 'Hamlet', 'Othello', 'King Lear', 'Macbeth'* (1904, second edition, 1905, repr. Macmillan, 1988), pp. 413–26; L.C. Knights, 'How Many Children Had Lady Macbeth? An Essay in the Theory and Practice of Shakespeare Criticism' (1933), in his *Explorations* (Chatto & Windus, 1946), pp. 1–39; *Macbeth*, ed. Dover Wilson, pp. xxxiv–xxxix; *Macbeth*, ed. Braunmuller, pp. 88–93; *Macbeth*, ed. Muir, pp. xxi–xxii; John Sutherland and Cedric Watts, *Henry V, War Criminal? and other Shakespeare Puzzles* (Oxford, 2000), pp. 65–8; and see our Textual Notes 28, 29, 37, 45, and 67 below.
72. See *Macbeth*, ed. Braunmuller, p. 66 n.4.
73. *Macbeth*, ed. Dover Wilson, pp. xxxvi–xxxvii. Wilson's argument depends upon the Folio 1.5 having been 'reconstructed', and the device of Lady Macbeth reading her husband's letter originally designed to paper over the cracks of Shakespeare's 1606 overhaul of his play.
74. *Macbeth*, ed. Dover Wilson, p. xxxvii.
75. *Macbeth*, ed. Muir, p. 72, paraphrasing John Dover Wilson.
76. *Macbeth*, ed. Dover Wilson, p. xxxix; John Masefield, *Thanks Before Going, with other gratitude for old delight including a 'Macbeth' Production* (William Heinemann Ltd, 1947), p. 172.
77. As editors of Shakespeare occasionally venture to supply, sometimes via cross-reference to a play's otherwise 'bad' Quarto edition (*Henry V*, 4.3: 'And say he had these scars on Crispin's Day'); sometimes via a play's known sources (*Richard II*, 2.1: 'The son of Richard, Earl of Arundel'. See our Shakespeare Folios edition, pp. 186–7); and sometimes with some inspired guesswork (*Henry V*, 5.0: 'But these now | We pass in silence over'. See our Shakespeare Folios edition, pp. 218–19). Sometimes, however, the wound is simply beyond surgery.
78. The Folio sequence of these scenes have accordingly been rearranged into the playing order 3.4, 4.1, 3.5, 3.6, 4.2 (in a Swedish production in 1880, presumably with cuts: see *Macbeth*, ed. Braunmuller, pp. 261–2), and 3.4, 3.5, 4.1, 3.6, 4.2 (as argued by G. Crosse, 'Spurious Passages in *Macbeth*', *Notes and Queries* 90 (1898), 321–2: see *Macbeth*, ed. Muir, pp. xxxi–xxxii). The confusion might be further minimized if Lennox's part in 3.6 were assigned to another anonymous lord.
79. *The Waste Land: A Facsimile and Transcript of the Original Drafts, Including the Annotations of Ezra Pound*, ed. Valerie Eliot (Faber and Faber, 1971), p. vii.
80. *The Waste Land: A Facsimile*, pp. 4–5.
81. *Macbeth*, ed. Braunmuller, p. 57.

82. 'The simplest explanation I can offer is that Shakespeare and Middleton collaborated on the revision' (*Macbeth*, ed. Brooke, p. 55). The forthcoming Oxford edition of Middleton's Works evidently rejects this view (see note 27 above). Eliot dedicated the published *Waste Land* (1922) to Pound as '*il miglior fabbro*' ('the better craftsman'); Shakespeare is unlikely to have paid the same compliment to Middleton.

83. 'The Macbeth Murder Mystery', in *My World and Welcome to It* (1942), reprinted in *The Thurber Carnival* (Penguin, 1953), pp. 46–9.

84. See our Textual Note 37 below.

85. As Nicola Wright comments, the influence worked both ways, since the whodunnit genre has also 'amused itself with discovering, only in the end to destroy, sundry lost Shakespearean manuscripts' (*The Oxford Companion to Shakespeare*, p. 138). For *Hamlet*'s enduring grip upon the form, look no further than the title of Agatha Christie's play *The Mousetrap*, which opened in London in 1952.

86. F.G. Fleay, 'On Metrical Tests as Applied to Dramatic Poetry' (1874), quoted in Gary Taylor, *Reinventing Shakespeare: A Cultural History from the Restoration to the Present* (Vintage, 1991), p. 166; Sherlock Holmes, quoted in Arthur Conan Doyle, *The Sign of the Four* (1890), ed. Christopher Roden (Oxford, 1993), p. 42.

87. See notes 1 and 52 above, and *Macbeth*, ed. Dover Wilson, pp. xxiii, xxxiii, and xxiv.

88. The trend found a stylish dead end in the 1955 gangster movie *Joe Macbeth* (1955).

89. John Sutherland (re-)tells the story in his *Where Was Rebecca Shot? Puzzles, Curiosities, and Conundrums in Modern Fiction* (Weidenfeld & Nicolson, 1998), p. 42, and then, much against the spirit of the thing, proposes a solution. See also note 71 above.

90. 'The play's the thing | Wherein I'll catch the conscience of the King' (*Hamlet*, 2.2).

91. *Macbeth*, ed. Dover Wilson, p. xxxiv.

92. Henrik Ibsen, *Peer Gynt* (1867), translated by Gerry Bamann and Irene B. Berman (TCG, 1992), p. 203.

93. See above, p. xxxiii.

94. *Macbeth*, ed. Brooke, p. 52.

95. As many as eight (perhaps nine) separate compositors are thought to have worked on typesetting the First Folio. They are known to scholarship by the initial letters A to H (or I), and distinguished by the distinct characteristics of their work. See Peter Blayney's Introduction to the second edition of Hinman's Norton Facsimile (1996), pp. xxxiv–xxxvii.

96. But not in the order in which we read it (*Macbeth*, ed. Braunmuller, p. 250).

97. *Macbeth*, ed. Brooke, p. 50; *Macbeth*, ed. Braunmuller, p. 251.

98. *Macbeth*, ed. Brooke, p. 51.

99. *Macbeth*, ed. Braunmuller, pp. 251–5.

100. Ornithology: *Field Guide to the Birds of Britain and Europe* (AA Publishing, 1998), p. 272. Palaeography: see the sample capital letters 'M' and 'B' reproduced in *Henry V*, ed. T.W. Craik (Arden, 1995), p. 104.

101. *Macbeth: A New Variorum Edition*, ed. H.H. Furness, rev. ed. H.H. Furness junior (Philadelphia, 1915), p. 88.

102. *Macbeth*, ed. Dover Wilson, p. xxii.

103. Nicholas Brooke's 1990 edition provides an evocative list of 'eight distinct forms of dramatic illusion' in the play (pp. 2–6).

104. See, for example, Cleanth Brooks, *The Well Wrought Urn: Studies in the Structure of Poetry* (Reynal & Hitchcock, 1947), pp. 21–46.

105. *Macbeth*, ed. Muir, p. xxviii.

106 See Anne Barton, *Essays, Mainly Shakespearean* (Cambridge, 1994), p. 235.

107. On the play's cues for music and sound-effects, see *Macbeth*, ed. Brooke, p. 36.

108. *The Virgin Film Guide* (8th edition, Virgin, 1999), p. 80.

109. 5.7 (pp. 154–5).

The Actors' Names
In Order of Appearance

Three WITCHES
King DUNCAN *of Scotland*
MALCOLM, *his elder son*
DONALBAIN, *his younger son*
The Thane of LENNOX
A bleeding CAPTAIN *in Duncan's army*
The Thane of ROSS
The Thane of ANGUS
MACBETH, *Thane of Glamis, later of Cawdor, subsequently King*
BANQUO, *later his ghost*
LADY MACBETH, *subsequently Queen*
MACDUFF, *Thane of Fife*
FLEANCE, *son of Banquo*
A PORTER *in Macbeth's castle*
An OLD MAN
Two MURDERERS
A third MURDERER
HECATE, *queen of the witches*
A Scottish LORD
Three other witches
Three APPARITIONS
LADY MACDUFF
SON *to Macduff*
A DOCTOR *to the English court*
A DOCTOR *of Physic to Macbeth's court*
A GENTLEWOMAN-*in-Waiting to Lady Macbeth*
The Thane of MENTEITH
The Thane of CAITHNESS
SEYTON, *servant to Macbeth*
SEYWARD, *Earl of Northumberland*
YOUNG SEYWARD, *his son*

MESSENGERS, SERVANTS, SOLDIERS, *attendants, lords,*
the apparition of eight kings, drums, colours

Macbeth

a parallel text

The Tragedie of Macbeth

The Tragedy of
Macbeth

1.1

Thunder and lightning. Enter three WITCHES

First Witch	When shall we three meet again?
	In thunder, lightning, or in rain?
Second Witch	When the hurly-burly's done,
	When the battle's lost and won.
Third Witch	That will be ere the set of sun.
First Witch	Where the place?
Second Witch	Upon the heath.
Third Witch	There to meet with Macbeth.
First Witch	I come, Graymalkin!
Second Witch	Paddock calls.
Third Witch	Anon!¹
All	Fair is foul, and foul is fair,
	Hover through the fog and filthy air.

Exeunt

1.2

Alarum within. Enter King DUNCAN, MALCOLM,
DONALBAIN, LENNOX, *with attendants,
meeting a bleeding* CAPTAIN

Duncan	What bloody man is that? He can report,
	As seemeth by his plight, of the revolt
	The newest state.

THE TRAGEDIE OF
MACBETH.

Actus Primus. Scœna Prima.

Thunder and Lightning. Enter three Witches.

I. When shall we three meet againe?
In Thunder, Lightning, or in Raine?
2. When the Hurley-burley's done,
When the Battaile's lost, and wonne.
3. That will be ere the set of Sunne.
I. Where the place?
2. Vpon the Heath.
3. There to meet with *Macbeth*.
I. I come, *Gray-Malkin*.
All. Padock calls anon: faire is foule, and foule is faire,
Houer through the fogge and filthie ayre.   *Exeunt.*

Scena Secunda.

*Alarum within. Enter King Malcome, Donal-
baine, Lenox, with attendants, meeting
a bleeding Captaine.*

King. What bloody man is that? he can report,
As seemeth by his plight, of the Reuolt
The newest state.

Malcolm	This is the sergeant
	Who like a good and hardy soldier fought
	'Gainst my captivity. – Hail, brave friend.
	Say to the King the knowledge of the broil
	As thou didst leave it.
Captain	Doubtful it stood,
	As two spent swimmers that do cling together
	And choke their art. The merciless Macdonald –
	Worthy to be a rebel, for to that
	The multiplying villainies of nature
	Do swarm upon him – from the Western Isles
	Of kerns and galloglasses is supplied,
	And Fortune on his damnèd quarry smiling,
	Show'd like a rebel's whore.[2] But all's too weak;
	For brave Macbeth (well he deserves that name),
	Disdaining Fortune, with his brandish'd steel,
	Which smok'd with bloody execution,
	Like Valour's minion carv'd out his passage
	Till he fac'd the slave,
	Which ne'er shook hands nor bade farewell to him
	Till he unseam'd him from the nave to th' chops,
	And fix'd his head upon our battlements.
Duncan	O valiant cousin, worthy gentleman!
Captain	As whence the sun 'gins his reflection,
	Ship-wrecking storms and direful thunders,[3]
	So from that spring whence comfort seem'd to come,
	Discomfort swells. Mark, King of Scotland, mark:
	No sooner justice had, with valour arm'd,
	Compell'd these skipping kerns to trust their heels,
	But the Norwegian lord, surveying vantage,
	With furbish'd arms and new supplies of men
	Began a fresh assault.
Duncan	Dismay'd not this our captains, Macbeth and Banquo?

Mal. This is the Serieant,
Who like a good and hardie Souldier fought
'Gainst my Captiuitie: Haile braue friend;
Say to the King, the knowledge of the Broyle,
As thou didst leaue it.

Cap. Doubtful it stood,
As two spent Swimmers, that doe cling together,
And choake thir Art: The mercilesse *Macdonwald*
(Worthie to be a Rebell, for to that
The multiplying Villanies of Nature
Doe swarme vpon him) from the Westerne Isles
Of Kernes and Gallowgrosses is supply'd,
And Fortune on his damned Quarry smiling,
Shew'd like a Rebells Whore: but all's too weake:
For braue *Macbeth* (well hee deserues that Name)
Disdayning Fortune, with his brandisht Steele,
Which smoak'd with bloody execution
(Like Valours Minion) caru'd out his passage,
Till hee fac'd the Slaue:
Which neu'r shooke hands, nor bad farwell to him,
Till he vnseam'd him from the Naue toth'Chops,
And fix'd his Head vpon our Battlements.

King. O valiant Cousin, worthy Gentleman.

Cap. As whence the Sunne 'gins his reflection,
Shipwracking Stormes, and direfull Thunders:
So from that Spring, whence comfort seem'd to come,
Discomfort swells: Marke King of Scotland, marke,
No sooner Iustice had, with Valour arm'd,
Compell'd these skipping Kernes to trust their heeles,
But the Norweyan Lord, surueying vantage,
With furbusht Armes, and new supplyes of men,
Began a fresh assault.

King. Dismay'd not this our Captaines, *Macbeth* and
Banquoh?

Captain   Yes, as sparrows, eagles, or the hare, the lion.
          If I say sooth, I must report they were
          As cannons over-charg'd with double cracks,
          So they doubly redoubled strokes upon the foe.
          Except they meant to bathe in reeking wounds
          Or memorize another Golgotha,
          I cannot tell –
          But I am faint, my gashes cry for help.
Duncan   So well thy words become thee as thy wounds;
          They smack of honour both. – Go get him surgeons.
                         [*Exit* CAPTAIN, *attended*]⁴
                   Enter ROSS *and* ANGUS
          Who comes here?
Malcolm   The worthy Thane of Ross.
Lennox   What a haste looks through his eyes! So should
                                                   he look
          That seems to speak things strange.
Ross   God save the King!
Duncan   Whence cam'st thou, worthy Thane?
Ross   From Fife, great King,
          Where the Norwegian banners flout the sky
          And fan our people cold.
          Norway himself, with terrible numbers,
          Assisted by that most disloyal traitor,
          The Thane of Cawdor, began a dismal conflict,
          Till that Bellona's bridegroom, lapp'd in proof,
          Confronted him with self-comparisons,
          Point against point, rebellious arm 'gainst arm,
          Curbing his lavish spirit; and to conclude,
          The victory fell on us –
Duncan   Great happiness!
Ross   – that now Sweno,
          The Norways' king, craves composition;
          Nor would we deign him burial of his men
          Till he disbursèd at Saint Colm's inch

 Cap. Yes, as Sparrowes, Eagles;
Or the Hare, the Lyon:
If I say sooth, I must report they were
As Cannons ouer-charg'd with double Cracks,
So they doubly redoubled stroakes vpon the Foe:
Except they meant to bathe in reeking Wounds,
Or memorize another *Golgotha*,
I cannot tell: but I am faint,
My Gashes cry for helpe.
 King. So well thy words become thee, as thy wounds,
They smack of Honor both: Goe get him Surgeons.

Enter Rosse and Angus.

Who comes here?
 Mal. The worthy *Thane* of Rosse.
 Lenox. What a haste lookes through his eyes?
So should he looke, that seemes to speake things strange.
 Rosse. God saue the King.
 King. Whence cam'st thou, worthy *Thane*?
 Rosse. From Fiffe, great King,
Where the Norweyan Banners flowt the Skie,
And fanne our people cold.
Norway himselfe, with terrible numbers,
Assisted by that most disloyall Traytor,
The *Thane* of Cawdor, began a dismall Conflict,
Till that *Bellona's* Bridegroome, lapt in proofe,
Confronted him with selfe-comparisons,
Point against Point, rebellious Arme 'gainst Arme,
Curbing his lauish spirit: and to conclude,
The Victorie fell on vs.
 King. Great happinesse.
 Rosse. That now, *Sweno*, the Norwayes King,
Craues composition:
Nor would we deigne him buriall of his men,
Till he disbursed, at Saint *Colmes* ynch,

	Ten thousand dollars to our general use.
Duncan	No more that Thane of Cawdor shall deceive
	Our bosom interest. Go pronounce his present death,
	And with his former title greet Macbeth.
Ross	I'll see it done.
Duncan	What he hath lost, noble Macbeth hath won.

Exeunt

1.3

Thunder. Enter the three WITCHES

First Witch	Where has thou been, sister?
Second Witch	Killing swine.
Third Witch	Sister, where thou?
First Witch	A sailor's wife had chestnuts in her lap,
	And munch'd, and munch'd, and munch'd. 'Give
	me,' quoth I.
	'Aroint thee, witch!' the rump-fed runnion cries.
	Her husband's to Aleppo gone, master o'th' *Tiger*.
	But in a sieve I'll thither sail,
	And like a rat without a tail
	I'll do, I'll do, and I'll do.
Second Witch	I'll give thee a wind.
First Witch	Thou'rt kind.
Third Witch	And I another.
First Witch	I myself have all the other,
	And the very ports they blow,
	All the quarters that they know
	I'th' shipman's card.
	I'll drain him dry as hay;
	Sleep shall neither night nor day
	Hang upon his penthouse lid;

Ten thousand Dollars, to our generall vse.

   King. No more that *Thane* of Cawdor shall deceiue
Our Bosome interest: Goe pronounce his present death,
And with his former Title greet *Macbeth.*

   Rosse. Ile see it done.

   King. What he hath lost, Noble *Macbeth* hath wonne.

Exeunt.

Scena Tertia.

Thunder. Enter the three Witches.

   1. Where has thou beene, Sister?

   2. Killing Swine.

   3. Sister, where thou?

   1. A Saylors Wife had Chestnuts in her Lappe,
And mouncht, & mouncht, and mouncht:
Giue me, quoth I.
Aroynt thee, Witch, the rumpe-fed Ronyon cryes.
Her Husband's to Aleppo gone, Master o'th'*Tiger*:
But in a Syue Ile thither sayle,
And like a Rat without a tayle,
Ile doe, Ile doe, and Ile doe.

   2. Ile giue thee a Winde.

   1. Th'art kinde.

   3. And I another.

   1. I my selfe haue all the other,
And the very Ports they blow,
All the Quarters that they know,
I'th'Ship-mans Card.
Ile dreyne him drie as Hay:
Sleepe shall neyther Night nor Day
Hang vpon his Pent-house Lid:

	He shall live a man forbid.
	Weary se'nnights, nine times nine,
	Shall he dwindle, peak, and pine.
	Though his bark cannot be lost,
	Yet it shall be tempest-toss'd.
	Look what I have.
Second Witch	Show me, show me.
First Witch	Here I have a pilot's thumb,
	Wreck'd as homeward he did come. *Drum within*
Third Witch	A drum, a drum:
	Macbeth doth come.
All	The weïrd sisters, hand in hand,
	Posters of the sea and land,
	Thus do go about, about,
	Thrice to thine, and thrice to mine,
	And thrice again, to make up nine.
	Peace! The charm's wound up.
	Enter MACBETH *and* BANQUO
Macbeth	So foul and fair a day I have not seen.
Banquo	How far is't call'd to Forres?[5] What are these,
	So wither'd, and so wild in their attire,
	That look not like th'inhabitants o'th'earth
	And yet are on't? – Live you, or are you aught
	That man may question? You seem to understand me,
	By each at once her choppy finger laying
	Upon her skinny lips. You should be women,
	And yet your beards forbid me to interpret
	That you are so.
Macbeth	Speak if you can. What are you?
First Witch	All hail, Macbeth! Hail to thee, Thane of Glamis!
Second Witch	All hail, Macbeth! Hail to thee, Thane of Cawdor!
Third Witch	All hail, Macbeth, that shalt be King hereafter!
Banquo	Good sir, why do you start, and seem to fear

He shall liue a man forbid:
Wearie Seu'nights, nine times nine,
Shall he dwindle, peake, and pine:
Though his Barke cannot be lost,
Yet it shall be Tempest-tost.
Looke what I haue.
   2. Shew me, shew me.
   1. Here I haue a Pilots Thumbe,
Wrackt, as homeward he did come.   *Drum within.*
   3. A Drumme, a Drumme:
Macbeth doth come.
   All. The weyward Sisters, hand in hand,
Posters of the Sea and Land,
Thus doe goe, about, about,
Thrice to thine, and thrice to mine,
And thrice againe, to make vp nine.
Peace, the Charme's wound vp.

Enter Macbeth and Banquo.

   Macb. So foule and faire a day I haue not seene.
   Banquo. How farre is't call'd to Soris? What are these,
So wither'd, and so wilde in their attyre,
That looke not like th'Inhabitants o'th'Earth,
And yet are on't? Liue you, or are you aught
That man may question? you seeme to vnderstand me,
By each at once her choppie finger laying
Vpon her skinnie Lips: you should be Women,
And yet your Beards forbid me to interprete
That you are so.
   Mac. Speake if you can: what are you?
   1. All haile *Macbeth*, haile to thee *Thane* of Glamis.
   2. All haile *Macbeth*, haile to thee *Thane* of Cawdor.
   3. All haile *Macbeth*, that shalt be King hereafter.
   Banq. Good Sir, why doe you start, and seeme to feare

Things that do sound so fair? – I'th' name of truth,
Are ye fantastical or that indeed
Which outwardly ye show? My noble partner
You greet with present grace, and great prediction
Of noble having and of royal hope,
That he seems rapt withal. To me you speak not.
If you can look into the seeds of time,
And say which grain will grow and which will not,
Speak then to me, who neither beg nor fear
Your favours nor your hate.

First Witch	Hail!
Second Witch	Hail!
Third Witch	Hail!
First Witch	Lesser than Macbeth, and greater.
Second Witch	Not so happy, yet much happier.
Third Witch	Thou shalt get kings, though thou be none.
	So all hail, Macbeth and Banquo!
First Witch	Banquo and Macbeth, all hail!
Macbeth	Stay, you imperfect speakers, tell me more.

By Finel's death I know I am Thane of Glamis,[6]
But how of Cawdor? The Thane of Cawdor lives
A prosperous gentleman, and to be king
Stands not within the prospect of belief,
No more than to be Cawdor. Say from whence
You owe this strange intelligence, or why
Upon this blasted heath you stop our way
With such prophetic greeting. Speak, I charge you.

                                        WITCHES *vanish*

Banquo	The earth hath bubbles as the water has,
	And these are of them. Whither are they vanish'd?
Macbeth	Into the air; and what seem'd corporal melted
	As breath into the wind. Would they had stay'd.
Banquo	Were such things here as we do speak about?
	Or have we eaten on the insane root

Things that doe sound so faire? i'th'name of truth
Are ye fantasticall, or that indeed
Which outwardly ye shew? My Noble Partner
You greet with present Grace, and great prediction
Of Noble hauing, and of Royall hope,
That he seemes wrapt withall: to me you speake not.
If you can looke into the Seedes of Time,
And say, which Graine will grow, and which will not,
Speake then to me, who neyther begge, nor feare
Your fauors, nor your hate.
   1. Hayle.
   2. Hayle.
   3. Hayle.
   1. Lesser then *Macbeth*, and greater.
   2. Not so happy, yet much happyer.
   3. Thou shalt get Kings, though thou be none:
So all haile *Macbeth*, and *Banquo*.
   1. *Banquo*, and *Macbeth*, all haile.
   Macb. Stay you imperfect Speakers, tell me more:
By *Sinells* death, I know I am *Thane* of Glamis,
But how, of Cawdor? the *Thane* of Cawdor liues
A prosperous Gentleman: And to be King,
Stands not within the prospect of beleefe,
No more then to be Cawdor. Say from whence
You owe this strange Intelligence, or why
Vpon this blasted Heath you stop our way
With such Prophetique greeting?
Speake, I charge you.   *Witches vanish.*
   Banq. The Earth hath bubbles, as the Water ha's,
And these are of them: whither are they vanish'd?
   Macb. Into the Ayre: and what seem'd corporall,
Melted, as breath into the Winde.
Would they had stay'd.
   Banq. Were such things here, as we doe speake about?
Or haue we eaten on the insane Root,

	That takes the reason prisoner?
Macbeth	Your children shall be kings.
Banquo	You shall be King.
Macbeth	And Thane of Cawdor too; went it not so?
Banquo	To th' self-same tune and words. Who's here?

Enter ROSS *and* ANGUS

Ross	The King hath happily receiv'd, Macbeth,
	The news of thy success, and when he reads
	Thy personal venture in the rebels' fight,[7]
	His wonders and praises do contend
	Which should be thine or his. Silenc'd with that,
	In viewing o'er the rest o'th' self-same day,
	He finds thee in the stout Norwegian ranks,
	Nothing afeard of what thyself didst make,
	Strange images of death. As thick as tale
	Came post with post,[8] and every one did bear
	Thy praises in his kingdom's great defence,
	And pour'd them down before him.
Angus	We are sent
	To give thee from our royal master thanks,
	Only to herald thee into his sight,
	Not pay thee.
Ross	And for an earnest of a greater honour,
	He bade me, from him, call thee Thane of Cawdor,
	In which addition, hail, most worthy Thane,
	For it is thine.
Banquo	What, can the devil speak true?
Macbeth	The Thane of Cawdor lives; why do you dress me
	In borrow'd robes?
Angus	Who was the Thane lives yet,
	But under heavy judgement bears that life
	Which he deserves to lose.
	Whether he was combin'd with those of Norway,

That takes the Reason Prisoner?
   Macb. Your Children shall be Kings.
   Banq. You shall be King.
   Macb. And *Thane* of Cawdor too: went it not so?
   Banq. Toth'selfe-same tunc, and words: who's here?

Enter Rosse and Angus.

   Rosse. The King hath happily receiu'd, *Macbeth*,
The newes of thy successe: and when he reades
Thy personall Venture in the Rebels fight,
His Wonders and Prayses doe contend,
Which should be thine, or his: silenc'd with that,
In viewing o're the rest o'th'selfe-same day,
He findes thee in the stout Norweyan Rankes,
Nothing afeard of what thy selfe didst make
Strange Images of death, as thick as Tale
Can post with post, and euery one did beare
Thy prayses in his Kingdomes great defence,
And powr'd them downe before him.
   Ang. Wee are sent,
To giue thee from our Royall Master thanks,
Onely to harrold thee into his sight,
Not pay thee.
   Rosse. And for an earnest of a greater Honor,
He bad me, from him, call thee *Thane* of Cawdor:
In which addition, haile most worthy *Thane*,
For it is thine.
   Banq. What, can the Deuill speake true?
   Macb. The *Thane* of Cawdor liues:
Why doe you dresse me in borrowed Robes?
   Ang. Who was the *Thane*, liues yet,
But vnder heauie Iudgement beares that Life,
Which he deserues to loose.
Whether he was combin'd with those of Norway,

Or did line the rebel with hidden help
And vantage; or that with both he labour'd
In his country's wrack, I know not.
But treasons capital, confess'd and prov'd,
Have overthrown him.

Macbeth   [*Aside*]   Glamis, and Thane of Cawdor?
The greatest is behind. – Thanks for your pains.
[*To* BANQUO]
Do you not hope your children shall be kings,
When those that gave the Thane of Cawdor to me
Promis'd no less to them?

Banquo   That, trusted home,
Might yet enkindle you unto the crown,
Besides the Thane of Cawdor. But 'tis strange,
And oftentimes, to win us to our harm,
The instruments of darkness tell us truths,
Win us with honest trifles, to betray's
In deepest consequence. –
Cousins, a word, I pray you.

Macbeth   [*Aside*]   Two truths are told
As happy Prologues to the swelling Act
Of the imperial theme. – I thank you, gentlemen.
[*Aside*] This supernatural soliciting
Cannot be ill, cannot be good. If ill,
Why hath it given me earnest of success,
Commencing in a truth? I am Thane of Cawdor.
If good, why do I yield to that suggestion
Whose horrid image doth unfix my hair
And make my seated heart knock at my ribs
Against the use of nature? Present fears
Are less than horrible imaginings.
My thought, whose murder yet is but fantastical,
Shakes so my single state of man that function
Is smother'd in surmise, and nothing is,
But what is not.

Banquo   Look how our partner's rapt.

Or did lyne the Rebell with hidden helpe,
And vantage; or that with both he labour'd
In his Countreyes wracke, I know not:
But Treasons Capitall, confess'd, and prou'd,
Haue ouerthrowne him.
   Macb. Glamys, and *Thane* of Cawdor:
The greatest is behinde. Thankes for your paines.
Doe you not hope your Children shall be Kings,
When those that gaue the *Thane* of Cawdor to me,
Promis'd no lesse to them.
   Banq. That trusted home,
Might yet enkindle you vnto the Crowne,
Besides the *Thane* of Cawdor. But 'tis strange:
And oftentimes, to winne vs to our harme,
The Instruments of Darknesse tell vs Truths,
Winne vs with honest Trifles, to betray's
In deepest consequence.
Cousins, a word, I pray you.
   Macb. Two Truths are told,
As happy Prologues to the swelling Act
Of the Imperiall Theame. I thanke you Gentlemen:
This supernaturall solliciting
Cannot be ill; cannot be good.
If ill? why hath it giuen me earnest of successe,
Commencing in a Truth? I am *Thane* of Cawdor.
If good? why doe I yeeld to that suggestion,
Whose horrid Image doth vnfixe my Heire,
And make my seated Heart knock at my Ribbes,
Against the vse of Nature? Present Feares
Are lesse then horrible Imaginings:
My Thought, whose Murther yet is but fantasticall,
Shakes so my single state of Man,
That Function is smother'd in surmise,
And nothing is, but what is not.
   Banq. Looke how our Partner's rapt.

Macbeth   [*Aside*] If chance will have me King, why chance
                                                    may crown me
            Without my stir.
Banquo   New honours come upon him,
            Like our strange garments, cleave not to their mould
            But with the aid of use.
Macbeth   [*Aside*]   Come what come may,
            Time and the hour runs through the roughest day.
Banquo   Worthy Macbeth, we stay upon your leisure.
Macbeth   Give me your favour. My dull brain was wrought
            With things forgotten. Kind gentlemen, your pains
            Are register'd where every day I turn
            The leaf to read them. Let us toward the King.
            [*To* BANQUO]
            Think upon what hath chanc'd, and at more time,
            The interim having weigh'd it, let us speak
            Our free hearts each to other.
Banquo   Very gladly.
Macbeth   Till then, enough. – Come, friends.   *Exeunt*

1.4

Flourish. Enter King DUNCAN, LENNOX, MALCOLM,
                DONALBAIN, *and attendants*
Duncan   Is execution done on Cawdor, or not
            Those in commission yet return'd?[9]
Malcolm   My liege,
            They are not yet come back. But I have spoke
            With one that saw him die, who did report
            That very frankly he confess'd his treasons,

Macb. If Chance will haue me King,
Why Chance may Crowne me,
Without my stirre.

Banq. New Honors come vpon him
Like our strange Garments, cleaue not to their mould,
But with the aid of vse.

Macb. Come what come may,
Time, and the Houre, runs through the roughest Day.

Banq. Worthy *Macbeth*, wee stay vpon your leysure.

Macb. Giue me your fauour:
My dull Braine was wrought with things forgotten.
Kinde Gentlemen, your paines are registred,
Where euery day I turne the Leafe,
To reade them.
Let vs toward the King: thinke vpon
What hath chanc'd: and at more time,
The *Interim* hauing weigh'd it, let vs speake
Our free Hearts each to other.

Banq. Very gladly.

Macb. Till then enough:
Come friends.   *Exeunt.*

Scena Quarta.

---

*Flourish. Enter King, Lenox, Malcolme,
Donalbaine, and Attendants.*

King. Is execution done on *Cawdor*?
Or not those in Commission yet return'd?

Mal. My Liege, they are not yet come back.
But I haue spoke with one that saw him die:
Who did report, that very frankly hee

Implor'd your highness' pardon, and set forth
A deep repentance. Nothing in his life
Became him like the leaving it. He died
As one that had been studied in his death
To throw away the dearest thing he ow'd
As 'twere a careless trifle.

Duncan   There's no art
To find the mind's construction in the face.
He was a gentleman on whom I built
An absolute trust.

Enter MACBETH, BANQUO, ROSS, *and* ANGUS
                              O worthiest cousin,
The sin of my ingratitude even now
Was heavy on me. Thou art so far before,
That swiftest wing of recompense is slow
To overtake thee. Would thou hadst less deserv'd,
That the proportion both of thanks and payment
Might have been mine. Only I have left to say,
More is thy due than more than all can pay.

Macbeth   The service and the loyalty I owe,
In doing it, pays itself.
Your highness' part is to receive our duties,
And our duties are to your throne and state
Children and servants, which do but what they should
By doing everything safe toward your love
And honour.

Duncan   Welcome hither.
I have begun to plant thee, and will labour
To make thee full of growing. Noble Banquo,
That hast no less deserv'd, nor must be known
No less to have done so, let me enfold thee
And hold thee to my heart.

Banquo   There if I grow,
The harvest is your own.

Confess'd his Treasons, implor'd your Highnesse Pardon,
And set forth a deepe Repentance:
Nothing in his Life became him,
Like the leauing it. Hee dy'de,
As one that had beene studied in his death,
To throw away the dearest thing he ow'd,
As 'twere a carelesse Trifle.
    King. There's no Art,
To finde the Mindes construction in the Face:
He was a Gentleman, on whom I built
An absolute Trust.
                Enter Macbeth, Banquo, Rosse, and Angus.
O worthyest Cousin,
The sinne of my Ingratitude euen now
Was heauie on me. Thou art so farre before,
That swiftest Wing of Recompence is slow,
To ouertake thee. Would thou hadst lesse deseru'd,
That the proportion both of thanks, and payment,
Might haue beene mine: onely I haue left to say,
More is thy due, then more then all can pay.
    Macb. The seruice, and the loyaltie I owe,
In doing it, payes it selfe.
Your Highnesse part, is to receiue our Duties:
And our Duties are to your Throne, and State,
Children, and Seruants; which doe but what they should,
By doing euery thing safe toward your Loue
And Honor.
    King. Welcome hither:
I haue begun to plant thee, and will labour
To make thee full of growing. Noble *Banquo*,
That hast no lesse deseru'd, nor must be knowne
No lesse to haue done so: Let me enfold thee,
And hold thee to my Heart.
    Banq. There if I grow,
The Haruest is your owne.

Duncan	My plenteous joys,
	Wanton in fullness, seek to hide themselves
	In drops of sorrow. Sons, kinsmen, thanes,
	And you whose places are the nearest, know
	We will establish our estate upon
	Our eldest, Malcolm, whom we name hereafter
	The Prince of Cumberland; which honour must
	Not unaccompanied invest him only,
	But signs of nobleness, like stars, shall shine
	On all deservers. From hence to Inverness,
	And bind us further to you.
Macbeth	The rest is labour, which is not us'd for you.
	I'll be myself the harbinger, and make joyful
	The hearing of my wife with your approach;
	So humbly take my leave.
Duncan	My worthy Cawdor.
Macbeth	[*Aside*] The Prince of Cumberland? That is a step
	On which I must fall down, or else o'er-leap,
	For in my way it lies. Stars, hide your fires,
	Let not light see my black and deep desires,
	The eye wink at the hand; yet let that be
	Which the eye fears, when it is done, to see. *Exit*
Duncan	True, worthy Banquo, he is full so valiant,
	And in his commendations I am fed;
	It is a banquet to me. Let's after him,
	Whose care is gone before to bid us welcome.
	It is a peerless kinsman. *Flourish. Exeunt*

King. My plenteous Ioyes,
Wanton in fulnesse, seeke to hide themselues
In drops of sorrow. Sonnes, Kinsmen, *Thanes*,
And you whose places are the nearest, know,
We will establish our Estate vpon
Our eldest, *Malcolme*, whom we name hereafter,
The Prince of Cumberland: which Honor must
Not vnaccompanied, inuest him onely,
But signes of Noblenesse, like Starres, shall shine
On all deseruers. From hence to Envernes,
And binde vs further to you.
    Macb. The Rest is Labor, which is not vs'd for you:
Ile be my selfe the Herbenger, and make ioyfull
The hearing of my Wife, with your approach:
So humbly take my leaue.
    King. My worthy *Cawdor.*
    Macb. The Prince of Cumberland: that is a step,
On which I must fall downe, or else o're-leape,
For in my way it lyes. Starres hide your fires,
Let not Light see my black and deepe desires:
The Eye winke at the Hand; yet let that bee,
Which the Eye feares, when it is done to see.   *Exit.*
    King. True, worthy *Banquo*: he is full so valiant,
And in his commendations, I am fed:
It is a Banquet to me. Let's after him,
Whose care is gone before, to bid vs welcome:
It is a peerelesse Kinsman.   *Flourish.*   *Exeunt.*

Enter LADY MACBETH *alone with a letter*

Lady Macbeth   [*Reads*] 'They met me in the day of success, and
I have learned by the perfectest report, they have
more in them than mortal knowledge. When
I burned in desire to question them further, they
made themselves air, into which they vanished.
Whiles I stood rapt in the wonder of it came
missives from the King, who all-hailed me Thane
of Cawdor, by which title before these weïrd sisters
saluted me, and referred me to the coming on
of time, with "Hail, King that shalt be!" This
have I thought good to deliver thee, my dearest
partner of greatness, that thou mightst not lose
the dues of rejoicing by being ignorant of what
greatness is promised thee. Lay it to thy heart,
and farewell.'
Glamis thou art, and Cawdor, and shalt be
What thou art promis'd; yet do I fear thy nature.
It is too full o'th' milk of human kindness
To catch the nearest way. Thou wouldst be great,
Art not without ambition, but without
The illness should attend it. What thou wouldst
                           highly,
That wouldst thou holily; wouldst not play false,
And yet wouldst wrongly win. Thou'dst have, great
                           Glamis,
That which cries, 'Thus thou must do,' if thou have it,
And that which rather thou dost fear to do
Than wishest should be undone. Hie thee hither,
That I may pour my spirits in thine ear,
And chastise with the valour of my tongue
All that impedes thee from the golden round
Which fate and metaphysical aid doth seem
To have thee crown'd withal.
           Enter MESSENGER

Scena Quinta.

Enter Macbeths Wife alone with a Letter.

Lady. *They met me in the day of successe: and I haue learn'd by the perfect'st report, they haue more in them, then mortall knowledge. When I burnt in desire to question them further, they made themselues Ayre, into which they vanish'd. Whiles I stood rapt in the wonder of it, came Missiues from the King, who all-hail'd me* Thane *of* Cawdor, *by which Title before, these weyward Sisters saluted me, and referr'd me to the comming on of time, with haile King that shalt be. This haue I thought good to deliuer thee (my dearest Partner of Greatnesse) that thou might'st not loose the dues of reioycing by being ignorant of what Greatnesse is promis'd thee. Lay it to thy heart, and farewell.*

Glamys thou art, and Cawdor, and shalt be
What thou art promis'd: yet doe I feare thy Nature,
It is too full o'th' Milke of humane kindnesse,
To catch the neerest way. Thou would'st be great,
Art not without Ambition, but without
The illnesse should attend it. What thou would'st highly,
That would'st thou holily: would'st not play false,
And yet would'st wrongly winne.
Thould'st haue, great Glamys, that which cryes,
Thus thou must doe, if thou haue it;
And that which rather thou do'st feare to doe,
Then wishest should be vndone. High thee hither,
That I may powre my Spirits in thine Eare,
And chastise with the valour of my Tongue
All that impeides thee from the Golden Round,
Which Fate and Metaphysicall ayde doth seeme
To haue thee crown'd withall.   *Enter Messenger.*

	What is your tidings?
Messenger	The King comes here tonight.
Lady Macbeth	Thou'rt mad to say it.

Is not thy master with him, who, were't so,
Would have inform'd for preparation?

Messenger So please you, it is true; our Thane is coming.
One of my fellows had the speed of him,
Who, almost dead for breath, had scarcely more
Than would make up his message.

Lady Macbeth   Give him tending,
He brings great news.   *Exit* MESSENGER
                            The raven himself is hoarse
That croaks the fatal entrance of Duncan
Under my battlements. Come, you spirits
That tend on mortal thoughts, unsex me here,
And fill me from the crown to the toe top-full
Of direst cruelty. Make thick my blood,
Stop up th'access and passage to remorse,
That no compunctious visitings of nature
Shake my fell purpose, nor keep peace between
Th'effect and it.[10] Come to my woman's breasts,
And take my milk for gall, you murdering ministers,
Wherever in your sightless substances
You wait on nature's mischief. Come, thick night,
And pall thee in the dunnest smoke of hell,
That my keen knife see not the wound it makes,
Nor heaven peep through the blanket of the dark
To cry, 'Hold, hold!'
                    Enter MACBETH
                        Great Glamis, worthy Cawdor,
Greater than both by the all-hail hereafter,
Thy letters have transported me beyond
This ignorant present, and I feel now
The future in the instant.

Macbeth   My dearest love,
Duncan comes here tonight.

What is your tidings?

   Mess. The King comes here to Night.

   Lady. Thou'rt mad to say it.

Is not thy Master with him? who, wer't so,

Would haue inform'd for preparation.

   Mess. So please you, it is true: our *Thane* is comming:

One of my fellowes had the speed of him;

Who almost dead for breath, had scarcely more

Then would make vp his Message.

   Lady. Giue him tending,

He brings great newes.   *Exit Messenger.*

The Rauen himselfe is hoarse,

That croakes the fatall entrance of *Duncan*

Vnder my Battlements. Come you Spirits,

That tend on mortall thoughts, vnsex me here,

And fill me from the Crowne to the Toe, top-full

Of direst Crueltie: make thick my blood,

Stop vp th'accesse, and passage to Remorse,

That no compunctious visitings of Nature

Shake my fell purpose, nor keepe peace betweene

Th'effect, and hit. Come to my Womans Brests,

And take my Milke for Gall, you murth'ring Ministers,

Where-euer, in your sightlesse substances,

You wait on Natures Mischiefe. Come thick Night,

And pall thee in the dunnest smoake of Hell,

That my keene Knife see not the Wound it makes,

Nor Heauen peepe through the Blanket of the darke,

To cry, hold, hold.   *Enter Macbeth.*

Great Glamys, worthy Cawdor,

Greater then both, by the all-haile hereafter,

Thy Letters haue transported me beyond

This ignorant present, and I feele now

The future in the instant.

   Macb. My dearest Loue,

Duncan comes here to Night.

Lady Macbeth	And when goes hence?
Macbeth	Tomorrow, as he purposes.
Lady Macbeth	O never

Shall sun that morrow see!
Your face, my Thane, is as a book where men
May read strange matters to beguile the time.
Look like the time:[11] bear welcome in your eye,
Your hand, your tongue; look like th'innocent flower,
But be the serpent under't. He that's coming
Must be provided for, and you shall put
This night's great business into my dispatch,
Which shall to all our nights and days to come
Give solely sovereign sway and masterdom.

Macbeth We will speak further.

Lady Macbeth Only look up clear;
To alter favour ever is to fear.
Leave all the rest to me.   *Exeunt*

1.6

Hautboys and torches.[12] *Enter King* DUNCAN,
MALCOLM, DONALBAIN, BANQUO, LENNOX,
MACDUFF, ROSS, ANGUS, *and attendants*

Duncan This castle hath a pleasant seat; the air
Nimbly and sweetly recommends itself
Unto our gentle senses.

Banquo This guest of summer,
The temple-haunting martlet, does approve,
By his lov'd masonry,[13] that the heavens' breath
Smells wooingly here. No jutty, frieze,
Buttress, nor coign of vantage, but this bird
Hath made his pendant bed and procreant cradle;
Where they must breed and haunt, I have observ'd,

Lady. And when goes hence?

Macb. To morrow, as he purposes.

Lady. O neuer,

Shall Sunne that Morrow see.

Your Face, my *Thane*, is as a Booke, where men

May reade strange matters, to beguile the time.

Looke like the time, beare welcome in your Eye,

Your Hand, your Tongue: looke like th'innocent flower,

But be the Serpent vnder't. He that's comming,

Must be prouided for: and you shall put

This Nights great Businesse into my dispatch,

Which shall to all our Nights, and Dayes to come,

Giue solely soueraigne sway, and Masterdome.

Macb. We will speake further.

Lady. Onely looke vp cleare:

To alter fauor, euer is to feare:

Leaue all the rest to me.   *Exeunt.*

Scena Sexta.

Hoboyes, and Torches. Enter King, Malcolme,
Donalbaine, Banquo, Lenox, Macduff,
Rosse, Angus, and Attendants.

King. This Castle hath a pleasant seat,

The ayre nimbly and sweetly recommends it selfe

Vnto our gentle sences.

Banq. This Guest of Summer,

The Temple-haunting Barlet does approue,

By his loued Mansonry, that the Heauens breath

Smells wooingly here: no Iutty frieze,

Buttrice, nor Coigne of Vantage, but this Bird

Hath made his pendant Bed, and procreant Cradle,

Where they must breed, and haunt: I haue obseru'd

The air is delicate.

Enter LADY MACBETH

Duncan   See, see, our honour'd hostess.
The love that follows us sometime is our trouble,
Which still we thank as love. Herein I teach you
How you shall bid God 'ield us for your pains,
And thank us for your trouble.

Lady Macbeth   All our service,
In every point twice done and then done double,
Were poor and single business to contend
Against those honours deep and broad wherewith
Your majesty loads our house. For those of old,
And the late dignities heap'd up to them,
We rest your hermits.

Duncan   Where's the Thane of Cawdor?
We cours'd him at the heels, and had a purpose
To be his purveyor; but he rides well,
And his great love, sharp as his spur, hath holp him
To his home before us. Fair and noble hostess,
We are your guest tonight.

Lady Macbeth   Your servants ever
Have theirs, themselves, and what is theirs in count
To make their audit at your highness' pleasure,
Still to return your own.

Duncan   Give me your hand.
Conduct me to mine host. We love him highly,
And shall continue our graces towards him.
By your leave, hostess.   *Exeunt*

The ayre is delicate.   *Enter Lady.*

    King. See, see, our honor'd Hostesse:
The Loue that followes vs, sometime is our trouble,
Which still we thanke as Loue. Herein I teach you,
How you shall bid God-eyld vs for your paines,
And thanke vs for your trouble.

    Lady. All our seruice,
In euery point twice done, and then done double,
Were poore, and single Businesse, to contend
Against those Honors deepe, and broad,
Wherewith your Maiestie loades our House:
For those of old, and the late Dignities,
Heap'd vp to them, we rest your Ermites.

    King. Where's the Thane of Cawdor?
We courst him at the heeles, and had a purpose
To be his Purueyor: But he rides well,
And his great Loue (sharpe as his Spurre) hath holp him
To his home before vs: Faire and Noble Hostesse
We are your guest to night.

    La. Your Seruants euer,
Haue theirs, themselues, and what is theirs in compt,
To make their Audit at your Highnesse pleasure,
Still to returne your owne.

    King. Giue me your hand:
Conduct me to mine Host we loue him highly,
And shall continue, our Graces towards him.
By your leaue Hostesse.   *Exeunt*

1.7

Hautboys. Torches. Enter a sewer and divers servants
with dishes and service over the stage [and exeunt]
Then enter MACBETH

Macbeth   If it were done when 'tis done, then 'twere well
It were done quickly. If th'assassination
Could trammel up the consequence, and catch
With his surcease, success; that but this blow
Might be the be-all and the end-all, here,
But here, upon this bank and school of time,14
We'd jump the life to come. But in these cases,
We still have judgement here, that we but teach
Bloody instructions which, being taught, return
To plague th'inventor. This even-handed justice
Commends th'ingredience of our poison'd chalice
To our own lips. He's here in double trust:
First, as I am his kinsman and his subject,
Strong both against the deed; then, as his host,
Who should against his murderer shut the door,
Not bear the knife myself. Besides, this Duncan
Hath borne his faculties so meek, hath been
So clear in his great office, that his virtues
Will plead like angels, trumpet-tongued against
The deep damnation of his taking-off;
And Pity, like a naked new-born babe
Striding the blast, or heaven's cherubim, hors'd
Upon the sightless couriers of the air,
Shall blow the horrid deed in every eye,
That tears shall drown the wind. I have no spur
To prick the sides of my intent, but only
Vaulting ambition, which o'er-leaps itself
And falls on th'other.
                    Enter LADY MACBETH

Scena Septima.

Ho-boyes.   Torches.
Enter a Sewer, and diuers Seruants with Dishes and Seruice
ouer the Stage. Then enter Macbeth.

Macb. If it were done, when 'tis done, then 'twer well,
It were done quickly: If th'Assassination
Could trammell vp the Consequence, and catch
With his surcease, Successe: that but this blow
Might be the be all, and the end all. Heere,
But heere, vpon this Banke and Schoole of time,
Wee'ld iumpe the life to come. But in these Cases,
We still haue iudgement heere, that we but teach
Bloody Instructions, which being taught, returne
To plague th'Inuenter, This euen-handed Iustice
Commends th'Ingredience of our poyson'd Challice
To our owne lips. Hee's heere in double trust;
First, as I am his Kinsman, and his Subiect,
Strong both against the Deed: Then, as his Host,
Who should against his Murtherer shut the doore,
Not beare the knife my selfe. Besides, this *Duncane*
Hath borne his Faculties so meeke; hath bin
So cleere in his great Office, that his Vertues
Will pleade like Angels, Trumpet-tongu'd against
The deepe damnation of his taking off:
And Pitty, like a naked New-borne-Babe,
Striding the blast, or Heauens Chrubin, hors'd
Vpon the sightlesse Curriors of the Ayre,
Shall blow the horrid deed in euery eye,
That teares shall drowne the winde. I haue no Spurre
To pricke the sides of my intent, but onely
Vaulting Ambition, which ore-leapes it selfe,
And falles on th'other.   *Enter Lady.*

	How now? What news?
Lady Macbeth	He has almost supp'd. Why have you left the chamber?
Macbeth	Hath he ask'd for me?
Lady Macbeth	Know you not he has?
Macbeth	We will proceed no further in this business.

He hath honour'd me of late, and I have bought
Golden opinions from all sorts of people,
Which would be worn now in their newest gloss,
Not cast aside so soon.

Lady Macbeth   Was the hope drunk
Wherein you dress'd yourself? Hath it slept since?
And wakes it now to look so green and pale
At what it did so freely? From this time,
Such I account thy love. Art thou afeard
To be the same in thine own act and valour
As thou art in desire? Wouldst thou have that
Which thou esteem'st the ornament of life,
And live a coward in thine own esteem,
Letting 'I dare not' wait upon 'I would',
Like the poor cat i'th'adage?

Macbeth   Prithee, peace.
I dare do all that may become a man;
Who dares do more is none.[15]

Lady Macbeth   What beast was't then
That made you break this enterprise to me?
When you durst do it, then you were a man;
And to be more than what you were, you would
Be so much more the man. Nor time nor place
Did then adhere, and yet you would make both.
They have made themselves, and that their fitness now
Does unmake you. I have given suck, and know
How tender 'tis to love the babe that milks me.
I would, while it was smiling in my face,
Have pluck'd my nipple from his boneless gums

How now? What Newes?

    La. He has almost supt: why haue you left the chamber?

    Mac. Hath he ask'd for me?

    La. Know you not, he ha's?

    Mac. We will proceed no further in this Businesse:

He hath Honour'd me of late, and I haue bought

Golden Opinions from all sorts of people,

Which would be worne now in their newest glosse,

Not cast aside so soone.

    La. Was the hope drunke,

Wherein you drest your selfe? Hath it slept since?

And wakes it now to looke so greene, and pale,

At what it did so freely? From this time,

Such I account thy loue. Art thou affear'd

To be the same in thine owne Act, and Valour,

As thou art in desire? Would'st thou haue that

Which thou esteem'st the Ornament of Life,

And liue a Coward in thine owne Esteeme?

Letting I dare not, wait vpon I would,

Like the poore Cat i'th'Addage.

    Macb. Prythee peace:

I dare do all that may become a man,

Who dares no more, is none.

    La. What Beast was't then

That made you breake this enterprize to me?

When you durst do it, then you were a man:

And to be more then what you were, you would

Be so much more the man. Nor time, nor place

Did then adhere, and yet you would make both:

They haue made themselues, and that their fitnesse now

Do's vnmake you. I haue giuen Sucke, and know

How tender 'tis to loue the Babe that milkes me,

I would, while it was smyling in my Face,

Haue pluckt my Nipple from his Bonelesse Gummes,

                    And dash'd the brains out, had I so sworn
                    As you have done to this.

Macbeth   If we should fail?

Lady Macbeth   We fail!¹⁶

                    But screw your courage to the sticking-place,
                    And we'll not fail. When Duncan is asleep –
                    Whereto the rather shall his day's hard journey
                    Soundly invite him – his two chamberlains
                    Will I with wine and wassail so convince
                    That memory, the warder of the brain,
                    Shall be a fume, and the receipt of reason
                    A limbeck only; when in swinish sleep
                    Their drenchèd natures lies as in a death,
                    What cannot you and I perform upon
                    Th'unguarded Duncan? What not put upon
                    His spongy officers, who shall bear the guilt
                    Of our great quell?

Macbeth   Bring forth men-children only,
                    For thy undaunted mettle should compose
                    Nothing but males. Will it not be receiv'd,
                    When we have mark'd with blood those sleepy two
                    Of his own chamber, and us'd their very daggers,
                    That they have done't?

Lady Macbeth   Who dares receive it other,
                    As we shall make our griefs and clamour roar
                    Upon his death?

Macbeth   I am settled, and bend up
                    Each corporal agent to this terrible feat.
                    Away, and mock the time with fairest show:
                    False face must hide what the false heart doth know.

                                                        Exeunt

And dasht the Braines out, had I so sworne
As you haue done to this.

    Macb. If we should faile?

    Lady. We faile?
But screw your courage to the sticking place,
And wee'le not fayle: when *Duncan* is asleepe,
(Whereto the rather shall his dayes hard Iourney
Soundly inuite him) his two Chamberlaines
Will I with Wine, and Wassell, so conuince,
That Memorie, the Warder of the Braine,
Shall be a Fume, and the Receit of Reason
A Lymbeck onely: when in Swinish sleepe,
Their drenched Natures lyes as in a Death,
What cannot you and I performe vpon
Th'vnguarded *Duncan*? What not put vpon
His spungie Officers? who shall beare the guilt
Of our great quell.

    Macb. Bring forth Men-Children onely:
For thy vndaunted Mettle should compose
Nothing but Males. Will it not be receiu'd,
When we haue mark'd with blood those sleepie two
Of his owne Chamber, and vs'd their very Daggers,
That they haue don't?

    Lady. Who dares receiue it other,
As we shall make our Griefes and Clamor rore,
Vpon his Death?

    Macb. I am settled, and bend vp
Each corporall Agent to this terrible Feat.
Away, and mock the time with fairest show,
False Face must hide what the false Heart doth know.

                               Exeunt.

2.1

Enter BANQUO *and* FLEANCE, *with a torch before him* [17]

Banquo	How goes the night, boy?
Fleance	The moon is down. I have not heard the clock.
Banquo	And she goes down at twelve.
Fleance	I take't 'tis later, sir.
Banquo	Hold, take my sword. There's husbandry in heaven,

Their candles are all out. Take thee that, too.
A heavy summons lies like lead upon me,
And yet I would not sleep. Merciful powers,
Restrain in me the cursèd thoughts that nature
Gives way to in repose.

Enter MACBETH *and a servant with a torch*

                       Give me my sword. –
Who's there?

Macbeth	A friend.
Banquo	What, sir, not yet at rest? The King's abed.

He hath been in unusual pleasure, and
Sent forth great largesse to your offices.
This diamond he greets your wife withal
By the name of 'most kind hostess', and shut up
In measureless content.

Macbeth   Being unprepar'd,
Our will became the servant to defect,
Which else should free have wrought.

Banquo   All's well.
I dreamt last night of the three weïrd sisters.
To you they have show'd some truth.

Macbeth   I think not of them;

Actus Secundus. Scena Prima.

Enter Banquo, and Fleance, with a Torch
before him.

Banq. How goes the Night, Boy?

Fleance. The Moone is downe: I haue not heard the Clock.

Banq. And she goes down at Twelue.

Fleance. I take't, 'tis later, Sir.

Banq. Hold, take my Sword:
There's Husbandry in Heauen,
Their Candles are all out: take thee that too.
A heauie Summons lyes like Lead vpon me,
And yet I would not sleepe:
Mercifull Powers, restraine in me the cursed thoughts
That Nature giues way to in repose.

Enter Macbeth, and a Seruant with a Torch.

Giue me my Sword: who's there?

Macb. A Friend.

Banq. What Sir, not yet at rest? the King's a bed.
He hath beene in vnusuall Pleasure,
And sent forth great Largesse to your Offices.
This Diamond he greetes your Wife withall,
By the name of most kind Hostesse,
And shut vp in measurelesse content.

Mac. Being vnprepar'd,
Our will became the seruant to defect,
Which else should free haue wrought.

Banq. All's well.
I dreamt last Night of the three weyward Sisters:
To you they haue shew'd some truth.

Macb. I thinke not of them:

Yet when we can entreat an hour to serve,
We would spend it in some words upon that business,
If you would grant the time.

Banquo   At your kind'st leisure.
Macbeth   If you shall cleave to my consent, when 'tis,
It shall make honour for you.

Banquo   So I lose none
In seeking to augment it, but still keep
My bosom franchis'd and allegiance clear,
I shall be counsell'd.

Macbeth   Good repose the while.
Banquo   Thanks, sir. The like to you.

                    Exeunt BANQUO [*and* FLEANCE]

Macbeth   Go bid thy mistress, when my drink is ready,
She strike upon the bell. Get thee to bed.

                                    Exit [SERVANT]

Is this a dagger which I see before me,
The handle toward my hand?

                                    Come, let me clutch thee!
I have thee not, and yet I see thee still.
Art thou not, fatal vision, sensible
To feeling as to sight? Or art thou but
A dagger of the mind, a false creation
Proceeding from the heat-oppressèd brain?
I see thee yet, in form as palpable
As this which now I draw.
Thou marshall'st me the way that I was going,
And such an instrument I was to use.
Mine eyes are made the fools o'th'other senses,
Or else worth all the rest. I see thee still,
And on thy blade and dudgeon gouts of blood,
Which was not so before. There's no such thing.
It is the bloody business which informs
Thus to mine eyes. Now o'er the one half-world
Nature seems dead, and wicked dreams abuse
The curtain'd sleep. Witchcraft celebrates

Yet when we can entreat an houre to serue,
We would spend it in some words vpon that Businesse,
If you would graunt the time.

    Banq. At your kind'st leysure.

    Macb. If you shall cleaue to my consent,
When 'tis, it shall make Honor for you.

    Banq. So I lose none,
In seeking to augment it, but still keepe
My Bosome franchis'd, and Allegeance cleare,
I shall be counsail'd.

    Macb. Good repose the while.

    Banq. Thankes Sir: the like to you.   *Exit Banquo.*

    Macb. Goe bid thy Mistresse, when my drinke is ready,
She strike vpon the Bell. Get thee to bed.   *Exit.*
Is this a Dagger, which I see before me,
The Handle toward my Hand? Come, let me clutch thee:
I haue thee not, and yet I see thee still.
Art thou not fatall Vision, sensible
To feeling, as to sight? or art thou but
A Dagger of the Minde, a false Creation,
Proceeding from the heat-oppressed Braine?
I see thee yet, in forme as palpable,
As this which now I draw.
Thou marshall'st me the way that I was going,
And such an Instrument I was to vse.
Mine Eyes are made the fooles o'th'other Sences,
Or else worth all the rest: I see thee still;
And on thy Blade, and Dudgeon, Gouts of Blood,
Which was not so before. There's no such thing:
It is the bloody Businesse, which informes
Thus to mine Eyes. Now o're the one halfe World
Nature seemes dead, and wicked Dreames abuse
The Curtain'd sleepe: Witchcraft celebrates

Pale Hecate's offerings, and wither'd Murder,
Alarum'd by his sentinel, the wolf,
Whose howl's his watch, thus with his stealthy pace,
With Tarquin's ravishing strides, towards his design
Moves like a ghost.[18] Thou sure and firm-set earth,
Hear not my steps, which way they walk, for fear
Thy very stones prate of my whereabout,[19]
And take the present horror from the time,
Which now suits with it. Whiles I threat, he lives:
Words to the heat of deeds too cold breath gives.

                                        A bell rings

I go, and it is done. The bell invites me.
Hear it not, Duncan, for it is a knell
That summons thee to heaven or to hell.   *Exit*

2.2

                    Enter LADY MACBETH
Lady Macbeth That which hath made them drunk hath
                                        made me bold;
            What hath quench'd them hath given me fire.
                                        Hark, peace!
            It was the owl that shriek'd, the fatal bell-man
            Which gives the stern'st good-night. He is about it.
            The doors are open, and the surfeited grooms
            Do mock their charge with snores. I have drugg'd
                                        their possets,
            That Death and Nature do contend about them
            Whether they live or die.
            Enter MACBETH [*with two daggers*] [20]
Macbeth   Who's there? What, ho?
Lady Macbeth Alack, I am afraid they have awak'd,
            And 'tis not done. Th'attempt and not the deed
            Confounds us. Hark! I laid their daggers ready,
            He could not miss 'em. Had he not resembled

Pale *Heccats* Offrings: and wither'd Murther,
Alarum'd by his Centinell, the Wolfe,
Whose howle's his Watch, thus with his stealthy pace,
With *Tarquins* rauishing sides, towards his designe
Moues like a Ghost. Thou sowre and firme-set Earth
Heare not my steps, which they may walke, for feare
Thy very stones prate of my where-about,
And take the present horror from the time,
Which now sutes with it. Whiles I threat, he liues:
Words to the heat of deedes too cold breath giues.
                    A Bell rings.
I goe, and it is done: the Bell inuites me.
Heare it not, *Duncan*, for it is a Knell,
That summons thee to Heauen, or to Hell.   *Exit.*

Scena Secunda.

Enter Lady.
La. That which hath made thē drunk, hath made me bold:
What hath quench'd them, hath giuen me fire.
Hearke, peace: it was the Owle that shriek'd,
The fatall Bell-man, which giues the stern'st good-night.
He is about it, the Doores are open:
And the surfeted Groomes doe mock their charge
With Snores. I haue drugg'd their Possets,
That Death and Nature doe contend about them,
Whether they liue, or dye.
                    Enter Macbeth.
  Macb. Who's there? what hoa?
  Lady. Alack, I am afraid they haue awak'd,
And 'tis not done: th'attempt, and not the deed,
Confounds vs: hearke: I lay'd their Daggers ready,
He could not misse 'em. Had he not resembled

	My father as he slept, I had done't. – My husband?
Macbeth	I have done the deed. Didst thou not hear a noise?
Lady Macbeth	I heard the owl scream, and the crickets cry.
	Did not you speak?

Macbeth   When?

Lady Macbeth   Now.

Macbeth   As I descended?

Lady Macbeth Ay.

Macbeth   Hark! Who lies i'th' second chamber?

Lady Macbeth Donalbain.

Macbeth   This is a sorry sight.

Lady Macbeth A foolish thought to say a sorry sight.

Macbeth   There's one did laugh in's sleep,
                                           and one cried 'Murder!'
That they did wake each other.
                              I stood, and heard them,
But they did say their prayers, and address'd them
Again to sleep.

Lady Macbeth   There are two lodg'd together.

Macbeth   One cried 'God bless us!' and 'Amen!' the other,
As they had seen me with these hangman's hands.
Listening their fear, I could not say 'Amen'
When they did say 'God bless us!'

Lady Macbeth Consider it not so deeply.

Macbeth   But wherefore could not I pronounce 'Amen'?
I had most need of blessing, and 'Amen'
Stuck in my throat.

Lady Macbeth   These deeds must not be thought
After these ways. So, it will make us mad.

Macbeth   Methought I heard a voice cry, 'Sleep no more!
Macbeth does murder sleep!' – the innocent sleep,
Sleep that knits up the ravell'd sleeve of care,
The death of each day's life, sore labour's bath,
Balm of hurt minds, great nature's second course,
Chief nourisher in life's feast –

My Father as he slept, I had don't.
My Husband?
    Macb. I haue done the deed:
Didst thou not heare a noyse?
    Lady. I heard the Owle schreame, and the Crickets cry.
Did not you speake?
    Macb. When?
    Lady. Now.
    Macb. As I descended?
    Lady. I.
    Macb. Hearke, who lyes i'th'second Chamber?
    Lady. Donalbaine.
    Mac. This is a sorry sight.
    Lady. A foolish thought, to say a sorry sight.
    Macb. There's one did laugh in's sleepe,
And one cry'd Murther, that they did wake each other:
I stood, and heard them: But they did say their Prayers,
And addrest them againe to sleepe.
    Lady. There are two lodg'd together.
    Macb. One cry'd God blesse vs, and Amen the other,
As they had seene me with these Hangmans hands:
Listning their feare, I could not say Amen,
When they did say God blesse vs.
    Lady. Consider it not so deepely.
    Mac. But wherefore could not I pronounce Amen?
I had most need of Blessing, and Amen stuck in my throat.
    Lady. These deeds must not be thought
After these wayes: so, it will make vs mad.
    Macb. Me thought I heard a voyce cry, Sleep no more:
Macbeth does murther Sleepe, the innocent Sleepe,
Sleepe that knits vp the rauel'd Sleeue of Care,
The death of each dayes Life, sore Labors Bath,
Balme of hurt Mindes, great Natures second Course,
Chiefe nourisher in Life's Feast.

Lady Macbeth	What do you mean?
Macbeth	Still it cried 'Sleep no more!' to all the house,
	'Glamis hath murder'd sleep, and therefore Cawdor
	Shall sleep no more, Macbeth shall sleep no more!'
Lady Macbeth	Who was it that thus cried? Why, worthy Thane,
	You do unbend your noble strength to think
	So brain-sickly of things. Go, get some water,
	And wash this filthy witness from your hand.
	Why did you bring these daggers from the place?
	They must lie there. Go, carry them, and smear
	The sleepy grooms with blood.
Macbeth	I'll go no more.
	I am afraid to think what I have done;
	Look on't again I dare not.
Lady Macbeth	Infirm of purpose!
	Give me the daggers. The sleeping and the dead
	Are but as pictures; 'tis the eye of childhood
	That fears a painted devil. If he do bleed,
	I'll gild the faces of the grooms withal,
	For it must seem their guilt. *Exit*

Knocking within 21

Macbeth	Whence is that knocking?
	How is't with me when every noise appals me?
	What hands are here? Ha, they pluck out mine eyes!
	Will all great Neptune's ocean wash this blood
	Clean from my hand? No, this my hand will rather
	The multitudinous seas incarnadine,
	Making the green one red.22

Enter LADY MACBETH

Lady Macbeth	My hands are of your colour, but I shame
	To wear a heart so white. *Knocking*
	I hear a knocking
	At the south entry. Retire we to our chamber.
	A little water clears us of this deed.

Lady. What doe you meane?

Macb. Still it cry'd, Sleepe no more to all the House:
Glamis hath murther'd Sleepe, and therefore *Cawdor*
Shall sleepe no more: *Macbeth* shall sleepe no more.

Lady. Who was it, that thus cry'd? why worthy *Thane*,
You doe vnbend your Noble strength, to thinke
So braine-sickly of things: Goe get some Water,
And wash this filthie Witnesse from your Hand.
Why did you bring these Daggers from the place?
They must lye there: goe carry them, and smeare
The sleepie Groomes with blood.

Macb. Ile goe no more:
I am afraid, to thinke what I haue done:
Looke on't againe, I dare not.

Lady. Infirme of purpose:
Giue me the Daggers: the sleeping, and the dead,
Are but as Pictures: 'tis the Eye of Child-hood,
That feares a painted Deuill. If he doe bleed,
Ile guild the Faces of the Groomes withall,
For it must seeme their Guilt.   *Exit.*
                              Knocke within.

Macb. Whence is that knocking?
How is't with me, when euery noyse appalls me?
What Hands are here? hah: they pluck out mine Eyes.
Will all great *Neptunes* Ocean wash this blood
Cleane from my Hand? no: this my Hand will rather
The multitudinous Seas incarnadine,
Making the Greene one, Red.

                    Enter Lady.

Lady. My Hands are of your colour: but I shame
To weare a Heart so white.   *Knocke.*
I heare a knocking at the South entry:
Retyre we to our Chamber:
A little Water cleares vs of this deed.

How easy is it then! Your constancy
Hath left you unattended.   *Knocking*
                            Hark, more knocking.
Get on your night-gown lest occasion call us
And show us to be watchers. Be not lost
So poorly in your thoughts.

Macbeth   To know my deed, 'twere best not know myself.
                                            Knocking

Wake Duncan with thy knocking;
                            I would thou couldst!
                                            Exeunt

2.3

Enter a PORTER. *Knocking within*

Porter   Here's a knocking indeed! If a man were porter of
hell-gate, he should have old turning the key.
(*Knocking within*) Knock, knock, knock! Who's
there, i'th' name of Beelzebub? Here's a farmer that
hanged himself on the expectation of plenty. Come
in time![23] Have napkins enough about you, here
you'll sweat for't. (*Knocking within*) Knock, knock!
Who's there, in th'other devil's name? Faith, here's
an equivocator that could swear in both the scales
against either scale, who committed treason enough
for God's sake, yet could not equivocate to heaven.
Oh, come in, equivocator. (*Knocking within*) Knock,
knock, knock! Who's there? Faith, here's an English
tailor come hither for stealing out of a French hose.
Come in, tailor. Here you may roast your goose.
(*Knocking within*) Knock, knock! Never at quiet.
What are you? But this place is too cold for hell.
I'll devil-porter it no further. I had thought to have
let in some of all professions that go the primrose
way to th'everlasting bonfire. (*Knocking within*)

How easie is it then? your Constancie
Hath left you vnattended.   *Knocke.*
Hearke, more knocking.
Get on your Night-Gowne, least occasion call vs,
And shew vs to be Watchers: be not lost
So poorely in your thoughts.
   Macb. To know my deed,   *Knocke.*
'Twere best not know my selfe.
Wake *Duncan* with thy knocking:
I would thou could'st.   *Exeunt.*

Scena Tertia.

Enter a Porter.

Knocking within.

   Porter. Here's a knocking indeede: if a man were
Porter of Hell Gate, hee should haue old turning the
Key.   *Knock.*   Knock, Knock, Knock. Who's there
i'th'name of *Belzebub*? Here's a Farmer, that hang'd
himselfe on th'expectation of Plentie: Come in time, haue
Napkins enow about you, here you'le sweat for't. *Knock.*
Knock, knock. Who's there in th'other Deuils Name?
Faith here's an Equiuocator, that could sweare in both
the Scales against eyther Scale, who committed Treason
enough for Gods sake, yet could not equiuocate to Hea-
uen: oh come in, Equiuocator.   *Knock.*   Knock,
Knock, Knock. Who's there? 'Faith here's an English
Taylor come hither, for stealing out of a French Hose:
Come in Taylor, here you may rost your Goose. *Knock.*
Knock, Knock. Neuer at quiet: What are you? but this
place is too cold for Hell. Ile Deuill-Porter it no further:
I had thought to haue let in some of all Professions, that
goe the Primrose way to th'euerlasting Bonfire. *Knock.*

Anon, anon! I pray you, remember the porter.

[Opens the door][24]

Enter MACDUFF *and* LENNOX

Macduff Was it so late, friend, ere you went to bed
That you do lie so late?

Porter Faith, sir, we were carousing till the second cock,
and drink, sir, is a great provoker of three things.

Macduff What three things does drink especially provoke?

Porter Marry, sir, nose-painting, sleep, and urine. Lechery,
sir, it provokes and unprovokes: it provokes the
desire, but it takes away the performance. Therefore
much drink may be said to be an equivocator with
lechery: it makes him, and it mars him; it sets him
on, and it takes him off; it persuades him, and
disheartens him; makes him stand to, and not stand
to; in conclusion, equivocates him in a sleep, and
giving him the lie, leaves him.

Macduff I believe drink gave thee the lie last night.

Porter That it did, sir, i' the very throat on me; but I
requited him for his lie, and, I think, being too
strong for him, though he took up my legs
sometime, yet I made a shift to cast him.

Enter MACBETH

Macduff Is thy master stirring?
Our knocking has awak'd him: here he comes.[25]

Lennox Good morrow, noble sir.

Macbeth   Good morrow, both.

Macduff Is the King stirring, worthy Thane?

Macbeth   Not yet.

Macduff He did command me to call timely on him.
I have almost slipp'd the hour.

Macbeth   I'll bring you to him.

Macduff I know this is a joyful trouble to you,

Anon, anon, I pray you remember the Porter.

Enter Macduff, and Lenox.

   Macd. Was it so late, friend, ere you went to Bed,
That you doe lye so late?
   Port. Faith Sir, we were carowsing till the second Cock:
And Drinke, Sir, is a great prouoker of three things.
   Macd. What three things does Drinke especially
prouoke?
   Port. Marry, Sir, Nose-painting, Sleepe, and Vrine.
Lecherie, Sir, it prouokes, and vnprouokes: it prouokes
the desire, but it takes away the performance. Therefore
much Drinke may be said to be an Equiuocator with Lecherie: it makes him, and it marres him; it sets him on,
and it takes him off; it perswades him, and dis-heartens
him; makes him stand too, and not stand too: in conclusion, equiuocates him in a sleepe, and giuing him the Lye,
leaues him.
   Macd. I beleeue, Drinke gaue thee the Lye last Night.
   Port. That it did, Sir, i'the very Throat on me: but I
requited him for his Lye, and (I thinke) being too strong
for him, though he tooke vp my Legges sometime, yet I
made a Shift to cast him.
                    Enter Macbeth.
   Macd. Is thy Master stirring?
Our knocking ha's awak'd him: here he comes.
   Lenox. Good morrow, Noble Sir.
   Macb. Good morrow both.
   Macd. Is the King stirring, worthy *Thane*?
   Macb. Not yet.
   Macd. He did command me to call timely on him,
I haue almost slipt the houre.
   Ma b. Ile bring you to him.
   Macd. I know this is a ioyfull trouble to you:

	But yet 'tis one.
Macbeth	The labour we delight in physics pain.
	This is the door.
Macduff	I'll make so bold to call,
	For 'tis my limited service. *Exit*
Lennox	Goes the King hence today?
Macbeth	He does; he did appoint so.
Lennox	The night has been unruly. Where we lay,
	Our chimneys were blown down, and, as they say,
	Lamentings heard i'th'air, strange screams of death,
	And prophesying, with accents terrible,
	Of dire combustion and confus'd events,
	New hatch'd to th' woeful time. The obscure bird 26
	Clamour'd the livelong night. Some say the earth
	Was feverous and did shake.
Macbeth	'Twas a rough night.
Lennox	My young remembrance cannot parallel
	A fellow to it.

Enter MACDUFF

Macduff	O horror, horror, horror!
	Tongue nor heart cannot conceive nor name thee!
Macbeth & Lennox	
	What's the matter?
Macduff	Confusion now hath made his masterpiece.
	Most sacrilegious murder hath broke ope
	The Lord's anointed temple, and stole thence
	The life o'th' building.
Macbeth	What is't you say? 'The life'?
Lennox	Mean you his majesty?
Macduff	Approach the chamber and destroy your sight
	With a new Gorgon. Do not bid me speak;
	See, and then speak yourselves.

Exeunt MACBETH *and* LENNOX

| | Awake, awake! |
| | Ring the alarum bell! Murder and treason! |

But yet 'tis one.

Macb. The labour we delight in, Physicks paine:
This is the Doore.

Macd. Ile make so bold to call, for'tis my limitted
seruice.   *Exit Macduffe.*

Lenox. Goes the King hence to day?

Macb. He does: he did appoint so.

Lenox. The Night ha's been vnruly:
Where we lay, our Chimneys were blowne downe,
And (as they say) lamentings heard i'th'Ayre;
Strange Schreemes of Death,
And Prophecying, with Accents terrible,
Of dyre Combustion, and confus'd Euents,
New hatch'd toth' wofull time.
The obscure Bird clamor'd the liue-long Night.
Some say, the Earth was feuorous,
And did shake.

Macb. 'Twas a rough Night.

Lenox. My young remembrance cannot paralell
A fellow to it.

Enter Macduff.

Macd. O horror, horror, horror,
Tongue nor Heart cannot conceiue, nor name thee.

Macb. and Lenox. What's the matter?

Macd. Confusion now hath made his Master-peece:
Most sacrilegious Murther hath broke ope
The Lords anoynted Temple, and stole thence
The Life o'th'Building.

Macb. What is't you say, the Life?

Lenox. Meane you his Maiestie?

Macd. Approch the Chamber, and destroy your sight
With a new *Gorgon.* Doe not bid me speake:
See, and then speake your selues: awake, awake,

Exeunt Macbeth and Lenox.

Ring the Alarum Bell: Murther, and Treason,

Banquo and Donalbain, Malcolm, awake!
Shake off this downy sleep, death's counterfeit,
And look on death itself! Up, up, and see
The great doom's image. Malcolm, Banquo,
As from your graves rise up, and walk like sprites
To countenance this horror. – Ring the bell.

Bell rings 27

Enter LADY MACBETH

Lady Macbeth What's the business, that such a hideous trumpet
Calls to parley the sleepers of the house?
Speak, speak.

Macduff   O gentle lady,
'Tis not for you to hear what I can speak:
The repetition in a woman's ear
Would murder as it fell.

Enter BANQUO

O Banquo, Banquo,
Our royal master's murder'd!

Lady Macbeth   Woe, alas!
What, in our house?

Banquo   Too cruel anywhere.
Dear Duff, I prithee contradict thyself,
And say it is not so.

Enter MACBETH, LENNOX, *and* ROSS 28

Macbeth   Had I but died an hour before this chance,
I had liv'd a blessèd time; for from this instant
There's nothing serious in mortality.
All is but toys; renown and grace is dead;
The wine of life is drawn, and the mere lees
Is left this vault to brag of.

Enter MALCOLM *and* DONALBAIN

Donalbain   What is amiss?

Macbeth   You are, and do not know't:

Banquo, and *Donalbaine*: *Malcolme* awake,
Shake off this Downey sleepe, Deaths counterfeit,
And looke on Death it selfe: vp, vp, and see
The great Doomes Image: *Malcolme, Banquo*,
As from your Graues rise vp, and walke like Sprights,
To countenance this horror. Ring the Bell.
                              Bell rings.   Enter Lady.
   Lady. What's the Businesse?
That such a hideous Trumpet calls to parley
The sleepers of the House? speake, speake.
   Macd. O gentle Lady,
'Tis not for you to heare what I can speake:
The repetition in a Womans eare,
Would murther as it fell.
                              Enter Banquo.
O *Banquo, Banquo*, Our Royall Master's murther'd.
   Lady. Woe, alas:
What, in our House?
   Ban. Too cruell, any where.
Deare *Duff*, I prythee contradict thy selfe,
And say, it is not so.

                Enter Macbeth, Lenox, and Rosse.

   Macb. Had I but dy'd an houre before this chance,
I had liu'd a blessed time: for from this instant,
There's nothing serious in Mortalitie:
All is but Toyes: Renowne and Grace is dead,
The Wine of Life is drawne, and the meere Lees
Is left this Vault, to brag of.

                Enter Malcolme and Donalbaine.

   Donal. What is amisse?
   Macb. You are, and doe not know't:

	The spring, the head, the fountain of your blood
	Is stopp'd, the very source of it is stopp'd.
Macduff	Your royal father's murder'd.
Malcolm	O! By whom?
Lennox	Those of his chamber, as it seem'd, had done't:
	Their hands and faces were all badg'd with blood;
	So were their daggers, which unwip'd we found
	Upon their pillows. They star'd, and were distracted;
	No man's life was to be trusted with them.
Macbeth	O, yet I do repent me of my fury,
	That I did kill them.
Macduff	Wherefore did you so?
Macbeth	Who can be wise, amaz'd, temperate and furious,
	Loyal and neutral, in a moment? No man.
	Th'expedition of my violent love
	Outran the pauser, reason. Here lay Duncan,
	His silver skin lac'd with his golden blood,
	And his gash'd stabs look'd like a breach in nature
	For ruin's wasteful entrance; there the murderers,
	Steep'd in the colours of their trade, their daggers
	Unmannerly breech'd with gore. Who could refrain,
	That had a heart to love, and in that heart
	Courage to make's love known?
Lady Macbeth	Help me hence, ho!
Macduff	Look to the lady.²⁹
Malcolm	[*Aside to* DONALBAIN]
	Why do we hold our tongues,
	That most may claim this argument for ours?
Donalbain	[*Aside to* MALCOLM]
	What should be spoken here, where our fate,
	Hid in an auger-hole, may rush and seize us?
	Let's away. Our tears are not yet brew'd.
Malcolm	[*Aside to* DONALBAIN]
	Nor our strong sorrow upon the foot of motion.
Banquo	Look to the lady.
	[*Exit* LADY MACBETH, *attended*]

The Spring, the Head, the Fountaine of your Blood
Is stopt, the very Source of it is stopt.

    Macd. Your Royall Father's murther'd.

    Mal. Oh, by whom?

    Lenox. Those of his Chamber, as it seem'd, had don't:
Their Hands, and Faces were all badg'd with blood,
So were their Daggers, which vnwip'd, we found
Vpon their Pillowes: they star'd, and were distracted,
No mans Life was to be trusted with them.

    Macb. O, yet I doe repent me of my furie,
That I did kill them.

    Macd. Wherefore did you so?

    Macb. Who can be wise, amaz'd, temp'rate, & furious,
Loyall, and Neutrall, in a moment? No man:
Th'expedition of my violent Loue
Out-run the pawser, Reason. Here lay *Duncan*,
His Siluer skinne, lac'd with his Golden Blood,
And his gash'd Stabs, look'd like a Breach in Nature,
For Ruines wastfull entrance: there the Murtherers,
Steep'd in the Colours of their Trade; their Daggers
Vnmannerly breech'd with gore: who could refraine,
That had a heart to loue; and in that heart,
Courage, to make's loue knowne?

    Lady. Helpe me hence, hoa.

    Macd. Looke to the Lady.

    Mal. Why doe we hold our tongues,
That most may clayme this argument for ours?

    Donal. What should be spoken here,
Where our Fate hid in an augure hole,
May rush, and seize vs? Let's away,
Our Teares are not yet brew'd.

    Mal. Nor our strong Sorrow
Vpon the foot of Motion.

    Banq. Looke to the Lady:

And when we have our naked frailties hid,
That suffer in exposure, let us meet
And question this most bloody piece of work
To know it further. Fears and scruples shake us.
In the great hand of God I stand, and thence
Against the undivulg'd pretence I fight
Off treasonous malice.

Macduff   And so do I.

All   So all.

Macbeth Let's briefly put on manly readiness,
And meet i'th' hall together.

All   Well contented.

Exeunt [all but MALCOLM and DONALBAIN]

Malcolm What will you do? Let's not consort with them.
To show an unfelt sorrow is an office
Which the false man does easy. I'll to England.

Donalbain To Ireland, I. Our separated fortune
Shall keep us both the safer. Where we are,
There's daggers in men's smiles; the near'r in blood,
The nearer bloody.

Malcolm   This murderous shaft that's shot
Hath not yet lighted, and our safest way
Is to avoid the aim. Therefore to horse,
And let us not be dainty of leave-taking,
But shift away. There's warrant in that theft
Which steals itself when there's no mercy left.

Exeunt

And when we haue our naked Frailties hid,
That suffer in exposure; let vs meet,
And question this most bloody piece of worke,
To know it further. Feares and scruples shake vs:
In the great Hand of God I stand, and thence,
Against the vndivulg'd pretence, I fight
Of Treasonous Mallice.

   Macd. And so doe I.

   All. So all.

   Macb. Let's briefely put on manly readinesse,
And meet i'th'Hall together.

   All. Well contented.   *Exeunt.*

   Malc. What will you doe?
Let's not consort with them:
To shew an vnfelt Sorrow, is an Office
Which the false man do's easie.
Ile to England.

   Don. To Ireland, I:
Our seperated fortune shall keepe vs both the safer:
Where we are, there's Daggers in mens Smiles;
The neere in blood, the neerer bloody.

   Malc. This murtherous Shaft that's shot,
Hath not yet lighted: and our safest way,
Is to auoid the ayme. Therefore to Horse,
And let vs not be daintie of leaue-taking,
But shift away: there's warrant in that Theft,
Which steales it selfe, when there's no mercie left.
                                   Exeunt.

2.4

                    Enter ROSS *with an* OLD MAN

Old Man   Three-score and ten I can remember well,
Within the volume of which time I have seen
Hours dreadful and things strange; but this sore night
Hath trifled former knowings.

Ross   Ha, good father,
Thou seest the heavens, as troubled with man's act,
Threatens his bloody stage. By th' clock 'tis day,
And yet dark night strangles the travailing lamp.[30]
Is't night's predominance or the day's shame
That darkness does the face of earth entomb
When living light should kiss it?

Old Man   'Tis unnatural,
Even like the deed that's done. On Tuesday last,
A falcon, towering in her pride of place,
Was by a mousing owl hawk'd at and kill'd.

Ross   And Duncan's horses – a thing most strange and
                                   certain –
Beauteous and swift, the minions of their race,
Turn'd wild in nature, broke their stalls, flung out,
Contending 'gainst obedience, as they would
Make war with mankind.

Old Man   'Tis said they ate each other.
Ross   They did so, to th'amazement of mine eyes
That look'd upon't.
                 Enter MACDUFF
                      Here comes the good Macduff.
How goes the world, sir, now?

Macduff   Why, see you not?
Ross   Is't known who did this more than bloody deed?
Macduff   Those that Macbeth hath slain.

Scena Quarta.

Enter Rosse, with an Old man.

Old man. Threescore and ten I can remember well,
Within the Volume of which Time, I haue seene
Houres dreadfull, and things strange: but this sore Night
Hath trifled former knowings.
    Rosse. Ha, good Father,
Thou seest the Heauens, as troubled with mans Act,
Threatens his bloody Stage: byth' Clock 'tis Day,
And yet darke Night strangles the trauailing Lampe:
Is't Nights predominance, or the Dayes shame,
That Darknesse does the face of Earth intombe,
When liuing Light should kisse it?
    Old man. 'Tis vnnaturall,
Euen like the deed that's done: On Tuesday last,
A Faulcon towring in her pride of place,
Was by a Mowsing Owle hawkt at, and kill'd.
    Rosse. And *Duncans* Horses,
(A thing most strange, and certaine)
Beauteous, and swift, the Minions of their Race,
Turn'd wilde in nature, broke their stalls, flong out,
Contending 'gainst Obedience, as they would
Make Warre with Mankinde.
    Old man. 'Tis said, they eate each other.
    Rosse. They did so:
To th'amazement of mine eyes that look'd vpon't.
              Enter Macduffe.
Heere comes the good *Macduffe.*
How goes the world Sir, now?
    Macd. Why see you not?
    Ross. Is't known who did this more then bloody deed?
    Macd. Those that *Macbeth* hath slaine.

Ross	Alas the day!
	What good could they pretend?
Macduff	They were suborn'd.
	Malcolm and Donalbain, the King's two sons,
	Are stol'n away and fled, which puts upon them
	Suspicion of the deed.
Ross	'Gainst nature still.
	Thriftless ambition, that will ravin up
	Thine own life's means! Then 'tis most like
	The sovereignty will fall upon Macbeth.
Macduff	He is already nam'd, and gone to Scone
	To be invested.
Ross	Where is Duncan's body?
Macduff	Carried to Colmekill,
	The sacred storehouse of his predecessors,
	And guardian of their bones.
Ross	Will you to Scone?
Macduff	No, cousin, I'll to Fife.
Ross	Well, I will thither.
Macduff	Well, may you see things well done there. Adieu,
	Lest our old robes sit easier than our new.
Ross	Farewell, father.
Old Man	God's benison go with you, and with those
	That would make good of bad, and friends of foes.

Exeunt

　　Ross. Alas the day,
What good could they pretend?
　　Macd. They were subborned,
Malcolme, and *Donalbaine* the Kings two Sonnes
Are stolne away and fled, which puts vpon them
Suspition of the deed.
　　Rosse. 'Gainst Nature still,
Thriftlesse Ambition, that will rauen vp
Thine owne liues meanes: Then 'tis most like,
The Soueraignty will fall vpon *Macbeth*.
　　Macd. He is already nam'd, and gone to Scone
To be inuested.
　　Rosse. Where is *Duncans* body?
　　Macd. Carried to Colmekill,
The Sacred Store-house of his Predecessors,
And Guardian of their Bones.
　　Rosse. Will you to Scone?
　　Macd. No Cosin, Ile to Fife.
　　Rosse· Well, I will thither.
　　Macd. Well may you see things wel done there: Adieu
Least our old Robes sit easier then our new.
　　Rosse. Farewell, Father.
　　Old M. Gods benyson go with you, and with those
That would make good of bad, and Friends of Foes.
　　　　　　　　　　　　　　　　　　Exeunt omnes

3.1

Enter BANQUO

Banquo   Thou hast it now: King, Cawdor, Glamis, all,
As the weïrd women promis'd; and, I fear,
Thou play'dst most foully for't. Yet it was said
It should not stand in thy posterity,
But that myself should be the root and father
Of many kings. If there come truth from them,
As upon thee, Macbeth, their speeches shine,
Why by the verities on thee made good
May they not be my oracles as well,
And set me up in hope? But hush, no more.

                                       Sennet sounded

Enter MACBETH *as King,* LADY MACBETH [*as Queen*],
LENNOX, ROSS, *lords,* [SERVANT,] *and attendants*

Macbeth   Here's our chief guest.

Lady Macbeth   If he had been forgotten,
It had been as a gap in our great feast,
And all-thing unbecoming.

Macbeth   Tonight we hold a solemn supper, sir,
And I'll request your presence.

Banquo   Let your highness
Command upon me, to the which my duties
Are with a most indissoluble tie
For ever knit.

Macbeth   Ride you this afternoon?

Banquo   Ay, my good lord.

Macbeth   We should have else desir'd your good advice,
Which still hath been both grave and prosperous,
In this day's council; but we'll take tomorrow.[31]
Is't far you ride?

Banquo   As far, my lord, as will fill up the time

Actus Tertius. Scena Prima.

Enter Banquo.

Banq. Thou hast it now, King, Cawdor, Glamis, all,
As the weyard Women promis'd, and I feare
Thou playd'st most fowly for't: yet it was saide
It should not stand in thy Posterity,
But that my selfe should be the Roote, and Father
Of many Kings. If there come truth from them,
As vpon thee *Macbeth*, their Speeches shine,
Why by the verities on thee made good,
May they not be my Oracles as well,
And set me vp in hope. But hush, no more.

Senit sounded. Enter Macbeth as King, Lady Lenox,
Rosse, Lords, and Attendants.

Macb. Heere's our chiefe Guest.
La. If he had beene forgotten,
It had bene as a gap in our great Feast,
And all-thing vnbecomming.
Macb. To night we hold a solemne Supper sir,
And Ile request your presence.
Banq. Let your Highnesse
Command vpon me, to the which my duties
Are with a most indissoluble tye
For euer knit.
Macb. Ride you this afternoone?
Ban. I, my good Lord.
Macb. We should haue else desir'd your good aduice
(Which still hath been both graue, and prosperous)
In this dayes Councell: but wee'le take to morrow.
Is't farre you ride?
Ban. As farre, my Lord, as will fill vp the time

'Twixt this and supper. Go not my horse the better,
I must become a borrower of the night
For a dark hour or twain.

Macbeth   Fail not our feast.
Banquo   My lord, I will not.
Macbeth   We hear our bloody cousins are bestow'd
In England and in Ireland, not confessing
Their cruel parricide, filling their hearers
With strange invention. But of that tomorrow,
When therewithal we shall have cause of state
Craving us jointly. Hie you to horse. Adieu,
Till you return at night. Goes Fleance with you?
Banquo   Ay, my good lord. Our time does call upon's.
Macbeth   I wish your horses swift and sure of foot,
And so I do commend you to their backs.
Farewell.   *Exit* BANQUO
Let every man be master of his time
Till seven at night. To make society
The sweeter welcome, we will keep ourself
Till supper-time alone. While then, God be with you.
                        Exeunt [*all but* MACBETH *and* SERVANT]
Sirrah, a word with you. Attend those men
Our pleasure?
Servant   They are, my lord, without the palace gate.
Macbeth   Bring them before us.   *Exit* SERVANT
                        To be thus is nothing,
But to be safely thus. Our fears in Banquo
Stick deep, and in his royalty of nature
Reigns that which would be fear'd. 'Tis much he
                                                        dares,
And to that dauntless temper of his mind
He hath a wisdom that doth guide his valour
To act in safety. There is none but he
Whose being I do fear, and under him

'Twixt this, and Supper. Goe not my Horse the better,
I must become a borrower of the Night,
For a darke houre, or twaine.

 Macb. Faile not our Feast.

 Ban. My Lord, I will not.

 Macb. We heare our bloody Cozens are bestow'd
In England, and in Ireland, not confessing
Their cruell Parricide, filling their hearers
With strange inuention. But of that to morrow,
When therewithall, we shall haue cause of State,
Crauing vs ioyntly. Hye you to Horse:
Adieu, till you returne at Night.
Goes *Fleance* with you?

 Ban. I, my good Lord: our time does call vpon's.

 Macb. I wish your Horses swift, and sure of foot:
And so I doe commend you to their backs.
Farwell.   *Exit Banquo.*
Let euery man be master of his time,
Till seuen at Night, to make societie
The sweeter welcome:
We will keepe our selfe till Supper time alone:
While then, God be with you.   *Exeunt Lords.*
Sirrha, a word with you: Attend those men
Our pleasure?

 Seruant. They are, my Lord, without the Pallace
Gate.

 Macb. Bring them before vs.   *Exit Seruant.*
To be thus, is nothing, but to be safely thus:
Our feares in *Banquo* sticke deepe,
And in his Royaltie of Nature reignes that
Which would be fear'd. 'Tis much he dares,
And to that dauntlesse temper of his Minde,
He hath a Wisdome, that doth guide his Valour,
To act in safetie. There is none but he,
Whose being I doe feare: and vnder him,

My genius is rebuk'd, as it is said,
Mark Antony's was by Caesar. He chid the sisters
When first they put the name of king upon me,
And bade them speak to him; then prophet-like
They hail'd him father to a line of kings.
Upon my head they plac'd a fruitless crown,
And put a barren sceptre in my grip,
Thence to be wrench'd with an unlineal hand,
No son of mine succeeding. If't be so,
For Banquo's issue have I fil'd my mind,
For them the gracious Duncan have I murder'd,
Put rancours in the vessel of my peace
Only for them, and mine eternal jewel
Given to the common enemy of man
To make them kings, the seeds of Banquo kings.
Rather than so, come, Fate, into the list
And champion me to th'utterance! – Who's there?

Enter SERVANT *and two* MURDERERS

Now go to the door, and stay there till we call.

Exit SERVANT

Was it not yesterday we spoke together?

Murderers	It was, so please your highness.[32]
Macbeth	Well then, now have you considered of my speeches?[33] Know that it was he, in the times past, which held you so under fortune, which you thought had been our innocent self. This I made good to you in our last conference, passed in probation with you how you were borne in hand, how crossed, the instruments, who wrought with them, and all things else that might to half a soul, and to a notion crazed, say, 'Thus did Banquo.'

My *Genius* is rebuk'd, as it is said
Mark Anthonies was by *Cæsar*. He chid the Sisters,
When first they put the Name of King vpon me,
And bad them speake to him. Then Prophet-like,
They hayl'd him Father to a Line of Kings.
Vpon my Head they plac'd a fruitlesse Crowne,
And put a barren Scepter in my Gripe,
Thence to be wrencht with an vnlineall Hand,
No Sonne of mine succeeding: if't be so,
For *Banquo's* Issue haue I fil'd my Minde,
For them, the gracious *Duncan* haue I murther'd,
Put Rancours in the Vessell of my Peace
Onely for them, and mine eternall Iewell
Giuen to the common Enemie of Man,
To make them Kings, the Seedes of *Banquo* Kings.
Rather then so, come Fate into the Lyst,
And champion me to th'vtterance.
Who's there?

Enter Seruant, and two Murtherers.

Now goe to the Doore, and stay there till we call.
                                            Exit Seruant.
Was it not yesterday we spoke together?
  Murth. It was, so please your Highnesse.
  Macb. Well then,
Now haue you consider'd of my speeches:
Know, that it was he, in the times past,
Which held you so vnder fortune,
Which you thought had been our innocent selfe.
This I made good to you, in our last conference,
Past in probation with you:
How you were borne in hand, how crost:
The Instruments: who wrought with them:
And all things else, that might
To halfe a Soule, and to a Notion craz'd,
Say, Thus did *Banquo.*

1 Murderer	You made it known to us.
Macbeth	I did so; and went further, which is now our point
	of second meeting. Do you find your patience so
	predominant in your nature that you can let this go?
	Are you so gospelled to pray for this good man and
	for his issue, whose heavy hand hath bowed you to
	the grave and beggared yours for ever?
1 Murderer	We are men, my liege.
Macbeth	Ay, in the catalogue ye go for men,
	As hounds and greyhounds, mongrels, spaniels, curs,
	Shoughs, water-rugs, and demi-wolves are clept
	All by the name of dogs. The valued file
	Distinguishes the swift, the slow, the subtle,
	The housekeeper, the hunter, every one
	According to the gift which bounteous nature
	Hath in him clos'd – whereby he does receive
	Particular addition from the bill
	That writes them all alike; and so of men.
	Now, if you have a station in the file
	Not i'th' worst rank of manhood, say't,
	And I will put that business in your bosoms,
	Whose execution takes your enemy off,
	Grapples you to the heart and love of us
	Who wear our health but sickly in his life,
	Which in his death were perfect.
2 Murderer	I am one, my liege,
	Whom the vile blows and buffets of the world
	Hath so incens'd that I am reckless what
	I do to spite the world.
1 Murderer	And I another,
	So weary with disasters, tugg'd with fortune,

1. *Murth.* You made it knowne to vs.

Macb. I did so:
And went further, which is now
Our point of second meeting.
Doe you finde your patience so predominant,
In your nature, that you can let this goe?
Are you so Gospell'd, to pray for this good man,
And for his Issue, whose heauie hand
Hath bow'd you to the Graue, and begger'd
Yours for euer?

1. *Murth.* We are men, my Liege.

Macb. I, in the Catalogue ye goe for men,
As Hounds, and Greyhounds, Mungrels, Spaniels, Curres,
Showghes, Water-Rugs, and Demy-Wolues are clipt
All by the Name of Dogges: the valued file
Distinguishes the swift, the slow, the subtle,
The House-keeper, the Hunter, euery one
According to the gift, which bounteous Nature
Hath in him clos'd: whereby he does receiue
Particular addition, from the Bill,
That writes them all alike: and so of men.
Now, if you haue a station in the file,
Not i'th' worst ranke of Manhood, say't,
And I will put that Businesse in your Bosomes,
Whose execution takes your Enemie off,
Grapples you to the heart; and loue of vs,
Who weare our Health but sickly in his Life,
Which in his Death were perfect.

2. *Murth.* I am one, my Liege,
Whom the vile Blowes and Buffets of the World
Hath so incens'd, that I am recklesse what I doe,
To spight the World.

1. *Murth.* And I another,
So wearie with Disasters, tugg'd with Fortune,

	That I would set my life on any chance
	To mend it or be rid on't.
Macbeth	Both of you
	Know Banquo was your enemy.
Murderers	True, my lord.
Macbeth	So is he mine, and in such bloody distance

So is he mine, and in such bloody distance
That every minute of his being thrusts
Against my near'st of life; and though I could
With bare-fac'd power sweep him from my sight
And bid my will avouch it, yet I must not,
For certain friends that are both his and mine,
Whose loves I may not drop, but wail his fall
Who I myself struck down. And thence it is
That I to your assistance do make love,
Masking the business from the common eye
For sundry weighty reasons.

2 Murderer   We shall, my lord,
Perform what you command us.

1 Murderer   Though our lives –

Macbeth Your spirits shine through you. Within this hour,
                                        at most,
I will advise you where to plant yourselves,
Acquaint you with the perfect spy o'th' time,
The moment on't, for't must be done tonight,
And something from the palace – always thought
That I require a clearness; and with him,
To leave no rubs nor botches in the work,
Fleance, his son, that keeps him company,
Whose absence is no less material to me
Than is his father's, must embrace the fate
Of that dark hour. Resolve yourselves apart;
I'll come to you anon.

Murderers   We are resolv'd, my lord.

Macbeth I'll call upon you straight. Abide within.
It is concluded: Banquo, thy soul's flight,
If it find heaven, must find it out tonight.   *Exeunt* [34]

That I would set my Life on any Chance,
To mend it, or be rid on't.

 Macb. Both of you know *Banquo* was your Enemie.

 Murth. True, my Lord.

 Macb. So is he mine: and in such bloody distance,
That euery minute of his being, thrusts
Against my neer'st of Life: and though I could
With bare-fac'd power sweepe him from my sight,
And bid my will auouch it; yet I must not,
For certaine friends that are both his, and mine,
Whose loues I may not drop, but wayle his fall,
Who I my selfe struck downe: and thence it is,
That I to your assistance doe make loue,
Masking the Businesse from the common Eye,
For sundry weightie Reasons.

 2. *Murth.* We shall, my Lord,
Performe what you command vs.

 1. *Murth.* Though our Liues--

 Macb. Your Spirits shine through you.
Within this houre, at most,
I will aduise you where to plant your selues,
Acquaint you with the perfect Spy o'th'time,
The moment on't, for't must be done to Night,
And something from the Pallace: always thought,
That I require a clearenesse; and with him,
To leaue no Rubs nor Botches in the Worke:
Fleans, his Sonne, that keepes him companie,
Whose absence is no lesse materiall to me,
Then is his Fathers, must embrace the fate
Of that darke houre: resolue your selues apart,
Ile come to you anon.

 Murth. We are resolu'd, my Lord.

 Macb. Ile call vpon you straight: abide within,
It is concluded: *Banquo*, thy Soules flight,
If it finde Heauen, must finde it out to Night.   *Exeunt.*

3.2

Enter LADY MACBETH *and a* SERVANT

Lady Macbeth	Is Banquo gone from court?
Servant	Ay, madam, but returns again tonight.
Lady Macbeth	Say to the King I would attend his leisure
	For a few words.
Servant	Madam, I will. *Exit*
Lady Macbeth	Nought's had, all's spent,

Where our desire is got without content.
'Tis safer to be that which we destroy
Than by destruction dwell in doubtful joy.

Enter MACBETH

How now, my lord, why do you keep alone,
Of sorriest fancies your companions making,
Using those thoughts which should indeed have died
With them they think on? Things without all remedy
Should be without regard: what's done is done.

Macbeth   We have scorch'd the snake, not kill'd it;35
She'll close, and be herself, whilst our poor malice
Remains in danger of her former tooth.
But let the frame of things disjoint, both the worlds
suffer,
Ere we will eat our meal in fear, and sleep
In the affliction of these terrible dreams
That shake us nightly. Better be with the dead,
Whom we, to gain our peace, have sent to peace,
Than on the torture of the mind to lie
In restless ecstasy. Duncan is in his grave;
After life's fitful fever he sleeps well;
Treason has done his worst; nor steel nor poison,
Malice domestic, foreign levy, nothing,
Can touch him further.

Scena Secunda.

Enter Macbeths Lady, and a Seruant.

Lady. Is *Banquo* gone from Court?

Seruant. I, Madame, but returnes againe to Night.

Lady. Say to the King, I would attend his leysure,
For a few words.

Seruant. Madame, I will.   *Exit.*

Lady. Nought's had, all's spent,
Where our desire is got without content:
'Tis safer, to be that which we destroy,
Then by destruction dwell in doubtfull ioy.

Enter Macbeth.

How now, my Lord, why doe you keepe alone?
Of sorryest Fancies your Companions making,
Vsing those Thoughts, which should indeed haue dy'd
With them they thinke on: things without all remedie
Should be without regard: what's done, is done.

Macb. We haue scorch'd the Snake, not kill'd it:
Shee'le close, and be her selfe, whilest our poore Mallice
Remaines in danger of her former Tooth.
But let the frame of things dis-ioynt,
Both the Worlds suffer,
Ere we will eate our Meale in feare, and sleepe
In the affliction of these terrible Dreames,
That shake vs Nightly: Better be with the dead,
Whom we, to gayne our peace, haue sent to peace,
Then on the torture of the Minde to lye
In restlesse extasie.
Duncane is in his Graue:
After Lifes fitfull Feuer, he sleepes well,
Treason ha's done his worst: nor Steele, nor Poyson,
Mallice domestique, forraine Leuie, nothing,
Can touch him further.

Lady Macbeth	Come on.
	Gentle my lord, sleek o'er your rugged looks,
	Be bright and jovial among your guests tonight.
Macbeth	So shall I, love, and so I pray be you.
	Let your remembrance apply to Banquo,
	Present him eminence both with eye and tongue;
	Unsafe the while, that we must lave our honours
	In these flattering streams, and make our faces
	Vizards to our hearts, disguising what they are.
Lady Macbeth	You must leave this.
Macbeth	O, full of scorpions is my mind, dear wife!
	Thou know'st that Banquo and his Fleance lives.
Lady Macbeth	But in them Nature's copy's not eterne.
Macbeth	There's comfort yet, they are assailable;
	Then be thou jocund. Ere the bat hath flown
	His cloister'd flight, ere to black Hecate's summons
	The shard-borne beetle with his drowsy hums 36
	Hath rung night's yawning peal, there shall be done
	A deed of dreadful note.
Lady Macbeth	What's to be done?
Macbeth	Be innocent of the knowledge, dearest chuck,
	Till thou applaud the deed. – Come, seeling night,
	Scarf up the tender eye of pitiful day,
	And with thy bloody and invisible hand
	Cancel and tear to pieces that great bond
	Which keeps me pale. Light thickens,
	And the crow makes wing to th' rooky wood;
	Good things of day begin to droop and drowse,
	Whiles night's black agents to their preys do rouse.
	– Thou marvell'st at my words, but hold thee still:
	Things bad begun make strong themselves by ill.
	So prithee go with me. *Exeunt*

Lady. Come on:
Gentle my Lord, sleeke o're your rugged Lookes,
Be bright and Iouiall among your Guests to Night.
    Macb. So shall I Loue, and so I pray be you:
Let your remembrance apply to *Banquo,*
Present him Eminence, both with Eye and Tongue:
Vnsafe the while, that wee must laue
Our Honors in these flattering streames,
And make our Faces Vizards to our Hearts,
Disguising what they are.
    Lady. You must leaue this.
    Macb. O, full of Scorpions is my Minde, deare Wife:
Thou know'st, that *Banquo* and his *Fleans* liues.
    Lady. But in them, Natures Coppie's not eterne.
    Macb. There's comfort yet, they are assaileable,
Then be iocund: ere the Bat hath flowne
His Cloyster'd flight, ere to black *Heccats* summons
The shard-borne Beetle, with his drowsie hums,
Hath rung Nights yawning Peale,
There shall be done a deed of dreadfull note.
    Lady. What's to be done?
    Macb. Be innocent of the knowledge, dearest Chuck,
Till thou applaud the deed: Come, seeling Night,
Skarfe vp the tender Eye of pittifull Day,
And with thy bloodie and inuisible Hand
Cancell and teare to pieces that great Bond,
Which keepes me pale. Light thickens,
And the Crow makes Wing toth'Rookie Wood:
Good things of Day begin to droope, and drowse,
Whiles Nights black Agents to their Prey's doe rowse.
Thou maruell'st at my words: but hold thee still,
Things bad begun, make strong themselues by ill:
So prythee goe with me.   *Exeunt.*

3.3

Enter three MURDERERS [37]

1 Murderer	But who did bid thee join with us?
3 Murderer	Macbeth.

2 Murderer He needs not our mistrust, since he delivers
Our offices and what we have to do
To the direction just.

1 Murderer   Then stand with us.
The west yet glimmers with some streaks of day;
Now spurs the lated traveller apace
To gain the timely inn, and near approaches [38]
The subject of our watch.

3 Murderer   Hark, I hear horses.

Banquo (*Within*) Give us a light there, ho!

2 Murderer   Then 'tis he; the rest
That are within the note of expectation
Already are i'th' court.

1 Murderer   His horses go about.

3 Murderer Almost a mile; but he does usually,
So all men do, from hence to th' palace gate
Make it their walk.

Enter BANQUO *and* FLEANCE, *with a torch*

2 Murderer   A light, a light!

3 Murderer   'Tis he.

1 Murderer Stand to't.

Banquo It will be rain tonight.

1 Murderer   Let it come down!

                               [*They attack*][39]

Banquo O, treachery! Fly, good Fleance, fly, fly, fly!
Thou mayst revenge. – O slave!

                         [*Dies. Exit* FLEANCE]

Scena Tertia.

Enter three Murtherers.

1. But who did bid thee ioyne with vs?
3. *Macbeth*.
2. He needes not our mistrust, since he deliuers
Our Offices, and what we haue to doe,
To the direction iust.
1. Then stand with vs:
The West yet glimmers with some streakes of Day.
Now spurres the lated Trauellcr apacc,
To gayne the timely Inne, end neere approches
The subiect of our Watch.
3. Hearke, I heare Horses.
Banquo within. Giue vs a Light there, hoa.
2. Then 'tis hee:
The rest, that are within the note of expectation,
Alreadie are i'th'Court.
1. His Horses goe about.
3. Almost a mile: but he does vsually,
So all men doe, from hence toth'Pallace Gate
Make it their Walke.

Enter Banquo and Fleans, with a Torch.

2. A Light, a Light.
3. 'Tis hee.
1. Stand too't.
Ban. It will be Rayne to Night.
1. Let it come downe.
Ban. O, Trecherie!
Flye good *Fleans*, flye, flye, flye,
Thou may'st reuenge. O Slaue!

3 Murderer	Who did strike out the light?
1 Murderer	Was't not the way?
3 Murderer	There's but one down; the son is fled.
2 Murderer	We have lost best half of our affair.
1 Murderer	Well, let's away, and say how much is done.

Exeunt

3.4

A banquet prepared. Enter MACBETH, LADY MACBETH, ROSS, LENNOX, *lords, and attendants*

Macbeth   You know your own degrees; sit down. At first and last, the hearty welcome.

Lords   Thanks to your majesty.

Macbeth   Ourself will mingle with society, and play the humble host. Our hostess keeps her state, but in best time we will require her welcome.

Lady Macbeth Pronounce it for me, sir, to all our friends, for my heart speaks they are welcome.

Enter first MURDERER

Macbeth   See, they encounter thee with their hearts' thanks.
Both sides are even. Here I'll sit i'th' midst.
Be large in mirth; anon we'll drink a measure
The table round.
[*To* MURDERER] There's blood upon thy face.

1 Murderer   'Tis Banquo's then.

Macbeth   'Tis better thee without than he within.
Is he dispatch'd?

1 Murderer   My lord, his throat is cut.
That I did for him.

Macbeth   Thou art the best o'th' cut-throats,
Yet he's good that did the like for Fleance;

3. Who did strike out the Light?
1. Was't not the way?
3. There's but one downe: the Sonne is fled.
2. We haue lost
Best halfe of our Affaire.
1. Well, let's away, and say how much is done.

Exeunt.

Scæna Quarta.

Banquet prepar'd. Enter Macbeth, Lady, Rosse, Lenox, Lords, and Attendants.

Macb. You know your owne degrees, sit downe:
At first and last, the hearty welcome.
Lords. Thankes to your Maiesty.
Macb. Our selfe will mingle with Society,
And play the humble Host:
Our Hostesse keepes her State, but in best time
We will require her welcome.
La. Pronounce it for me Sir, to all our Friends,
For my heart speakes, they are welcome.
Enter first Murtherer.
Macb. See they encounter thee with their harts thanks
Both sides are euen: heere Ile sit i'th'mid'st,
Be large in mirth, anon wee'l drinke a Measure
The Table round. There's blood vpon thy face.
Mur. 'Tis *Banquo's* then.
Macb. 'Tis better thee without, then he within.
Is he dispatch'd?
Mur. My Lord his throat is cut, that I did for him.
Mac. Thou art the best o'th'Cut-throats,
Yet hee's good that did the like for *Fleans:*

	If thou didst it, thou art the nonpareil.
1 Murderer	Most royal sir –
	Fleance is scap'd.
Macbeth	Then comes my fit again!

I had else been perfect,
Whole as the marble, founded as the rock,
As broad and general as the casing air,
But now I am cabin'd, cribb'd, confin'd, bound in
To saucy doubts and fears. But Banquo's safe?

| 1 Murderer | Ay, my good lord: safe in a ditch he bides, |

With twenty trenchèd gashes on his head,
The least a death to nature.

| Macbeth | Thanks for that. |

There the grown serpent lies; the worm that's fled
Hath nature that in time will venom breed,
No teeth for th' present. Get thee gone; tomorrow
We'll hear ourselves again.

Exit first MURDERER

| Lady Macbeth | My royal lord, |

You do not give the cheer. The feast is sold
That is not often vouch'd while 'tis a-making.
'Tis given, with welcome. To feed were best at home;
From thence, the sauce to meat is ceremony,
Meeting were bare without it.

Enter the ghost of BANQUO, *and sits in* MACBETH's *place* 40

| Macbeth | Sweet remembrancer! |

Now good digestion wait on appetite,
And health on both.

| Lennox | May't please your highness sit? |
| Macbeth | Here had we now our country's honour roof'd, |

Were the grac'd person of our Banquo present;
Who may I rather challenge for unkindness
Than pity for mischance.

| Ross | His absence, sir, |

Lays blame upon his promise. Please't your highness

If thou did'st it, thou art the Non-pareill.

    Mur. Most Royall Sir
Fleans is scap'd.

    Macb. Then comes my Fit againe:
I had else beene perfect;
Whole as the Marble, founded as the Rocke,
As broad, and generall, as the casing Ayre:
But now I am cabin'd crib'd, confin'd, bound in
To sawcy doubts, and feares. But *Banquo*'s safe?

    Mur. I, my good Lord: safe in a ditch he bides,
With twenty trenched gashes on his head;
The least a Death to Nature.

    Macb. Thankes for that:
There the growne Serpent lyes, the worme that's fled
Hath Nature that in time will Venom breed,
No teeth for th'present. Get thee gone, to morrow
Wee'l heare our selues againe.   *Exit Murderer.*

    Lady. My Royall Lord,
You do not giue the Cheere, the Feast is sold
That is not often vouch'd, while 'tis a making:
'Tis giuen, with welcome: to feede were best at home:
From thence, the sawce to meate is Ceremony,
Meeting were bare without it.

    Enter the Ghost of Banquo, and sits in Macbeths place.

    Macb. Sweet Remembrancer:
Now good digestion waite on Appetite,
And health on both.

    Lenox. May't please your Highnesse sit.

    Macb. Here had we now our Countries Honor, roof'd,
Were the grac'd person of our *Banquo* present:
Who, may I rather challenge for vnkindnesse,
Then pitty for Mischance.

    Rosse. His absence (Sir)
Layes blame vpon his promise. Pleas't your Highnesse

	To grace us with your royal company?
Macbeth	The table's full.
Lennox	Here is a place reserv'd, sir.
Macbeth	Where?
Lennox	Here, my good lord. What is't that moves your
	highness?
Macbeth	Which of you have done this?
Lords	What, my good lord?
Macbeth	Thou canst not say I did it. – Never shake
	Thy gory locks at me.
Ross	Gentlemen, rise, his highness is not well.
Lady Macbeth	Sit, worthy friends. My lord is often thus,
	And hath been from his youth. Pray you keep seat,
	The fit is momentary; upon a thought
	He will again be well. If much you note him,
	You shall offend him and extend his passion.
	Feed, and regard him not.
	[*Aside to* MACBETH] Are you a man?
Macbeth	Ay, and a bold one, that dare look on that
	Which might appal the devil.
Lady Macbeth	O proper stuff!
	This is the very painting of your fear;
	This is the air-drawn dagger which you said
	Led you to Duncan. O, these flaws and starts,
	Impostors to true fear, would well become
	A woman's story at a winter's fire,
	Authoriz'd by her grandam. Shame itself,
	Why do you make such faces! When all's done,
	You look but on a stool.
Macbeth	Prithee see there:
	Behold, look, lo! – How say you?
	Why, what care I? If thou canst nod, speak too.
	If charnel-houses and our graves must send
	Those that we bury back, our monuments
	Shall be the maws of kites.
	[*Exit* BANQUO's *ghost*][41]

To grace vs with your Royall Company?

    Macb. The Table's full.

    Lenox. Heere is a place reseru'd Sir.

    Macb. Where?

    Lenox. Heere my good Lord.

What is't that moues your Highnesse?

    Macb. Which of you haue done this?

    Lords. What, my good Lord?

    Macb. Thou canst not say I did it: neuer shake
Thy goary lockes at me.

    Rosse. Gentlemen rise, his Highnesse is not well.

    Lady. Sit worthy Friends: my Lord is often thus,
And hath beene from his youth. Pray you keepe Seat,
The fit is momentary, vpon a thought
He will againe be well. If much you note him
You shall offend him, and extend his Passion,
Feed, and regard him not. Arc you a man?

    Macb. I, and a bold one, that dare looke on that
Which might appall the Diuell.

    La. O proper stuffe:
This is the very painting of your feare:
This is the Ayre-drawne-Dagger which you said
Let you to *Duncan.* O, these flawes and starts
(Impostors to true feare) would well become
A womans story, at a Winters fire
Authoriz'd by her Grandam: shame it selfe,
Why do you make such faces? When all's done
You looke but on a stoole.

    Macb. Prythee see there:
Behold, looke, loe, how say you:
Why what care I, if thou canst nod, speake too.
If Charnell houses, and our Graues must send
Those that we bury, backe; our Monuments
Shall be the Mawes of Kytes.

Lady Macbeth	What, quite unmann'd in folly?
Macbeth	If I stand here, I saw him.
Lady Macbeth	Fie, for shame!
Macbeth	Blood hath been shed ere now, i'th'olden time,

Ere human statute purg'd the gentle weal;
Ay, and since too, murders have been perform'd
Too terrible for the ear. The times has been
That when the brains were out, the man would die,
And there an end; but now they rise again
With twenty mortal murders on their crowns,
And push us from our stools. This is more strange
Than such a murder is.

Lady Macbeth   My worthy lord,
Your noble friends do lack you.

Macbeth   I do forget.
Do not muse at me, my most worthy friends:
I have a strange infirmity, which is nothing
To those that know me. Come, love and health to all.
Then I'll sit down. – Give me some wine, fill full.

Enter the ghost of BANQUO

I drink to th' general joy o'th' whole table,
And to our dear friend Banquo, whom we miss.
Would he were here! To all, and him, we thirst,
And all to all.

Lords   Our duties, and the pledge.

Macbeth   [*To the ghost*]
Avaunt, and quit my sight! Let the earth hide thee!
Thy bones are marrowless, thy blood is cold;
Thou hast no speculation in those eyes
Which thou dost glare with!

Lady Macbeth   Think of this, good peers,
But as a thing of custom; 'tis no other,
Only it spoils the pleasure of the time.

Macbeth   What man dare, I dare:
Approach thou like the ruggèd Russian bear,

La. What? quite vnmann'd in folly.

Macb. If I stand heere, I saw him.

La. Fie for shame.

Macb. Blood hath bene shed ere now, i'th'olden time
Ere humane Statute purg'd the gentle Weale:
I, and since too, Murthers haue bene perform'd
Too terrible for the eare. The times has bene,
That when the Braines were out, the man would dye,
And there an end: But now they rise againe
With twenty mortall murthers on their crownes,
And push vs from our stooles. This is more strange
Then such a murther is.

La. My worthy Lord
Your Noble Friends do lacke you.

Macb. I do forget:
Do not muse at me my most worthy Friends,
I haue a strange infirmity, which is nothing
To those that know me. Come, loue and health to all,
Then Ile sit downe: Giue me some Wine, fill full:

Enter Ghost.

I drinke to th'generall ioy o'th'whole Table,
And to our deere Friend *Banquo*, whom we misse:
Would he were heere: to all, and him we thirst,
And all to all.

Lords. Our duties, and the pledge.

Mac. Auant, & quit my sight, let the earth hide thee:
Thy bones are marrowlesse, thy blood is cold:
Thou hast no speculation in those eyes
Which thou dost glare with.

La. Thinke of this good Peeres
But as a thing of Custome: 'Tis no other,
Onely it spoyles the pleasure of the time.

Macb. What man dare, I dare:
Approach thou like the rugged Russian Beare,

The arm'd rhinoceros, or th'Hyrcan tiger,
Take any shape but that, and my firm nerves
Shall never tremble. Or be alive again,
And dare me to the desert with thy sword;
If trembling I inhabit then, protest me
The baby of a girl. Hence, horrible shadow!
Unreal mockery, hence!   [*Exit the ghost*]
                                        Why so, being gone,
I am a man again. – Pray you sit still.

Lady Macbeth   You have displac'd the mirth, broke the good meeting,
With most admir'd disorder.

Macbeth   Can such things be,
And overcome us like a summer's cloud,
Without our special wonder? You make me strange
Even to the disposition that I owe,
When now I think you can behold such sights
And keep the natural ruby of your cheeks,
When mine is blanch'd with fear.

Ross   What sights, my lord?

Lady Macbeth   I pray you speak not. He grows worse and worse;
Question enrages him. At once, good night.
Stand not upon the order of your going,
But go at once.

Lennox   Good night, and better health
Attend his majesty.

Lady Macbeth   A kind good night to all.
                Exeunt [*all but* MACBETH *and* LADY MACBETH]

Macbeth   It will have blood, they say: blood will have blood.
Stones have been known to move, and trees to speak;
Augures and understood relations have
By maggot-pies and choughs and rooks brought forth
The secret'st man of blood. What is the night?

Lady Macbeth   Almost at odds with morning, which is which.

Macbeth   How sayst thou that Macduff denies his person
At our great bidding?

Lady Macbeth   Did you send to him, sir?

The arm'd Rhinoceros, or th'Hircan Tiger,
Take any shape but that, and my firme Nerues
Shall neuer tremble. Or be aliue againe,
And dare me to the Desart with thy Sword:
If trembling I inhabit then, protest mee
The Baby of a Girle. Hence horrible shadow,
Vnreall mock'ry hence. Why so, being gone
I am a man againe: pray you sit still.

    La. You haue displac'd the mirth,
Broke the good meeting, with most admir'd disorder.

    Macb. Can such things be,
And ouercome vs like a Summers Clowd,
Without our speciall wonder? You make me strange
Euen to the disposition that I owe,
When now I thinke you can behold such sights,
And keepe the naturall Rubie of your Cheekes,
When mine is blanch'd with feare.

    Rosse. What sights, my Lord?

    La. I pray you speake not: he growes worse & worse
Question enrages him: at once, goodnight.
Stand not vpon the order of your going,
But go at once.

    Len. Good night, and better health
Attend his Maiesty.

    La. A kinde goodnight to all.   *Exit Lords.*

    Macb. It will haue blood they say:
Blood will haue Blood:
Stones haue beene knowne to moue, & Trees to speake:
Augures, and vnderstood Relations, haue
By Maggot Pyes, & Choughes, & Rookes brought forth
The secret'st man of Blood. What is the night?

    La. Almost at oddes with morning, which is which.

    Macb. How say'st thou that *Macduff* denies his person
At our great bidding.

    La: Did you send to him Sir?

Macbeth	I hear it by the way; but I will send.
	There's not a one of them but in his house
	I keep a servant fee'd. I will tomorrow –
	And betimes I will – to the weïrd sisters.
	More shall they speak; for now I am bent to know,
	By the worst means, the worst. For mine own good,
	All causes shall give way.⁴² I am in blood
	Stepp'd in so far that, should I wade no more,
	Returning were as tedious as go o'er.
	Strange things I have in head that will to hand,
	Which must be acted ere they may be scann'd.
Lady Macbeth	You lack the season of all natures, sleep.
Macbeth	Come, we'll to sleep. My strange and self-abuse
	Is the initiate fear that wants hard use.
	We are yet but young in deed. *Exeunt*

3.5

Thunder. Enter the three WITCHES, *meeting* HECATE

1 Witch	Why, how now, Hecate? You look angrily.
Hecate	Have I not reason, beldams as you are?
	Saucy and over-bold, how did you dare
	To trade and traffic with Macbeth
	In riddles and affairs of death?
	And I the mistress of your charms,
	The close contriver of all harms,
	Was never call'd to bear my part
	Or show the glory of our art?
	And, which is worse, all you have done
	Hath been but for a wayward son,
	Spiteful and wrathful, who, as others do,

Macb. I heare it by the way: But I will send:
There's not a one of them but in his house
I keepe a Seruant Feed. I will to morrow
(And betimes I will) to the weyard Sisters.
More shall they speake: for now I am bent to know
By the worst meanes, the worst, for mine owne good,
All causes shall giue way. I am in blood
Stept in so farre, that should I wade no more,
Returning were as tedious as go ore:
Strange things I haue in head, that will to hand,
Which must be acted, ere they may be scand.
　　La. You lacke the season of all Natures, sleepe.
　　Macb. Come, wee'l to sleepe: My strange & self-abuse
Is the initiate feare, that wants hard vse:
We are yet but yong indeed. 　　　　　　　　*Exeunt.*

Scena Quinta.

Thunder. 　*Enter the three Witches, meeting*
Hecat.

　I. Why how now *Hecat*, you looke angerly?
　Hec. Haue I not reason (Beldams) as you are?
Sawcy, and ouer-bold, how did you dare
To Trade, and Trafficke with *Macbeth*,
In Riddles, and Affaires of death;
And I the Mistris of your Charmes,
The close contriuer of all harmes,
Was neuer call'd to beare my part,
Or shew the glory of our Art?
And which is worse, all you haue done
Hath bene but for a wayward Sonne,
Spightfull, and wrathfull, who (as others do)

Loves for his own ends, not for you.
But make amends now. Get you gone,
And at the pit of Acheron
Meet me i'th' morning; thither he
Will come to know his destiny.
Your vessels and your spells provide,
Your charms and every thing beside;
I am for th'air: this night I'll spend
Unto a dismal and a fatal end.
Great business must be wrought ere noon.
Upon the corner of the moon
There hangs a vap'rous drop profound:
I'll catch it ere it come to ground,
And, that distill'd by magic sleights,
Shall raise such artificial sprites
As by the strength of their illusion
Shall draw him on to his confusion.
He shall spurn fate, scorn death, and bear
His hopes 'bove wisdom, grace, and fear.
And you all know, security
Is mortals' chiefest enemy.

Music, and a song within:
'Come away, come away.'[43]

Hark, I am call'd. My little spirit, see,
Sits in a foggy cloud, and stays for me.   [*Exit*]

1 Witch   Come, let's make haste, she'll soon be back again.
Exeunt

Loues for his owne ends, not for you.
But make amends now: Get you gon,
And at the pit of Acheron
Meete me i'th'Morning: thither he
Will come, to know his Destinie.
Your Vessels, and your Spels prouide,
Your Charmes, and euery thing beside;
I am for th'Ayre: This night Ile spend
Vnto a dismall, and a Fatall end.
Great businesse must be wrought ere Noone.
Vpon the Corner of the Moone
There hangs a vap'rous drop, profound,
Ile catch it ere it come to ground;
And that distill'd by Magicke slights,
Shall raise such Artificiall Sprights,
As by the strength of their illusion,
Shall draw him on to his Confusion.
He shall spurne Fate, scorne Death, and beare
His hopes 'boue Wisedome, Grace, and Feare:
And you all know, Security
Is Mortals cheefest Enemie.
　　　　　　　Musicke, and a Song.
Hearke, I am call'd: my little Spirit see
Sits in a Foggy cloud, and stayes for me.
　　　　　　Sing within. Come away, come away, &c.
　1　Come, let's make hast, shee'l soone be
Backe againe.　　　　　　　　　　　*Exeunt.*

3.6

Enter LENNOX *and another* LORD

Lennox	My former speeches have but hit your thoughts

Which can interpret further; only I say
Things have been strangely borne. The gracious
                                        Duncan
Was pitied of Macbeth: marry, he was dead;
And the right valiant Banquo walk'd too late,
Whom you may say, if't please you, Fleance kill'd,
For Fleance fled. Men must not walk too late.
Who cannot want the thought how monstrous
It was for Malcolm and for Donalbain
To kill their gracious father? Damnèd fact,
How it did grieve Macbeth! Did he not straight
In pious rage the two delinquents tear,
That were the slaves of drink and thralls of sleep?
Was not that nobly done? Ay, and wisely too,
For 'twould have anger'd any heart alive
To hear the men deny't. So that I say,
He has borne all things well, and I do think
That had he Duncan's sons under his key –
As, an't please heaven he shall not – they should find
What 'twere to kill a father. So should Fleance.
But peace; for from broad words, and 'cause he fail'd
His presence at the tyrant's feast, I hear
Macduff lives in disgrace. Sir, can you tell
Where he bestows himself?

Lord	The son of Duncan,[44]

From whom this tyrant holds the due of birth,
Lives in the English court, and is receiv'd
Of the most pious Edward with such grace
That the malevolence of fortune nothing

Scæna Sexta.

Enter Lenox, and another Lord.

Lenox. My former Speeches,
Haue but hit your Thoughts
Which can interpret farther: Onely I say
Things haue bin strangely borne. The gracious *Duncan*
Was pittied of *Macbeth*: marry he was dead:
And the right valiant *Banquo* walk'd too late,
Whom you may say (if't please you) *Fleans* kill'd,
For *Fleans* fled: Men must not walke too late.
Who cannot want the thought, how monstrous
It was for *Malcolme*, and for *Donalbane*
To kill their gracious Father? Damned Fact,
How it did greeue *Macbeth*? Did he not straight
In pious rage, the two delinquents teare,
That were the Slaues of drinke, and thralles of sleepe?
Was not that Nobly done? I, and wisely too:
For 'twould haue anger'd any heart aliue
To heare the men deny't. So that I say,
He ha's borne all things well, and I do thinke,
That had he *Duncans* Sonnes vnder his Key,
(As, and't please Heauen he shall not) they should finde
What 'twere to kill a Father: So should *Fleans*.
But peace; for from broad words, and cause he fayl'd
His presence at the Tyrants Feast, I heare
Macduffe liues in disgrace. Sir, can you tell
Where he bestowes himselfe?
   Lord. The Sonnes of *Duncane*
(From whom this Tyrant holds the due of Birth)
Liues in the English Court, and is receyu'd
Of the most Pious *Edward*, with such grace,
That the maleuolence of Fortune, nothing

Takes from his high respect. Thither Macduff
Is gone, to pray the holy King upon his aid
To wake Northumberland and warlike Seyward,
That by the help of these, with Him above
To ratify the work, we may again
Give to our tables meat, sleep to our nights,
Free from our feasts and banquets bloody knives,
Do faithful homage and receive free honours,
All which we pine for now. And this report
Hath so exasperate their King, that he
Prepares for some attempt of war.[45]

Lennox   Sent he to Macduff?

Lord   He did; and with an absolute 'Sir, not I',
The cloudy messenger turns me his back,
And hums, as who should say, 'You'll rue the time
That clogs me with this answer.'

Lennox   And that well might
Advise him to a caution, t'hold what distance
His wisdom can provide. Some holy angel
Fly to the court of England, and unfold
His message ere he come, that a swift blessing
May soon return to this our suffering country,
Under a hand accurs'd!

Lord   I'll send my prayers with him.

                                Exeunt

4.1

         Thunder. Enter the three WITCHES

1 Witch   Thrice the brinded cat hath mew'd.

2 Witch   Thrice, and once the hedge-pig whin'd.

3 Witch   Harpier cries, ''Tis time, 'tis time.'

1 Witch   Round about the cauldron go,

Takes from his high respect. Thither *Macduffe*
Is gone, to pray the Holy King, vpon his ayd
To wake Northumberland, and warlike *Seyward*,
That by the helpe of these (with him aboue)
To ratifie the Worke) we may againe
Giue to our Tables meate, sleepe to our Nights:
Free from our Feasts, and Banquets bloody kniues;
Do faithfull Homage, and receiue free Honors,
All which we pine for now. And this report
Hath so exasperate their King, that hee
Prepares for some attempt of Warre.

    Len. Sent he to *Macduffe*?

    Lord. He did: and with an absolute Sir, not I
The clowdy Messenger turnes me his backe,
And hums; as who should say, you'l rue the time
That clogges me with this Answer.

    Lenox. And that well might
Aduise him to a Caution, t hold what distance
His wisedome can prouide. Some holy Angell
Flye to the Court of England, and vnfold
His Message ere he come, that a swift blessing
May soone returne to this our suffering Country,
Vnder a hand accurs'd.

    Lord. Ile send my Prayers with him.   *Exeunt*

Actus Quartus.   *Scena Prima.*

Thunder.   *Enter the three Witches.*

1   Thrice the brinded Cat hath mew'd
2   Thrice, and once the Hedge-Pigge whin'd.
3   Harpier cries, 'tis time, 'tis time.
1   Round about the Caldron go:

In the poison'd entrails throw.
Toad, that under cold stone
Days and nights has thirty-one,
Swelter'd venom sleeping got,
Boil thou first i'th' charmèd pot.

All Witches Double, double, toil and trouble,
Fire burn, and cauldron bubble.

2 Witch Fillet of a fenny snake
In the cauldron boil and bake;
Eye of newt, and toe of frog,
Wool of bat, and tongue of dog,
Adder's fork, and blind-worm's sting,
Lizard's leg, and owlet's wing:
For a charm of powerful trouble,
Like a hell-broth boil and bubble.

All Witches Double, double, toil and trouble,
Fire burn, and cauldron bubble.

3 Witch Scale of dragon, tooth of wolf,
Witch's mummy, maw and gulf
Of the ravin'd salt-sea shark,
Root of hemlock digg'd i'th' dark,
Liver of blaspheming Jew,
Gall of goat, and slips of yew
Sliver'd in the moon's eclipse,
Nose of Turk, and Tartar's lips,
Finger of birth-strangled babe,
Ditch-deliver'd by a drab:
Make the gruel thick and slab.
Add thereto a tiger's chawdron,
For th'ingredience of our cauldron.

All Witches Double, double, toil and trouble,
Fire burn, and cauldron bubble.

2 Witch Cool it with a bàboon's blood,
Then the charm is firm and good.

In the poysond Entrailes throw
Toad, that vnder cold stone,
Dayes and Nights, ha's thirty one:
Sweltred Venom, sleeping got,
Boyle thou first i'th'charmed pot.
 All. Double, double, toile and trouble;
Fire burne, and Cauldron bubble.
 2 Fillet of a Fenny Snake,
In the Cauldron boyle and bake:
Eye of Newt, and Toe of Frogge,
Wooll of Bat, and Tongue of Dogge:
Adders Forke, and Blinde-wormes Sting,
Lizards legge, and Howlets wing:
For a Charme of powrefull trouble,
Like a Hell-broth, boyle and bubble.
 All. Double, double, toyle and trouble,
Fire burne, and Cauldron bubble.
 3 Scale of Dragon, Tooth of Wolfe,
Witches Mummey, Maw, and Gulfe
Of the rauin'd salt Sea sharke:
Roote of Hemlocke, digg'd i'th'darke:
Liuer of Blaspheming Iew,
Gall of Goate, and Slippes of Yew,
Sliuer'd in the Moones Ecclipse:
Nose of Turke, and Tartars lips:
Finger of Birth-strangled Babe,
Ditch-deliuer'd by a Drab,
Make the Grewell thicke, and slab.
Adde thereto a Tigers Chawdron,
For th'Ingredience of our Cawdron.
 All. Double, double, toyle and trouble,
Fire burne, and Cauldron bubble.
 2 Coole it with a Baboones blood,
Then the Charme is firme and good.

Enter HECATE *and the other three witches*

Hecate   O, well done! I commend your pains,
And everyone shall share i'th' gains.
And now about the cauldron sing
Like elves and fairies in a ring,
Enchanting all that you put in.

Music and a song:
'Black spirits and white, red spirits and grey.'
[*Exeunt* HECATE *and the other three witches*]46

2 Witch   By the pricking of my thumbs,
Something wicked this way comes.
Open, locks, whoever knocks.

Enter MACBETH

Macbeth   How now, you secret, black, and midnight hags?
What is't you do?

All Witches   A deed without a name.

Macbeth   I conjure you, by that which you profess,
Howe'er you come to know it, answer me.
Though you untie the winds, and let them fight
Against the churches; though the yeasty waves
Confound and swallow navigation up;
Though bladed corn be lodg'd, and trees blown down;
Though castles topple on their warders' heads;
Though palaces and pyramids do slope
Their heads to their foundations; though the treasure
Of nature's germen tumble all together,47
Even till destruction sicken: answer me
To what I ask you.

1 Witch   Speak.
2 Witch   Demand.
3 Witch   We'll answer.
1 Witch   Say if thou'dst rather hear it from our mouths
Or from our masters.

Macbeth   Call 'em, let me see 'em.
1 Witch   Pour in sow's blood, that hath eaten
Her nine farrow; grease that's sweaten

Enter Hecat, and the other three Witches.

Hec. O well done: I commend your paines,
And euery one shall share i'th'gaines:
And now about the Cauldron sing
Like Elues and Fairies in a Ring,
Inchanting all that you put in.
                    Musicke and a Song. Blacke Spirits, &c.
  2 By the pricking of my Thumbes,
Something wicked this way comes:
Open Lockes, who euer knockes.
                    Enter Macbeth.
Macb. How now you secret, black, & midnight Hags?
What is't you do?
All. A deed without a name.
Macb. I coniure you, by that which you Professe,
(How ere you come to know it) answer me:
Though you vntye the Windes, and let them fight
Against the Churches: Though the yesty Waues
Confound and swallow Nauigation vp:
Though bladed Corne be lodg'd, & Trees blown downe,
Though Castles topple on their Warders heads:
Though Pallaces, and Pyramids do slope
Their heads to their Foundations: Though the treasure
Of Natures Germaine, tumble altogether,
Euen till destruction sicken: Answer me
To what I aske you.
  1 Speake.
  2 Demand.
  3 Wee'l answer.
  1 Say, if th'hadst rather heare it from our mouthes,
Or from our Masters.
Macb. Call 'em: let me see 'em.
  1 Powre in Sowes blood, that hath eaten
Her nine Farrow: Greaze that's sweaten

From the murderer's gibbet throw
Into the flame.

All Witches   Come, high or low:
Thy self and office deftly show.   *Thunder*

Enter the first APPARITION: *an armed head*

Macbeth   Tell me, thou unknown power –

1 Witch   He knows thy thought:
Hear his speech, but say thou nought.

1 Apparition   Macbeth, Macbeth, Macbeth: beware Macduff,
Beware the Thane of Fife. Dismiss me. Enough.

                                          He descends

Macbeth   Whate'er thou art, for thy good caution, thanks.
Thou hast harp'd my fear aright. But one word more –

1 Witch   He will not be commanded. Here's another,
More potent than the first.   *Thunder*

Enter the second APPARITION: *a bloody child*

2 Apparition   Macbeth, Macbeth, Macbeth.

Macbeth   Had I three ears, I'd hear thee.

2 Apparition   Be bloody, bold, and resolute. Laugh to scorn
The power of man, for none of woman born
Shall harm Macbeth.   *Descends*

Macbeth   Then live, Macduff; what need I fear of thee?
But yet I'll make assurance double sure,
And take a bond of fate. Thou shalt not live,
That I may tell pale-hearted fear it lies,
And sleep in spite of thunder.   *Thunder*

Enter the third APPARITION: *a child crowned, with a tree in his hand*

                                  What is this,
That rises like the issue of a king
And wears upon his baby-brow the round
And top of sovereignty?

All Witches   Listen, but speak not to't.

3 Apparition   Be lion-mettled, proud, and take no care
Who chafes, who frets, or where conspirers are.

From the Murderers Gibbet, throw
Into the Flame.
    All. Come high or low:
Thy Selfe and Office deaftly show.   *Thunder.*
                  1. *Apparation, an Armed Head.*
    Macb. Tell me, thou vnknowne power.
    1 He knowes thy thought:
Heare his speech, but say thou nought.
    1 *Appar.*   *Macbeth, Macbeth, Macbeth*:
Beware *Macduffe*,
Beware the Thane of Fife: dismisse me. Enough.
                          He Descends.
    Macb. What ere thou art, for thy good caution, thanks
Thou hast harp'd my feare aright. But one word more.
    1 He will not be commanded: heere's another
More potent then the first.   *Thunder.*
                 2 *Apparition, a Bloody Childe.*
    2 *Appar.* *Macbeth, Macbeth, Macbeth.*
    Macb. Had I three eares, Il'd heare thee.
    2 *Appar.* Be bloody, bold, & resolute:
Laugh to scorne
The powre of man: For none of woman bornc
Shall harme *Macbeth.*   *Descends.*
    Mac. Then liue *Macduffe*: what nccd I feare of thee?
But yet Ile make assurance: double sure,
And take a Bond of Fate: thou shalt not liue,
That I may tell pale-hearted Feare, it lies;
And sleepe in spight of Thunder.   *Thunder*
        3 *Apparition, a Childe Crowned, with a Tree in his hand.*
What is this, that rises like the issue of a King,
And weares vpon his Baby-brow, the round
And top of Soueraignty?
    All. Listen, but speake not too't.
    3 *Appar.* Be Lyon metled, proud, and take no care:
Who chafes, who frets, or where Conspirers are:

	Macbeth shall never vanquish'd be until
	Great Birnam Wood to high Dunsinane Hill
	Shall come against him. *Descends*
Macbeth	That will never be.
	Who can impress the forest, bid the tree
	Unfix his earth-bound root? Sweet bodements, good!
	Rebellious dead, rise never till the Wood
	Of Birnam rise, and our high-plac'd Macbeth
	Shall live the lease of nature, pay his breath
	To time and mortal custom. Yet my heart
	Throbs to know one thing: tell me, if your art
	Can tell so much, shall Banquo's issue ever
	Reign in this kingdom?
All Witches	Seek to know no more.
Macbeth	I will be satisfied. Deny me this,
	And an eternal curse fall on you. Let me know.
	[*The cauldron descends;*] *hautboys play*
	Why sinks that cauldron? And what noise is this?
1 Witch	Show.
2 Witch	Show.
3 Witch	Show.
All Witches	Show his eyes, and grieve his heart;
	Come like shadows, so depart.

Enter a show of eight kings in procession,
the last with a glass in his hand, followed by Banquo's ghost 48

Macbeth	Thou art too like the spirit of Banquo. Down!
	Thy crown does sear mine eyeballs. And thy hair,
	Thou other gold-bound-brow, is like the first.
	A third is like the former. – Filthy hags,
	Why do you show me this? – A fourth? Start, eyes!
	What, will the line stretch out to th' crack of doom?
	Another yet? A seventh? I'll see no more,
	And yet the eighth appears, who bears a glass
	Which shows me many more; and some I see
	That two-fold balls and treble sceptres carry.
	Horrible sight! Now I see 'tis true,

Macbeth shall neuer vanquish'd be, vntill
Great Byrnam Wood, to high Dunsmane Hill
Shall come against him.   *Descend.*
   Macb. That will neuer bee:
Who can impresse the Forrest, bid the Tree
Vnfixe his earth-bound Root? Sweet boadments, good:
Rebellious dead, rise neuer till the Wood
Of Byrnan rise, and our high plac'd *Macbeth*
Shall liue the Lease of Nature, pay his breath
To time, and mortall Custome. Yet my Hart
Throbs to know one thing: Tell me, if your Art
Can tell so much: Shall *Banquo*'s issue euer
Reigne in this Kingdome?
   All. Seeke to know no more.
   Macb. I will be satisfied. Deny me this,
And an eternall Curse fall on you: Let me know.
Why sinkes that Caldron? & what noise is this?   *Hoboyes*
   1 Shew.
   2 Shew.
   3 Shew.
   All. Shew his Eyes, and greeue his Hart,
Come like shadowes, so depart.
       A shew of eight Kings, and Banquo last, with a glasse
         in his hand.
   Macb. Thou art too like the Spirit of *Banquo*: Down:
Thy Crowne do's seare mine Eye-bals. And thy haire
Thou other Gold-bound-brow, is like the first:
A third, is like the former. Filthy Hagges,
Why do you shew me this? ——A fourth? Start eyes!
What will the Line stretch out to'th'cracke of Doome?
Another yet? A scauenth? Ile see no more:
And yet the eight appeares, who beares a glasse,
Which shewes me many more: and some I see,
That two-fold Balles, and trebble Scepters carry.
Horrible sight: Now I see 'tis true,

	For the blood-bolter'd Banquo smiles upon me,
	And points at them for his.
	[*Exit the show of kings with Banquo's ghost*]
	What? Is this so?
1 Witch	Ay, sir, all this is so. But why
	Stands Macbeth thus amazedly?
	Come, sisters, cheer we up his sprites,
	And show the best of our delights.
	I'll charm the air to give a sound,
	While you perform your antic round,
	That this great King may kindly say
	Our duties did his welcome pay. *Music*
	The WITCHES *dance, and vanish*
Macbeth	Where are they? Gone? Let this pernicious hour
	Stand aye accursèd in the calendar!
	Come in, without there!
	Enter LENNOX
Lennox	What's your grace's will?
Macbeth	Saw you the weïrd sisters?
Lennox	No, my lord.
Macbeth	Came they not by you?
Lennox	No indeed, my lord.
Macbeth	Infected be the air whereon they ride,
	And damn'd all those that trust them! I did hear
	The galloping of horse. Who was't came by?
Lennox	'Tis two or three, my lord, that bring you word:
	Macduff is fled to England.
Macbeth	Fled to England?
Lennox	Ay, my good lord.
Macbeth	[*Aside*] Time, thou anticipat'st my dread exploits.
	The flighty purpose never is o'ertook
	Unless the deed go with it. From this moment,
	The very firstlings of my heart shall be
	The firstlings of my hand. And even now,
	To crown my thoughts with acts, be it thought and
	done.

For the Blood-bolter'd *Banquo* smiles vpon me,
And points at them for his. What? is this so?

 ı I Sir, all this is so. But why
Stands *Macbeth* thus amazedly?
Come Sisters, cheere we vp his sprights,
And shew the best of our delights.
Ile Charme the Ayre to giue a sound,
While you performe your Antique round:
That this great King may kindly say,
Our duties, did his welcome pay.   *Musicke.*
    The Witches Dance, and vanish.

 Macb. Where are they? Gone?
Let this pernitious houre,
Stand aye accursed in the Kalender.
Come in, without there.   *Enter Lenox.*

 Lenox. What's your Graces will.
 Macb. Saw you the Weyard Sisters?
 Lenox. No my Lord.
 Macb. Came they not by you?
 Lenox. No indeed my Lord.
 Macb. Infected be the Ayre whereon they ride,
And damn'd all those that trust them. I did heare
The gallopping of Horse. Who was't came by?
 Len. 'Tis two or three my Lord, that bring you word:
Macduff is fled to England.
 Macb. Fled to England?
 Len. I, my good Lord.
 Macb. Time, thou anticipat'st my dread exploits:
The flighty purpose neuer is o're-tooke
Vnlesse the deed go with it. From this moment,
The very firstlings of my heart shall be
The firstlings of my hand. And euen now
To Crown my thoughts with Acts: be it thoght & done:

The castle of Macduff I will surprise,
Seize upon Fife, give to th'edge o'th' sword
His wife, his babes, and all unfortunate souls
That trace him in his line. No boasting like a fool;
This deed I'll do before this purpose cool.
But no more sights. – Where are these gentlemen?
Come bring me where they are.   *Exeunt*

4.2

Enter LADY MACDUFF, *her* SON, *and* ROSS

Lady Macduff	What had he done, to make him fly the land?
Ross	You must have patience, madam.
Lady Macduff	He had none;

His flight was madness. When our actions do not,
Our fears do make us traitors.

Ross	You know not

Whether it was his wisdom or his fear.

Lady Macduff Wisdom? To leave his wife, to leave his babes,
His mansion, and his titles, in a place
From whence himself does fly? He loves us not,
He wants the natural touch; for the poor wren,
The most diminutive of birds, will fight,
Her young ones in her nest, against the owl.
All is the fear, and nothing is the love;
As little is the wisdom, where the flight
So runs against all reason.

Ross   My dearest coz,
I pray you school yourself. But for your husband,
He is noble, wise, judicious, and best knows
The fits o'th' season. I dare not speak much further,
But cruel are the times when we are traitors

The Castle of *Macduff*, I will surprize,
Seize vpon Fife; giue to th'edge o'th'Sword
His Wife, his Babes, and all vnfortunate Soules
That trace him in his Line. No boasting like a Foole,
This deed Ile do, before this purpose coolc,
But no more sights. Where are these Gentlemen?
Come bring me where they are.   *Exeunt*

Scena Secunda.

Enter Macduffes Wife, her Son, and Rosse.

Wife. What had he done, to make him fly the Land?
Rosse. You must haue patience Madam.
Wife. He had none:
His flight was madnesse: when our Actions do not,
Our feares do make vs Traitors.
Rosse. You know not
Whether it was his wisedome, or his feare.
Wife. Wisedom? to leaue his wife, to leaue his Babes,
His Mansion, and his Titles, in a place
From whence himselfe do's flye? He loues vs not,
He wants the naturall touch. For the poore Wren
(The most diminitiue of Birds) will fight,
Her yong ones in her Nest, against the Owle:
All is the Feare, and nothing is the Loue;
As little is the Wisedome, where the flight
So runnes against all reason.
Rosse. My deerest Cooz,
I pray you schoole your selfe. But for your Husband,
He is Noble, Wise, Iudicious, and best knowes
The fits o'th'Season. I dare not speake much further,
But cruell are the times, when we are Traitors

And do not know ourselves; when we hold rumour
From what we fear, yet know not what we fear,
But float upon a wild and violent sea
Each way and move.[49] I take my leave of you;
Shall not be long but I'll be here again.
Things at the worst will cease, or else climb upward
To what they were before.
[*To* SON]   My pretty cousin,
Blessing upon you.

Lady Macduff   Father'd he is, and yet he's fatherless.

Ross   I am so much a fool, should I stay longer
It would be my disgrace and your discomfort.
I take my leave at once.   *Exit*

Lady Macduff   Sirrah, your father's dead,
And what will you do now? How will you live?

Son   As birds do, mother.

Lady Macduff   What, with worms and flies?

Son   With what I get, I mean, and so do they.

Lay Macduff   Poor bird, thou'dst never fear the net, nor lime, the
pit-fall, nor the gin.

Son   Why should I, mother? Poor birds they are not set for;
My father is not dead for all your saying.

Lady Macduff   Yes, he is dead. How wilt thou do for a father?

Son   Nay, how will you do for a husband?

Lady Macduff   Why, I can buy me twenty at any market.

Son   Then you'll buy 'em to sell again.

Lady Macduff   Thou speak'st with all thy wit, and yet i'faith with
wit enough for thee.

Son   Was my father a traitor, mother?

Lady Macduff   Ay, that he was.

Son   What is a 'traitor'?

Lady Macduff   Why, one that swears and lies.

And do not know our selues: when we hold Rumor
From what we feare, yet know not what we feare,
But floate vpon a wilde and violent Sea
Each way, and moue. I take my leaue of you:
Shall not be long but Ile be heere againe:
Things at the worst will cease, or else climbe vpward,
To what they were before. My pretty Cosine,
Blessing vpon you.

 Wife. Father'd he is,
And yet hee's Father-lesse.

 Rosse. I am so much a Foole, should I stay longer
It would be my disgrace, and your discomfort.
I take my leaue at once.   *Exit Rosse.*

 Wife. Sirra, your Fathers dead,
And what will you do now? How will you liue?

 Son. As Birds do Mother.

 Wife. What with Wormes, and Flyes?

 Son. With what I get I meane, and so do they.

 Wife. Poore Bird,
Thou'dst neuer Feare the Net, nor Lime,
The Pitfall, nor the Gin.

 Son. Why should I Mother?
Poore Birds they are not set for:
My Father is not dead for all your saying.

 Wife. Yes, he is dead:
How wilt thou do for a Father?

 Son. Nay how will you do for a Husband?

 Wife. Why I can buy me twenty at any Market.

 Son. Then you'l by 'em to sell againe.

 Wife. Thou speak'st withall thy wit,
And yet I'faith with wit enough for thee.

 Son. Was my Father a Traitor, Mother?

 Wife. I, that he was.

 Son. What is a Traitor?

 Wife. Why one that sweares, and lyes.

Son	And be all traitors that do so?
Lady Macduff	Everyone that does so is a traitor, and must be hanged.
Son	And must they all be hanged that swear and lie?
Lady Macduff	Every one.
Son	Who must hang them?
Lady Macduff	Why, the honest men.
Son	Then the liars and swearers are fools: for there are liars and swearers enough to beat the honest men, and hang up them.
Lady Macduff	Now God help thee, poor monkey! But how wilt thou do for a father?
Son	If he were dead, you'd weep for him; if you would not, it were a good sign that I should quickly have a new father.
Lady Macduff	Poor prattler, how thou talk'st!

Enter a MESSENGER

Messenger	Bless you, fair dame. I am not to you known,
	Though in your state of honour I am perfect.
	I doubt some danger does approach you nearly.
	If you will take a homely man's advice,
	Be not found here; hence with your little ones.
	To fright you thus, methinks I am too savage;
	To do worse to you were fell cruelty,
	Which is too nigh your person. Heaven preserve you,
	I dare abide no longer. *Exit*
Lady Macduff	Whither should I fly?
	I have done no harm. But I remember now
	I am in this earthly world, where to do harm
	Is often laudable, to do good sometime
	Accounted dangerous folly. Why then, alas,
	Do I put up that womanly defence,
	To say I have done no harm?

Son. And be all Traitors, that do so.

Wife. Euery one that do's so, is a Traitor,
And must be hang'd.

Son. And must they all be hang'd, that swear and lye?

Wife. Euery one.

Son. Who must hang them?

Wife. Why, the honest men.

Son. Then the Liars and Swearers are Fools: for there
are Lyars and Swearers enow, to beate the honest men,
and hang vp them.

Wife. Now God helpe thee, poore Monkie:
But how wilt thou do for a Father?

Son. If he were dead, youl'd weepe for him: if you
would not, it were a good signe, that I should quickely
haue a new Father.

Wife. Poore pratler, how thou talk'st?

Enter a Messenger.

Mes. Blesse you faire Dame: I am not to you known,
Though in your state of Honor I am perfect;
I doubt some danger do's approach you neerely.
If you will take a homely mans aduice,
Be not found heere: Hence with your little ones
To fright you thus. Me thinkes I am too sauage:
To do worse to you, were fell Cruelty,
Which is too nie your person. Heauen preserue you,
I dare abide no longer.   *Exit Messenger*

Wife. Whether should I flye?
I haue done no harme. But I remember now
I am in this earthly world: where to do harme
Is often laudable, to do good sometime
Accounted dangerous folly. Why then (alas)
Do I put vp that womanly defence,
To say I haue done no harme?
What are these faces?

Enter MURDERERS

                                      What are these faces?

Murderer   Where is your husband?

Lady Macduff I hope in no place so unsanctified
Where such as thou mayst find him.

Murderer   He's a traitor.

Son   Thou liest, thou shag-ear'd villain!50

Murderer   What, you egg!
Young fry of treachery!   [*Stabs him*]

Son   He has kill'd me, mother,
Run away, I pray you!   [*Dies*]

            Exit [LADY MACDUFF] *crying* 'Murder!'
                  [*pursued by the* MURDERERS
                  with the body of her SON]

4.3

Enter MALCOLM *and* MACDUFF

Malcolm   Let us seek out some desolate shade, and there
Weep our sad bosoms empty.

Macduff   Let us rather
Hold fast the mortal sword, and like good men
Bestride our downfall birthdom.51 Each new morn,
New widows howl, new orphans cry, new sorrows
Strike heaven on the face, that it resounds
As it felt with Scotland, and yell'd out
Like syllable of dolour.

Malcolm   What I believe, I'll wail;
What know, believe; and what I can redress,
As I shall find the time to friend, I will.
What you have spoke, it may be so perchance.
This tyrant, whose sole name blisters our tongues,
Was once thought honest; you have lov'd him well,
He hath not touch'd you yet. I am young, but
                                 something
You may discern of him through me,52 and wisdom
To offer up a weak, poor, innocent lamb

Enter Murtherers.

Mur. Where is your Husband?

Wife. I hope in no place so vnsanctified,
Where such as thou may'st finde him.

Mur. He's a Traitor.

Son. Thou ly'st thou shagge-ear'd Villaine.

Mur. What you Egge?
Yong fry of Treachery?

Son. He ha's kill'd me Mother,
Run away I pray you.   *Exit crying Murther.*

Scæna Tertia.

Enter Malcolme and Macduffe.

Mal. Let vs seeke out some desolate shade, & there
Weepe our sad bosomes empty.

Macd. Let vs rather
Hold fast the mortall Sword: and like good men,
Bestride our downfall Birthdome: each new Morne,
New Widdowes howle, new Orphans cry, new sorowes
Strike heauen on the face, that it resounds
As it felt with Scotland, and yell'd out
Like Syllable of Dolour.

Mal. What I beleeue, Ile waile;
What know, beleeue; and what I can redresse,
As I shall finde the time to friend: I wil.
What you haue spoke, it may be so perchance.
This Tyrant, whose sole name blisters our tongues,
Was once thought honest: you haue lou'd him well,
He hath not touch'd you yet. I am yong, but something
You may discerne of him through me, and wisedome
To offer vp a weake, poore innocent Lambe

T'appease an angry god.

Macduff   I am not treacherous.

Malcolm   But Macbeth is.
A good and virtuous nature may recoil
In an imperial charge. But I shall crave your pardon.
That which you are, my thoughts cannot transpose;
Angels are bright still, though the brightest fell.
Though all things foul would wear the brows of grace,
Yet grace must still look so.

Macduff   I have lost my hopes.

Malcolm   Perchance even there where I did find my doubts.
Why in that rawness left you wife and child,
Those precious motives, those strong knots of love,
Without leave-taking? I pray you,
Let not my jealousies be your dishonours,
But mine own safeties. You may be rightly just,
Whatever I shall think.

Macduff   Bleed, bleed, poor country!
Great tyranny, lay thou thy basis sure,
For goodness dare not check thee; wear thou thy
                                                    wrongs,
The title is affeer'd.⁵³ Fare thee well, lord,
I would not be the villain that thou think'st
For the whole space that's in the tyrant's grasp,
And the rich East to boot.

Malcolm   Be not offended;
I speak not as in absolute fear of you.
I think our country sinks beneath the yoke;
It weeps, it bleeds, and each new day a gash
Is added to her wounds. I think withal
There would be hands uplifted in my right,
And here from gracious England have I offer
Of goodly thousands. But for all this,
When I shall tread upon the tyrant's head,
Or wear it on my sword, yet my poor country

T'appease an angry God.
    Macd. I am not treacherous.
    Malc. But *Macbeth* is.
A good and vertuous Nature may recoyle
In an Imperiall charge. But I shall craue your pardon:
That which you are, my thoughts cannot transpose;
Angels are bright still, though the brightest fell.
Though all things foule, would wear the brows of grace
Yet Grace must still looke so.
    Macd. I haue lost my Hopes.
    Malc. Perchance euen there
Where I did finde my doubts.
Why in that rawnesse left you Wife, and Childe?
Those precious Motiues, those strong knots of Loue,
Without leaue-taking. I pray you,
Let not my Iealousies, be your Dishonors,
But mine owne Safeties: you may be rightly iust,
What euer I shall thinke.
    Macd. Bleed, bleed poore Country,
Great Tyranny, lay thou thy basis sure,
For goodnesse dare not check thee: wear ẙ thy wrongs,
The Title, is affear'd. Far thee well Lord,
I would not be the Villaine that thou think'st,
For the whole Space that's in the Tyrants Graspe,
And the rich East to boot.
    Mal. Be not offended:
I speake not as in absolute feare of you:
I thinke our Country sinkes beneath the yoake,
It weepes, it bleeds, and each new day a gash
Is added to her wounds. I thinke withall,
There would be hands vplifted in my right:
And heere from gracious England haue I offer
Of goodly thousands. But for all this,
When I shall treade vpon the Tyrants head,
Or weare it on my Sword; yet my poore Country

Shall have more vices than it had before,
More suffer, and more sundry ways than ever,
By him that shall succeed.

Macduff   What should he be?

Malcolm It is myself I mean; in whom I know
All the particulars of vice so grafted
That when they shall be open'd, black Macbeth
Will seem as pure as snow, and the poor state
Esteem him as a lamb, being compar'd
With my confineless harms.

Macduff   Not in the legions
Of horrid hell can come a devil more damn'd
In evils to top Macbeth.

Malcolm   I grant him bloody,
Luxurious, avaricious, false, deceitful,
Sudden, malicious, smacking of every sin
That has a name. But there's no bottom, none,
In my voluptuousness. Your wives, your daughters,
Your matrons, and your maids, could not fill up
The cistern of my lust; and my desire
All continent impediments would o'erbear
That did oppose my will. Better Macbeth
Than such an one to reign.

Macduff   Boundless intemperance
In nature is a tyranny. It hath been
Th'untimely emptying of the happy throne,
And fall of many kings. But fear not yet
To take upon you what is yours; you may
Convey your pleasures in a spacious plenty,
And yet seem cold. The time you may so hoodwink.
We have willing dames enough; there cannot be
That vulture in you to devour so many
As will to greatness dedicate themselves,
Finding it so inclin'd.

Malcolm   With this, there grows

Shall haue more vices then it had before,
More suffer, and more sundry wayes then euer,
By him that shall succeede.

    Macd. What should he be?

    Mal. It is my selfe I meane: in whom I know
All the particulars of Vice so grafted,
That when they shall be open'd, blacke *Macbeth*
Will seeme as pure as Snow, and the poore State
Esteeme him as a Lambe, being compar'd
With my confinelesse harmes.

    Macd. Not in the Legions
Of horrid Hell, can come a Diuell more damn'd
In euils, to top *Macbeth*.

    Mal. I grant him Bloody,
Luxurious, Auaricious, False, Deceitfull,
Sodaine, Malicious, smacking of euery sinne
That ha's a name. But there's no bottome, none
In my Voluptuousnesse: Your Wiues, your Daughters,
Your Matrons, and your Maides, could not fill vp
The Cesterne of my Lust, and my Desire
All continent Impediments would ore-beare
That did oppose my will. Better *Macbeth*,
Then such an one to reigne.

    Macd. Boundlesse intemperance
In Nature is a Tyranny: It hath beene
Th'vntimely emptying of the happy Throne,
And fall of many Kings. But feare not yet
To take vpon you what is yours: you may
Conuey your pleasures in a spacious plenty,
And yet seeme cold. The time you may so hoodwinke:
We haue willing Dames enough: there cannot be
That Vulture in you, to deuoure so many
As will to Greatnesse dedicate themselues,
Finding it so inclinde.

    Mal. With this, there growes

In my most ill-compos'd affection such
A stanchless avarice that, were I King,
I should cut off the nobles for their lands,
Desire his jewels, and this other's house,
And my more-having would be as a sauce
To make me hunger more, that I should forge
Quarrels unjust against the good and loyal,
Destroying them for wealth.

Macduff   This avarice
Sticks deeper, grows with more pernicious root
Than summer-seeming lust, and it hath been
The sword of our slain kings. Yet do not fear,
Scotland hath foisons to fill up your will
Of your mere own. All these are portable,
With other graces weigh'd.

Malcolm   But I have none. The king-becoming graces,
As justice, verity, temperance, stableness,
Bounty, persèverance, mercy, lowliness,
Devotion, patience, courage, fortitude –
I have no relish of them, but abound
In the division of each several crime,
Acting it many ways. Nay, had I power, I should
Pour the sweet milk of concord into hell,
Uproar the universal peace, confound
All unity on earth.

Macduff   O Scotland, Scotland!
Malcolm   If such a one be fit to govern, speak.
I am as I have spoken.

Macduff   Fit to govern?
No, not to live. O nation miserable!
With an untitled tyrant, bloody-sceptred,
When shalt thou see thy wholesome days again,
Since that the truest issue of thy throne
By his own interdiction stands accus'd,[54]
And does blaspheme his breed? Thy royal father
Was a most sainted king; the queen that bore thee.

In my most ill-compos'd Affection, such
A stanchlesse Auarice, that were I King,
I should cut off the Nobles for their Lands,
Desire his Iewels, and this others House,
And my more-hauing, would be as a Sawce
To make me hunger more, that I should forge
Quarrels vniust against the Good and Loyall,
Destroying them for wealth.

    Macd. This Auarice
stickes deeper: growes with more pernicious roote
Then Summer-seeming Lust: and it hath bin
The Sword of our slaine Kings: yet do not feare,
Scotland hath Foysons, to fill vp your will
Of your meere Owne. All these are portable,
With other Graces weigh'd.

    Mal. But I haue none. The King-becoming Graces,
As Iustice, Verity, Temp'rance, Stablenesse,
Bounty, Perseuerance, Mercy, Lowlinesse,
Deuotion, Patience, Courage, Fortitude,
I haue no rellish of them, but abound
In the diuision of each seuerall Crime,
Acting it many wayes. Nay, had I powre, I should
Poure the sweet Milke of Concord, into Hell,
Vprore the vniuersall peace, confound
All vnity on earth.

    Macd. O Scotland, Scotland.

    Mal. If such a one be fit to gouerne, speake:
I am as I haue spoken.

    Mac. Fit to gouern? No not to liue. O Natiō miserable!
With an vntitled Tyrant, bloody Sceptred,
When shalt thou see thy wholsome dayes againe?
Since that the truest Issue of thy Throne
By his owne Interdiction stands accust,
And do's blaspheme his breed? Thy Royall Father
Was a most Sainted-King: the Queene that bore thee,

Oft'ner upon her knees than on her feet,
Died every day she liv'd. Fare thee well,
These evils thou repeat'st upon thyself
Hath banish'd me from Scotland. O my breast,
Thy hope ends here!

Malcolm   Macduff, this noble passion,
Child of integrity, hath from my soul
Wip'd the black scruples, reconcil'd my thoughts
To thy good truth and honour. Devilish Macbeth
By many of these trains hath sought to win me
Into his power, and modest wisdom plucks me
From over-credulous haste. But God above
Deal between thee and me; for even now
I put myself to thy direction, and
Unspeak mine own detraction; here abjure
The taints and blames I laid upon myself,
For strangers to my nature. I am yet
Unknown to woman, never was forsworn,
Scarcely have coveted what was mine own,
At no time broke my faith, would not betray
The devil to his fellow, and delight
No less in truth than life. My first false speaking
Was this upon myself. What I am truly
Is thine, and my poor country's, to command:
Whither indeed, before thy here-approach,⁵⁵
Old Seyward with ten thousand warlike men
Already at a point was setting forth;
Now we'll together, and the chance of goodness
Be like our warranted quarrel. Why are you silent?

Macduff   Such welcome and unwelcome things at once
'Tis hard to reconcile.

Enter a DOCTOR [*of the English court*]

Malcolm   Well, more anon. –
Comes the King forth, I pray you?

Doctor   Ay, sir; there are a crew of wretched souls

Oftner vpon her knees, then on her feet,
Dy'de euery day she liu'd. Fare thee well,
These Euils thou repeat'st vpon thy selfe,
Hath banish'd me from Scotland. O my Brest,
Thy hope ends heere.

   Mal. Macduff, this Noble passion
Childe of integrity, hath from my soule
Wip'd the blacke Scruples, reconcil'd my thoughts
To thy good Truth, and Honor. Diuellish *Macbeth*,
By many of these traines, hath sought to win me
Into his power: and modest Wisedome pluckes me
From ouer-credulous hast: but God aboue
Deale betweene thee and me; For euen now
I put my selfe to thy Direction, and
Vnspeake mine owne detraction. Heere abiure
The taints, and blames I laide vpon my selfe,
For strangers to my Nature. I am yet
Vnknowne to Woman, neuer was forsworne,
Scarsely haue coueted what was mine owne.
At no time broke my Faith, would not betray
The Deuill to his Fellow, and delight
No lesse in truth then life. My first false speaking
Was this vpon my selfe. What I am truly
Is thine, and my poore Countries to command:
Whither indeed, before they heere approa:h
Old *Seyward* with ten thousand warlike men
Already at a point, was setting foorth:
Now wee'l together, and the chance of goodnesse
Be like our warranted Quarrell. Why are you silent?

   Macd. Such welcome, and vnwelcom things at once
'Tis hard to reconcile.

Enter a Doctor.

   Mal. Well, more anon. Comes the King forth
I pray you?

   Doct. I Sir: there are a crew of wretched Soules

	That stay his cure. Their malady convinces
	The great assay of art, but at his touch,
	Such sanctity hath heaven given his hand,
	They presently amend.
Malcolm	I thank you, doctor.
	Exit DOCTOR
Macduff	What's the disease he means?
Malcolm	'Tis call'd the Evil:
	A most miraculous work in this good King,
	Which often since my here-remain in England
	I have seen him do. How he solicits heaven
	Himself best knows, but strangely visited people,
	All swoll'n and ulcerous, pitiful to the eye,
	The mere despair of surgery, he cures,
	Hanging a golden stamp about their necks
	Put on with holy prayers; and 'tis spoken,
	To the succeeding royalty he leaves
	The healing benediction. With this strange virtue
	He hath a heavenly gift of prophecy,
	And sundry blessings hang about his throne
	That speak him full of grace.
	Enter ROSS
Macduff	See who comes here.
Malcolm	My countryman; but yet I know him not.[56]
Macduff	My ever gentle cousin, welcome hither.
Malcolm	I know him now. – Good God betimes remove
	The means that make us strangers!
Ross	Sir, amen.
Macduff	Stands Scotland where it did?
Ross	Alas, poor country,
	Almost afraid to know itself. It cannot
	Be call'd our mother, but our grave – where nothing
	But who knows nothing is once seen to smile;
	Where sighs and groans and shrieks that rend the air
	Are made, not mark'd; where violent sorrow seems
	A modern ecstasy. The dead man's knell

That stay his Cure: their malady conuinces
The great assay of Art. But at his touch,
Such sanctity hath Heauen giuen his hand,
They presently amend. *Exit.*

    Mal. I thanke you Doctor.
    Macd. What's the Disease he meanes?
    Mal. Tis call'd the Euill.
A most myraculous worke in this good King,
Which often since my heere remaine in England,
I haue seene him do: How he solicites heauen
Himselfe best knowes: but strangely visited people
All swolne and Vlcerous, pittifull to the eye,
The meere dispaire of Surgery, he cures,
Hanging a golden stampe about their neckes,
Put on with holy Prayers, and 'tis spoken
To the succeeding Royalty he leaues
The healing Benediction. With this strange vertue,
He hath a heauenly guift of Prophesie,
And sundry Blessings hang about his Throne,
That speake him full of Grace.

               Enter Rosse.

    Macd. See who comes heere.
    Malc. My Countryman: but yet I know him nor.
    Macd. My euer gentle Cozen, welcome hither.
    Malc. I know him now. Good God betimes remoue
The meanes that make vs Strangers.
    Rosse. Sir, Amen.
    Macd. Stands Scotland where it did?
    Rosse. Alas poore Countrey,
Almost affraid to know it selfe. It cannot
Be call'd our Mother, but our Graue; where nothing
But who knowes nothing, is once scene to smile:
Where sighes, and groanes, and shrieks that rent the ayre
Are made, not mark'd: Where violent sorrow seemes
A Moderne extasie: The Deadmans knell,

Is there scarce ask'd for who, and good men's lives
Expire before the flowers in their caps,
Dying or ere they sicken.

Macduff   O relation
Too nice, and yet too true!

Malcolm   What's the newest grief?

Ross   That of an hour's age doth hiss the speaker,
Each minute teems a new one.

Macduff   How does my wife?

Ross   Why, well.

Macduff   And all my children?

Ross   Well, too.

Macduff   The tyrant has not batter'd at their peace?

Ross   No, they were well at peace when I did leave 'em.

Macduff   Be not a niggard of your speech. How goes't?

Ross   When I came hither to transport the tidings
Which I have heavily borne, there ran a rumour
Of many worthy fellows that were out,
Which was to my belief witness'd the rather
For that I saw the tyrant's power afoot.
Now is the time of help. Your eye in Scotland
Would create soldiers, make our women fight,
To doff their dire distresses.

Malcolm   Be't their comfort
We are coming thither. Gracious England hath
Lent us good Seyward and ten thousand men –
An older and a better soldier none
That Christendom gives out.

Ross   Would I could answer
This comfort with the like. But I have words
That would be howl'd out in the desert air,
Where hearing should not latch them.

Macduff   What concern they?
The general cause, or is it a fee-grief
Due to some single breast?

Ross   No mind that's honest

Is there scarse ask'd for who, and good mens liues
Expire before the Flowers in their Caps,
Dying, or ere they sicken.

    Macd. Oh Relation; too nice, and yet too true.

    Malc. What's the newest griefe?

    Rosse. That of an houres age, doth hisse the speaker,
Each minute teemes a new one.

    Macd. How do's my Wife?

    Rosse. Why well.

    Macd. And all my Children?

    Rosse. Well too.

    Macd. The Tyrant ha's not batter'd at their peace?

    Rosse. No, they were wel at peace, when I did leaue 'em

    Macd. Be not a niggard of your speech: How gos't?

    Rosse. When I came hither to transport the Tydings
Which I haue heauily borne, there ran a Rumour
Of many worthy Fellowes, that were out,
Which was to my beleefe witnest the rather,
For that I saw the Tyrants Power a-foot.
Now is the time of helpe: your eye in Scotland
Would create Soldiours, make our women fight,
To doffe their dire distresses.

    Malc. Bee't their comfort
We are comming thither: Gracious England hath
Lent vs good *Seyward*, and ten thousand men,
An older, and a better Souldier, none
That Christendome giues out.

    Rosse. Would I could answer
This comfort with the like. But I haue words
That would be howl'd out in the desert ayre,
Where hearing should not latch them.

    Macd. What concerne they,
The generall cause, or is it a Fee-griefe
Due to some single brest?

    Rosse. No minde that's honest

	But in it shares some woe, though the main part

But in it shares some woe, though the main part
Pertains to you alone.

Macduff   If it be mine,
Keep it not from me; quickly let me have it.

Ross   Let not your ears despise my tongue forever
Which shall possess them with the heaviest sound
That ever yet they heard.

Macduff   H'm! I guess at it.

Ross   Your castle is surpris'd; your wife and babes
Savagely slaughter'd. To relate the manner
Were on the quarry of these murder'd deer
To add the death of you.

Malcolm   Merciful heaven!
What, man, ne'er pull your hat upon your brows:
Give sorrow words. The grief that does not speak
Whispers the o'er-fraught heart, and bids it break.

Macduff   My children too?

Ross   Wife, children, servants, all
That could be found.

Macduff   And I must be from thence!
My wife kill'd too?

Ross   I have said.

Malcolm   Be comforted.
Let's make us medicines of our great revenge
To cure this deadly grief.

Macduff   He has no children. All my pretty ones?
Did you say all? O, hell-kite! All?
What, all my pretty chickens and their dam
At one fell swoop?

Malcolm   Dispute it like a man.

Macduff   I shall do so;
But I must also feel it as a man.
I cannot but remember such things were
That were most precious to me. Did heaven look on,
And would not take their part? Sinful Macduff,
They were all struck for thee. Naught that I am,

But in it shares some woe, though the maine part
Pertaines to you alone.

    Macd. If it be mine
Keepe it not from me, quickly let me haue it.

    Rosse. Let not your cares dispise my tongue for euer,
Which shall possesse them with the heauiest sound
That euer yet they heard.

    Macd. Humh: I guesse at it.

    Rosse, Your Castle is surpriz'd: your Wife, and Babes
Sauagely slaughter'd: To relate the manner
Were on the Quarry of these murther'd Deere
To adde the death of you.

    Malc. Mercifull Heauen:
What man, ne're pull your hat vpon your browes:
Giue sorrow words; the griefe that do's not speake,
Whispers the o're-fraught heart, and bids it breake.

    Macd. My Children too?

    Ro. Wife, Children, Seruants, all that could be found.

    Macd. And I must be from thence? My wife kil'd too?

    Rosse. I haue said.

    Malc. Be comforted.
Let's make vs Med'cines of our great Reuenge,
To cure this deadly greefe.

    Macd. He ha's no Children. All my pretty ones?
Did you say All? Oh Hell-Kite! All?
What, All my pretty Chickens, and their Damme
At one fell swoope?

    Malc. Dispute it like a man.

    Macd. I shall do so:
But I must also feele it as a man;
I cannot but remember such things were
That were most precious to me: Did heauen looke on,
And would not take their part? Sinfull *Macduff,*
They were all strooke for thee: Naught that I am,

                    Not for their own demerits but for mine,
                    Fell slaughter on their souls. Heaven rest them now.
Malcolm   Be this the whetstone of your sword; let grief
                    Convert to anger. Blunt not the heart: enrage it.
Macduff   O, I could play the woman with mine eyes,
                    And braggart with my tongue. But, gentle heavens,
                    Cut short all intermission: front to front
                    Bring thou this fiend of Scotland and myself,
                    Within my sword's length set him. If he scape,
                    Heaven forgive him too.
Malcolm   This time goes manly. 57
                    Come, go we to the King; our power is ready,
                    Our lack is nothing but our leave. Macbeth
                    Is ripe for shaking, and the powers above
                    Put on their instruments. Receive what cheer you
                                                                    may:
                    The night is long that never finds the day.
                                                            Exeunt

5.1

        Enter a DOCTOR *of physic* [*to Macbeth's court*]
                *and a waiting-*GENTLEWOMAN
Doctor   I have two nights watched with you, but can
                    perceive no truth in your report. When was it she
                    last walked?
Gentlewoman   Since his majesty went into the field, I have seen
                    her rise from her bed, throw her night-gown upon
                    her, unlock her closet, take forth paper, fold it, write
                    upon't, read it, afterwards seal it, and again return to
                    bed – yet all this while in a most fast sleep.
Doctor   A great perturbation in nature, to receive at once the
                    benefit of sleep, and do the effects of watching. In
                    this slumbery agitation, besides her walking and
                    other actual performances, what at any time have
                    you heard her say?

Not for their owne demerits, but for mine
Fell slaughter on their soules: Heauen rest them now.

  Mal. Be this the Whetstone of your sword, let griefe
Conuert to anger: blunt not the heart, enrage it.

  Macd. O I could play the woman with mine eyes,
And Braggart with my tongue. But gentle Heauens,
Cut short all intermission: Front to Front,
Bring thou this Fiend of Scotland, and my selfe
Within my Swords length set him, if he scape
Heauen forgiue him too.

  Mal. This time goes manly:
Come go we to the King, our Power is ready,
Our lacke is nothing but our leaue. *Macbeth*
Is ripe for shaking, and the Powres aboue
Put on their Instruments: Receiue what cheere you may,
The Night is long, that neuer findes the Day.   *Exeunt*

Actus Quintus.   *Scena Prima.*

Enter a Doctor of Physicke, and a Wayting
Gentlewoman.

  Doct. I haue too Nights watch'd with you, but can perceiue no truth in your report. When was it shee last walk'd?

  Gent. Since his Maiesty went into the Field, I haue seene her rise from her bed, throw her Night-Gown vppon her, vnlocke her Closset, take foorth paper, folde it, write vpon't, read it, afterwards Seale it, and againe returne to bed; yet all this while in a most fast sleepe.

  Doct. A great perturbation in Nature, to receyue at once the benefit of sleep, and do the effects of watching. In this slumbry agitation, besides her walking, and other actuall performances, what (at any time) haue you heard her say?

Gentlewoman	That, sir, which I will not report after her.
Doctor	You may to me, and 'tis most meet you should.
Gentlewoman	Neither to you nor anyone, having no witness to confirm my speech.

Enter LADY MACBETH *with a taper*

	Lo you, here she comes. This is her very guise, and upon my life, fast asleep. Observe her, stand close.
Doctor	How came she by that light?
Gentlewoman	Why, it stood by her. She has light by her continually; 'tis her command.
Doctor	You see her eyes are open.
Gentlewoman	Ay, but their sense are shut.
Doctor	What is it she does now? Look how she rubs her hands.
Gentlewoman	It is an accustomed action with her to seem thus washing her hands. I have known her continue in this a quarter of an hour.
Lady Macbeth	Yet here's a spot.
Doctor	Hark, she speaks. I will set down what comes from her, to satisfy my remembrance the more strongly.
Lady Macbeth	Out, damned spot! Out, I say! One, two – why then 'tis time to do't. Hell is murky. Fie, my lord, fie! A soldier, and afeard? What need we fear? Who knows it, when none can call our power to account?[58] Yet who would have thought the old man to have had so much blood in him?
Doctor	Do you mark that?
Lady Macbeth	The Thane of Fife had a wife. Where is she now? What, will these hands ne'er be clean? No more o' that, my lord, no more o' that. You mar all with this starting.
Doctor	Go to, go to. You have known what you should not.
Gentlewoman	She has spoke what she should not, I am sure of that. Heaven knows what she has known.

Gent. That Sir, which I will not report after her.

Doct. You may to me, and 'tis most meet you should.

Gent. Neither to you, nor any one, hauing no witnesse to confirme my speech.   *Enter Lady, with a Taper.* Lo you, heere she comes: This is her very guise, and vpon my life fast asleepe: obserue her, stand close.

Doct. How came she by that light?

Gent. Why it stood by her: she ha's light by her continually, 'tis her command.

Doct. You see her eyes are open.

Gent. I but their sense are shut.

Doct. What is it she do's now? Looke how she rubbes her hands.

Gent. It is an accustom'd action with her, to seeme thus washing her hands: I haue knowne her continue in this a quarter of an houre.

Lad. Yet heere's a spot.

Doct. Heark, she speaks, I will set downe what comes from her, to satisfie my remembrance the more strongly.

La. Out damned spot: out I say. One: Two: Why then 'tis time to doo't: Hell is murky. Fye, my Lord, fie, a Souldier, and affear'd? what need we feare? who knowes it, when none can call our powre to accompt: yet who would haue thought the olde man to haue had so much blood in him.

Doct. Do you marke that?

Lad. The Thane of Fife, had a wife: where is she now? What will these hands ne're be cleane? No more o'that my Lord, no more o'that: you marre all with this starting.

Doct. Go too, go too: You haue knowne what you should not.

Gent. She ha's spoke what shee should not, I am sure of that: Heauen knowes what she ha's knowne.

Lady Macbeth	Here's the smell of the blood still. All the perfumes of Arabia will not sweeten this little hand. Oh – oh – oh!
Doctor	What a sigh is there! The heart is sorely charged.
Gentlewoman	I would not have such a heart in my bosom, for the dignity of the whole body.
Doctor	Well, well, well.
Gentlewoman	Pray God it be, sir.
Doctor	This disease is beyond my practice; yet I have known those which have walked in their sleep who have died holily in their beds.
Lady Macbeth	Wash your hands, put on your night-gown, look not so pale. I tell you yet again: Banquo's buried, he cannot come out on's grave.
Doctor	Even so?
Lady Macbeth	To bed, to bed. There's knocking at the gate. Come, come, come, come, give me your hand. What's done cannot be undone. To bed, to bed, to bed. *Exit*
Doctor	Will she go now to bed?
Gentlewoman	Directly.
Doctor	Foul whisperings are abroad; unnatural deeds Do breed unnatural troubles; infected minds To their deaf pillows will discharge their secrets. More needs she the divine than the physician. God, God, forgive us all. Look after her, Remove from her the means of all annoyance, And still keep eyes upon her. So, good night; My mind she has mated, and amaz'd my sight. I think, but dare not speak.
Gentlewoman	Good night, good doctor.

Exeunt

La. Heere's the smell of the blood still: all the perfumes of Arabia will not sweeten this little hand.
Oh, oh, oh.

Doct. What a sigh is there? The hart is sorely charg'd.

Gent. I would not hauc such a heart in my bosome, for the dignity of the whole body.

Doct. Well, well, well.

Gent. Pray God it be sir.

Doct. This disease is beyond my practise: yet I haue knowne those which haue walkt in their sleep, who haue dyed holily in their beds.

Lad. Wash your hands, put on your Night-Gowne, looke not so pale: I tell you yet againe *Banquo*'s buried; he cannot come out on's graue.

Doct. Euen so?

Lady. To bed, to bed: there's knocking at the gate: Come, come, come, come, giue me your hand: What's done, cannot be vndone. To bed, to bed, to bed.

Exit Lady.

Doct. Will she go now to bed?

Gent. Directly.

Doct. Foule whisp'rings are abroad: vnnaturall deeds
Do breed vnnaturall troubles: infected mindes
To their deafe pillowes will discharge their Secrets:
More needs she the Diuine, then the Physitian:
God, God forgiue vs all. Looke after her,
Remoue from her the meanes of all annoyance,
And still keepe eyes vpon her: So goodnight,
My minde she ha's mated, and amaz'd my sight.
I thinke, but dare not speake.

Gent. Good night good Doctor.   *Exeunt.*

5.2

Drum and colours. Enter MENTEITH, CAITHNESS,
         ANGUS, LENNOX, *and soldiers*

Menteith   The English power is near, led on by Malcolm,
                His uncle Seyward, and the good Macduff.
                Revenges burn in them, for their dear causes
                Would to the bleeding and the grim alarm
                Excite the mortified man.
Angus   Near Birnam Wood
                Shall we well meet them; that way are they coming.
Caithness   Who knows if Donalbain be with his brother?
Lennox   For certain, sir, he is not. I have a file
                Of all the gentry; there is Seyward's son,
                And many unrough youths that even now
                Protest their first of manhood.
Menteith   What does the tyrant?
Caithness   Great Dunsinane he strongly fortifies.
                Some say he's mad; others, that lesser hate him,
                Do call it valiant fury, but for certain
                He cannot buckle his distemper'd cause
                Within the belt of rule.
Angus   Now does he feel
                His secret murders sticking on his hands,
                Now, minutely, revolts upbraid his faith-breach.
                Those he commands move only in command,
                Nothing in love; now does he feel his title
                Hang loose about him, like a giant's robe
                Upon a dwarfish thief.
Menteith   Who then shall blame
                His pester'd senses to recoil and start,
                When all that is within him does condemn
                Itself for being there?

Scena Secunda.

Drum and Colours. Enter Menteth, Cathnes,
Angus, Lenox, Soldiers.

Ment. The English powre is neere, led on by *Malcolm,*
His Vnkle *Seyward,* and the good *Macduff.*
Reuenges burne in them: for their deere causes
Would to the bleeding, and the grim Alarme
Excite the mortified man.
   Ang. Neere Byrnan wood
Shall we well meet them, that way are they comming.
   Cath. Who knowes if *Donalbane* be with his brother?
   Len. For certaine Sir, he is not: I haue a File
Of all the Gentry; there is *Seywards* Sonne,
And many vnruffe youths, that euen now
Protest their first of Manhood.
   Ment. What do's the Tyrant.
   Cath. Great Dunsinane he strongly Fortifies:
Some say hee's mad: Others, that lesser hate him,
Do call it valiant Fury, but for certaine
He cannot buckle his distemper'd cause
Within the belt of Rule.
   Ang. Now do's he feele
His secret Murthers sticking on his hands,
Now minutely Reuolts vpbraid his Faith-breach:
Those he commands, moue onely in command,
Nothing in loue: Now do's he feele his Title
Hang loose about him, like a Giants Robe
Vpon a dwarfish Theefe.
   Ment. Who then shall blame
His pester'd Senses to recoyle, and start,
When all that is within him, do's condemne
It selfe, for being there.

Caithness   Well, march we on
                    To give obedience where 'tis truly ow'd.
                    Meet we the medicine of the sickly weal,
                    And with him pour we in our country's purge,
                    Each drop of us.
Lennox   Or so much as it needs
                    To dew the sovereign flower and drown the weeds.
                    Make we our march towards Birnam.

                                        Exeunt marching

5.3

                    Enter MACBETH, DOCTOR, and attendants
Macbeth   Bring me no more reports, let them fly all.
                    Till Birnam Wood remove to Dunsinane,
                    I cannot taint with fear. What's the boy Malcolm?
                    Was he not born of woman? The spirits that know
                    All mortal consequences have pronounc'd me thus:
                    'Fear not, Macbeth, no man that's born of woman
                    Shall e'er have power upon thee.' Then fly, false
                                                                    thanes,
                    And mingle with the English epicures.
                    The mind I sway by and the heart I bear
                    Shall never sag with doubt nor shake with fear.
                            Enter SERVANT
                    The devil damn thee black, thou cream-fac'd loon!
                    Where got'st thou that goose-look?
Servant   There is ten thousand –
Macbeth   Geese, villain?
Servant   Soldiers, sir.
Macbeth   Go prick thy face, and over-red thy fear,
                    Thou lily-liver'd boy. What soldiers, patch?
                    Death of thy soul, those linen cheeks of thine
                    Are counsellors to fear. What soldiers, whey-face?

Cath. Well, march we on,
To giue Obedience, where 'tis truly ow'd:
Meet we the Med'cine of the sickly Weale,
And with him poure we in our Countries purge,
Each drop of vs.
    Lenox. Or so much as it needes,
To dew the Soueraigne Flower, and drowne the Weeds:
Make we our March towards Birnan.   *Exeunt marching.*

Scæna Tertia.

Enter Macbeth, Doctor, and Attendants.

    Macb. Bring me no more Reports, let them flye all:
Till Byrnane wood remoue to Dunsinane,
I cannot taint with Feare. What's the Boy *Malcolme*?
Was he not borne of woman? The Spirits that know
All mortall Consequences, haue pronounc'd me thus:
Feare not *Macbeth*, no man that's borne of woman
Shall ere haue power vpon thee. Then fly false Thanes,
And mingle with the English Epicures,
The minde I sway by, and the heart I beare,
Shall neuer sagge with doubt, nor shake with feare.
                     Enter Seruant.
The diuell damne thee blacke, thou cream-fac'd Loone:
Where got'st thou that Goose-looke.
    Ser. There is ten thousand·
    Macb. Geese Villaine?
    Ser. Souldiers Sir.
    Macb. Go pricke thy face, and ouer-red thy feare
Thou Lilly-liuer'd Boy. What Soldiers, Patch?
Death of thy Soule, those Linnen cheekes of thine
Are Counsailers to feare. What Soldiers Whay-face?

Servant	The English force, so please you.
Macbeth	Take thy face hence! [*Exit* SERVANT]
	Seyton! – I am sick at heart
	When I behold – Seyton, I say! – This push
	Will cheer me ever, or dis-seat me now. 59
	I have liv'd long enough. My way of life
	Is fallen into the sere, the yellow leaf, 60
	And that which should accompany old age,
	As honour, love, obedience, troops of friends,
	I must not look to have; but in their stead,
	Curses, not loud but deep, mouth-honour, breath
	Which the poor heart would fain deny, and dare not.
	Seyton!

Enter SEYTON

Seyton	What's your gracious pleasure?
Macbeth	What news more?
Seyton	All is confirm'd, my lord, which was reported.
Macbeth	I'll fight till from my bones my flesh be hack'd.
	Give me my armour.
Seyton	'Tis not needed yet.
Macbeth	I'll put it on.
	Send out more horses, skirr the country round;
	Hang those that talk of fear. Give me mine armour. –
	How does your patient, doctor?
Doctor	Not so sick, my lord,
	As she is troubled with thick-coming fancies
	That keep her from her rest.
Macbeth	Cure her of that.61
	Canst thou not minister to a mind diseas'd,
	Pluck from the memory a rooted sorrow,
	Raze out the written troubles of the brain,
	And with some sweet oblivious antidote
	Cleanse the stuff'd bosom of that perilous stuff 62
	Which weighs upon the heart?
Doctor	Therein the patient
	Must minister to himself.

Ser. The English Force, so please you.

Macb. Take thy face hence. *Seyton*, I am sick at hart,
When I behold: *Seyton*, I say, this push
Will cheere me euer, or dis-eate me now.
I haue liu'd long enough: my way of life
Is falne into the Seare, the yellow Leafe,
And that which should accompany Old-Age,
As Honor, Loue, Obedience, Troopes of Friends,
I must not looke to haue: but in their steed,
Curses, not lowd but deepe, Mouth-honor, breath
Which the poore heart would faine deny, and dare not.
Seyton?

Enter Seyton.

Sey. What's your gracious pleasure?

Macb. What Newes more?

Sey. All is confirm'd my Lord, which was reported.

Macb. Ile fight, till from my bones, my flesh be hackt.
Giue me my Armor.

Seyt. 'Tis not needed yet.

Macb. Ile put it on:
Send out moe Horses, skirre the Country round,
Hang those that talke of Feare. Giue me mine Armor:
How do's your Patient, Doctor?

Doct. Not so sicke my Lord,
As she is troubled with thicke-comming Fancies
That keepe her from her rest.

Macb. Cure of that:
Can'st thou not Minister to a minde diseas'd,
Plucke from the Memory a rooted Sorrow,
Raze out the written troubles of the Braine,
And with some sweet Obliuious Antidote
Cleanse the stufft bosome, of that perillous stuffe
Which weighes vpon the heart?

Doct. Therein the Patient
Must minister to himselfe.

Macbeth	Throw physic to the dogs, I'll none of it! –
	Come, put mine armour on. Give me my staff.
	Seyton, send out. Doctor, the thanes fly from me. –
	Come sir, dispatch. – If thou couldst, doctor, cast
	The water of my land, find her disease,
	And purge it to a sound and pristine health,
	I would applaud thee to the very echo
	That should applaud again. – Pull't off, I say. –
	What rhubarb, senna, or what purgative drug [63]
	Would scour these English hence? Hear'st thou
	of them?
Doctor	Ay, my good lord; your royal preparation
	Makes us hear something.
Macbeth	Bring it after me.
	I will not be afraid of death and bane
	Till Birnam Forest come to Dunsinane.
	[*Exeunt all but* DOCTOR] [64]
Doctor	Were I from Dunsinane away, and clear,
	Profit again should hardly draw me here. *Exit*

5.4

Drum and colours. Enter MALCOLM, SEYWARD,
MACDUFF, YOUNG SEYWARD, MENTEITH,
CAITHNESS, ANGUS, *and* SOLDIERS *marching* [65]

Malcolm	Cousins, I hope the days are near at hand
	That chambers will be safe.
Menteith	We doubt it nothing.
Seyward	What wood is this before us?
Menteith	The Wood of Birnam.
Malcolm	Let every soldier hew him down a bough,
	And bear't before him; thereby shall we shadow
	The numbers of our host, and make discovery
	Err in report of us.

Macb. Throw Physicke to the Dogs, Ile none of it.
Come, put mine Armour on: giue me my Staffe:
Seyton, send out: Doctor, the Thanes flye from me:
Come sir, dispatch. If thou could'st Doctor, cast
The Water of my Land, finde her Disease,
And purge it to a sound and pristiue Health,
I would applaud thee to the very Eccho,
That should applaud againe. Pull't off I say,
What Rubarb, Cyme, or what Purgatiue drugge
Would scowre these English hence: hear'st ẙ of them?
    Doct. I my good Lord: your Royall Preparation
Makes vs heare something.
    Macb. Bring it after me:
I will not be affraid of Death and Bane,
Till Birnane Forrest come to Dunsinane.
    Doct. Were I from Dunsinane away, and cleere,
Profit againe should hardly draw me heere.   *Exeunt*

Scena Quarta.

Drum and Colours. Enter Malcolme, Seyward, Macduffe,
Seywards Sonne, Menteth, Cathnes, Angus,
and Soldiers Marching.

Malc. Cosins, I hope the dayes are neere at hand
That Chambers will be safe.
    Ment. We doubt it nothing.
    Syew. What wood is this before vs?
    Ment. The wood of Birnane.
    Malc, Let euery Souldier hew him downe a Bough,
And bear't before him, thereby shall we shadow
The numbers of our Hoast, and make discouery
Erre in report of vs.

Soldier	It shall be done.
Seyward	We learn no other but the confident tyrant
	Keeps still in Dunsinane, and will endure
	Our setting down before't.
Malcolm	'Tis his main hope,
	For where there is advantage to be given,
	Both more and less have given him the revolt,[66]
	And none serve with him but constrainèd things
	Whose hearts are absent too.
Macduff	Let our just censures
	Attend the true event, and put we on
	Industrious soldiership.
Seyward	The time approaches
	That will with due decision make us know
	What we shall say we have and what we owe;
	Thoughts speculative their unsure hopes relate,
	But certain issue strokes must arbitrate;
	Towards which, advance the war.

Exeunt marching

5.5

Enter MACBETH, SEYTON, *and soldiers, with drum and colours*

Macbeth	Hang out our banners on the outward walls.
	The cry is still, 'They come.' Our castle's strength
	Will laugh a siege to scorn; here let them lie
	Till famine and the ague eat them up.
	Were they not forc'd with those that should be ours,
	We might have met them dareful, beard to beard,
	And beat them backward home.

A cry within of women [67]

	What is that noise?
Seyton	It is the cry of women, my good lord.

Sold. It shall be done.

Syw. We learne no other, but the confident Tyrant
Keepes still in Dunsinane, and will indure
Our setting downe befor't.

Malc. 'Tis his maine hope:
For where there is aduantage to be giuen,
Both more and lesse haue giuen him the Reuolt,
And none serue with him, but constrained things,
Whose hearts are absent too.

Macd. Let our iust Censures
Attend the true euent, and put we on
Industrious Souldiership.

Sey. The time approaches,
That will with due decision make vs know
What we shall say we haue, and what we owe:
Thoughts speculatiue, their vnsure hopes relate,
But certaine issue, stroakes must arbitrate,
Towards which, aduance the warre.   *Exeunt marching*

Scena Quinta.

Enter Macbeth, Seyton, & Souldiers, with
Drum and Colours.

Macb. Hang out our Banners on the outward walls,
The Cry is still, they come: our Castles strength
Will laugh a Siedge to scorne: Heere let them lye,
Till Famine and the Ague eate them vp:
Were they not forc'd with those that should be ours,
We might haue met them darefull, beard to beard,
And beate them backward home. What is that noyse?
                 A Cry within of Women.
Sey. It is the cry of women, my good Lord.

Macbeth	I have almost forgot the taste of fears.
	The time has been, my senses would have cool'd
	To hear a night-shriek, and my fell of hair
	Would at a dismal treatise rouse and stir
	As life were in't. I have supp'd full with horrors;
	Direness familiar to my slaughterous thoughts
	Cannot once start me. Wherefore was that cry?
Seyton	The Queen, my lord, is dead.
Macbeth	She should have died hereafter;
	There would have been a time for such a word.
	Tomorrow, and tomorrow, and tomorrow,
	Creeps in this petty pace from day to day,
	To the last syllable of recorded time;
	And all our yesterdays have lighted fools
	The way to dusty death. Out, out, brief candle!
	Life's but a walking shadow, a poor player
	That struts and frets his hour upon the stage,
	And then is heard no more. It is a tale
	Told by an idiot, full of sound and fury,
	Signifying nothing.

Enter a MESSENGER

	Thou com'st to use thy tongue: thy story quickly.
Messenger	Gracious my lord,
	I should report that which I say I saw,
	But know not how to do't.
Macbeth	Well, say, sir.
Messenger	As I did stand my watch upon the hill,
	I look'd toward Birnam, and anon methought
	The wood began to move.
Macbeth	Liar and slave!
Messenger	Let me endure your wrath if't be not so.
	Within this three mile may you see it coming:
	I say, a moving grove.
Macbeth	If thou speak'st false,[68]
	Upon the next tree shall thou hang alive
	Till famine cling thee. If thy speech be sooth,

Macb. I haue almost forgot the taste of Feares:
The time ha's beene, my sences would haue cool'd
To heare a Night-shrieke, and my Fell of haire
Would at a dismall Treatise rowze, and stirre
As life were in't. I haue supt full with horrors,
Direnesse familiar to my slaughterous thoughts
Cannot once start me. Wherefore was that cry?

Sey. The Queene (my Lord) is dead.

Macb. She should haue dy'de heereafter;
There would haue beene a time for such a word:
To morrow, and to morrow, and to morrow,
Creepes in this petty pace from day to day,
To the last Syllable of Recorded time:
And all our yesterdayes, haue lighted Fooles
The way to dusty death. Out, out, breefe Candle,
Life's but a walking Shadow, a poore Player,
That struts and frets his houre vpon the Stage,
And then is heard no more. It is a Tale
Told by an Ideot, full of sound and fury
Signifying nothing.   *Enter a Messenger.*
Thou com'st to vse thy Tongue: thy Story quickly.

Mes. Gracious my Lord,
I should report that which I say I saw,
But know not how to doo't.

Macb. Well, say sir.

Mes. As I did stand my watch vpon the Hill
I look'd toward Byrnane, and anon me thought
The Wood began to moue.

Macb. Lyar, and Slaue.

Mes. Let me endure your wrath, if't be not so:
Within this three Mile may you see it comming.
I say, a mouing Groue.

Macb. If thou speak'st fhlse,
Vpon the next Tree shall thou hang aliue
Till Famine cling thee: If thy speech be sooth,

I care not if thou dost for me as much.
I pull in resolution, and begin
To doubt th'equivocation of the fiend,
That lies like truth: 'Fear not till Birnam Wood
Do come to Dunsinane' – and now a wood
Comes toward Dunsinane. – Arm, arm, and out! –
If this which he avouches does appear,
There is nor flying hence nor tarrying here.
I 'gin to be a-weary of the sun,
And wish th'estate o'th' world were now undone.
Ring the alarum bell! Blow wind, come wrack:
At least we'll die with harness on our back!

                                            Exeunt

5.6

        Drum and colours. Enter MALCOLM, SEYWARD,
           MACDUFF, *and their army, with boughs*

Malcolm   Now near enough; your leafy screens throw down,
                  And show like those you are. – You, worthy uncle,
                  Shall with my cousin, your right noble son,
                  Lead our first battle. Worthy Macduff and we
                  Shall take upon's what else remains to do,
                  According to our order.

Seyward   Fare you well.
                  Do we but find the tyrant's power tonight,
                  Let us be beaten if we cannot fight.

Macduff   Make all our trumpets speak, give them all breath,
                  Those clamorous harbingers of blood and death.

                                            Exeunt
                               Alarums continued

I care not if thou dost for me as much.
I pull in Resolution, and begin
To doubt th'Equiuocation of the Fiend,
That lies like truth. Feare not, till Byrnane Wood
Do come to Dunsinane, and now a Wood
Comes toward Dunsinane. Arme, Arme, and out,
If this which he auouches, do's appeare,
There is nor flying hence, nor tarrying here.
I 'ginne to be a-weary of the Sun,
And wish th'estate o'th'world were now vndon.
Ring the Alarum Bell, blow Winde, come wracke,
At least wee'l dye with Harnesse on our backe.   *Exeunt*

Scena Sexta.

Drumme and Colours.
Enter Malcolme, Seyward, Macduffe, and their Army,
with Boughes.

   Mal. Now neere enough:
Your leauy Skreenes throw downe,
And shew like those you are: You (worthy Vnkle)
Shall with my Cosin your right Noble Sonne
Leade our first Battell. Worthy *Macduffe*, and wee
Shall take vpon's what else remaines to do,
According to our order.
   Sey. Fare you well:
Do we but finde the Tyrants power to night,
Let vs be beaten, if we cannot fight.
   Macd. Make all our Trumpets speak, giue thē all breath
Those clamorous Harbingers of Blood, & Death.   *Exeunt*
                                Alarums continued.

5.7 [69]

                        Enter MACBETH
Macbeth   They have tied me to a stake; I cannot fly,
                   But bear-like I must fight the course. What's he
                   That was not born of woman? Such a one
                   Am I to fear, or none.
                        Enter YOUNG SEYWARD
Young Seyward   What is thy name?
Macbeth   Thou'lt be afraid to hear it.
Young Seyward   No, though thou call'st thyself a hotter name
                   Than any is in hell.
Macbeth   My name's Macbeth.
Young Seyward   The devil himself could not pronounce a title
                   More hateful to mine ear.
Macbeth   No, nor more fearful.
Young Seyward   Thou liest, abhorrèd tyrant! With my sword
                   I'll prove the lie thou speak'st.
                        They fight, and YOUNG SEYWARD *slain*
Macbeth   Thou wast born of woman.
                   But swords I smile at, weapons laugh to scorn,
                   Brandish'd by man that's of a woman born.   *Exit*
                                                       Alarums
                        Enter MACDUFF
Macduff   That way the noise is. Tyrant, show thy face!
                   If thou be'st slain, and with no stroke of mine,
                   My wife and children's ghosts will haunt me still.
                   I cannot strike at wretched kerns whose arms
                   Are hir'd to bear their staves. Either thou, Macbeth,
                   Or else my sword with an unbatter'd edge
                   I sheathe again undeeded. There thou shouldst be.
                   By this great clatter, one of greatest note
                   Seems bruited. Let me find him, Fortune,
                   And more I beg not!   *Exit*
                                                       Alarums

Scena Septima.

Enter Macbeth.

Macb. They haue tied me to a stake, I cannot flye,
But Beare-like I must fight the course. What's he
That was not borne of Woman? Such a one
Am I to feare, or none.

Enter young Seyward.

Y. Sey. What is thy name?

Macb. Thou'lt be affraid to heare it.

Y. Sey. No: though thou call'st thy selfe a hoter name
Then any is in hell.

Macb. My name's *Macbeth*.

Y. Sey. The diuell himselfe could not pronounce a Title
More hatefull to mine eare.

Macb. No: nor more fearefull.

Y. Sey. Thou lyest abhorred Tyrant, with my Sword
Ile proue the lye thou speak st.

Fight, and young Seyward slaine.

Macb. Thou was't borne of woman;
But Swords I smile at, Weapons laugh to scorne,
Brandish'd by man that's of a Woman borne.   *Exit.*

Alarums.   *Enter Macduffe.*

Macd. That way the noise is: Tyrant shew thy face,
If thou beest slaine, and with no stroake of mine,
My Wife and Childrens Ghosts will haunt me still:
I cannot strike at wretched Kernes, whose armes
Are hyr'd to beare their Staues; either thou *Macbeth*,
Or else my Sword with an vnbattered edge
I sheath againe vndeeded. There thou should'st be,
By this great clatter, one of greatest note
Seemes bruited. Let me finde him Fortune,
And more I begge not.   *Exit.*   *Alarums.*

Enter MALCOLM *and* SEYWARD

Seyward This way, my lord; the castle's gently render'd.
The tyrant's people on both sides do fight;
The noble thanes do bravely in the war.
The day almost itself professes yours,
And little is to do.

Malcolm   We have met with foes
That strike beside us.

Seyward   Enter, sir, the castle.   *Exeunt*
                                                        Alarum

Enter MACBETH

Macbeth Why should I play the Roman fool, and die
On mine own sword? Whiles I see lives, the gashes
Do better upon them.

Enter MACDUFF

Macduff   Turn, hell-hound, turn!

Macbeth Of all men else I have avoided thee –
But get thee back, my soul is too much charg'd
With blood of thine already.

Macduff   I have no words,
My voice is in my sword, thou bloodier villain
Than terms can give thee out.   *Fight*
                                                      Alarum

Macbeth   Thou losest labour.
As easy mayst thou the intrenchant air
With thy keen sword impress as make me bleed.
Let fall thy blade on vulnerable crests:
I bear a charmèd life which must not yield
To one of woman born.

Macduff   Despair thy charm,
And let the angel whom thou still hast serv'd
Tell thee, Macduff was from his mother's womb
Untimely ripp'd.

Macbeth Accursèd be that tongue that tells me so,
For it hath cow'd my better part of man!
And be these juggling fiends no more believ'd,

Enter Malcolme and Seyward.

Sey. This way my Lord, the Castles gently rendred:
The Tyrants people, on both sides do fight,
The Noble Thanes do brauely in the Warre,
The day almost it selfe professes yours,
And little is to do.
   Malc. We haue met with Foes
That strike beside vs.
   Sey. Enter Sir, the Castle.   *Exeunt.*   *Alarum*
                    Enter Macbeth.
   Macb. Why should I play the Roman Foole, and dye
On mine owne sword? whiles I see liues, the gashes
Do better vpon them.
                    Enter Macduffe.
   Macd. Turne Hell-hound, turne.
   Macb. Of all men else I haue auoyded thee:
But get thee backe, my soule is too much charg'd
With blood of thine already.
   Macd. I haue no words,
My voice is in my Sword, thou bloodier Villaine
Then tearmes can giue thee out.   *Fight: Alarum*
   Macb. Thou loosest labour
As easie may'st thou the intrenchant Ayre
With thy keene Sword impresse, as make me bleed:
Let fall thy blade on vulnerable Crests,
I beare a charmed Life, which must not yeeld
To one of woman borne.
   Macd. Dispaire thy Charme,
And let the Angell whom thou still hast seru'd
Tell thee, *Macduffe* was from his Mothers womb
Vntimely ript.
   Macb. Accursed be that tongue that tels mee so;
For it hath Cow'd my better part of man:
And be these Iugling Fiends no more beleeu'd,

	That palter with us in a double sense,
	That keep the word of promise to our ear
	And break it to our hope. I'll not fight with thee.
Macduff	Then yield thee, coward,
	And live to be the show and gaze o'th' time!
	We'll have thee as our rarer monsters are,
	Painted upon a pole, and under writ:
	'Here may you see the tyrant.'
Macbeth	I will not yield
	To kiss the ground before young Malcolm's feet,
	And to be baited with the rabble's curse.
	Though Birnam Wood be come to Dunsinane,
	And thou oppos'd, being of no woman born,
	Yet I will try the last. Before my body
	I throw my warlike shield. Lay on, Macduff,
	And damn'd be him that first cries, 'Hold, enough!'

                                              Exeunt fighting
                                                    Alarums

Enter [MACDUFF *and* MACBETH] *fighting,*
and MACBETH *slain*

[*Exeunt.*] *Retreat and flourish* 70
Enter with drum and colours, MALCOLM, SEYWARD,
ROSS, *thanes, and soldiers*

Malcolm	I would the friends we miss were safe arriv'd.
Seyward	Some must go off; and yet by these I see,
	So great a day as this is cheaply bought.
Malcolm	Macduff is missing, and your noble son.
Ross	Your son, my lord, has paid a soldier's debt;
	He only liv'd but till he was a man,
	The which no sooner had his prowess confirm'd
	In the unshrinking station where he fought,
	But like a man he died.
Seyward	Then he is dead?
Ross	Ay, and brought off the field. Your cause of sorrow
	Must not be measur'd by his worth, for then
	It hath no end.

That palter with vs in a double sence,
That keepe the word of promise to our eare,
And breake it to our hope. Ile not fight with thee.
    Macd. Then yeeld thee Coward,
And liue to be the shew, and gaze o'th'time.
Wee'l haue thee, as our rarer Monsters are
Painted vpon a pole, and vnder-writ,
Heere may you see the Tyrant.
    Macb. I will not yeeld
To kisse the ground before young *Malcolmes* feet,
And to be baited with the Rabbles curse.
Though Byrnane wood be come to Dunsinane,
And thou oppos'd, being of no woman borne,
Yet I will try the last. Before my body,
I throw my warlike Shield: Lay on *Macduffe*,
And damn'd be him, that first crics hold, enough.
                        Exeunt fighting.   *Alarums.*

      Enter Fighting, and Macbeth slaine.

   Retreat, and Flourish. Enter with Drumme and Colours,
     Malcolm, Seyward, Rosse, Thanes, & Soldiers.
    Mal. I would the Friends we misse, were safe arriu'd·
    Sey. Some must go off: and yet by these I see,
So great a day as this is cheaply bought.
    Mal. Macduffe is missing, and your Noble Sonne.
    Rosse. Your son my Lord, ha's paid a souldiers debt,
He onely liu'd but till he was a man,
The which no sooner had his Prowesse confirm'd
In the vnshrinking station where he fought,
But like a man he dy'de.
    Sey. Then he is dead?
    Rosse. 1, and brought off the field: your cause of sorrow
Must not be measur'd by his worth, for then
It hath no end.

Seyward	Had he his hurts before?
Ross	Ay, on the front.
Seyward	Why then, God's soldier be he.

Had I as many sons as I have hairs,
I would not wish them to a fairer death.
And so his knell is knoll'd.

Malcolm   He's worth more sorrow,
And that I'll spend for him.

Seyward   He's worth no more:
They say he parted well, and paid his score,
And so God be with him. Here comes newer comfort.

Enter MACDUFF *with Macbeth's head*

Macduff   Hail, King, for so thou art. Behold where stands
Th'usurper's cursèd head. The time is free.
I see thee compass'd with thy kingdom's pearl,
That speak my salutation in their minds,
Whose voices I desire allow'd with mine.
Hail, King of Scotland!

All   Hail, King of Scotland!

Flourish

Malcolm   We shall not spend a large expense of time
Before we reckon with your several loves,
And make us even with you. My thanes and kinsmen,
Henceforth be earls, the first that ever Scotland
In such an honour nam'd. What's more to do
Which would be planted newly with the time –
As calling home our exil'd friends abroad
That fled the snares of watchful tyranny,
Producing forth the cruel ministers
Of this dead butcher and his fiend-like queen
Who, as 'tis thought, by self and violent hands
Took off her life – this, and what needful else
That calls upon us, by the grace of Grace,
We will perform in measure, time, and place.

Sey. Had he his hurts before?

Rosse. I, on the Front.

Sey. Why then, Gods Soldier be he:
Had I as many Sonnes, as I haue haires,
I would not wish them to a fairer death:
And so his Knell is knoll'd.

Mal. Hee's worth more sorrow,
And that Ile spend for him.

Sey. He's worth no more,
They say he parted well, and paid his score,
And so God be with him. Here comes newer comfort.

> *Enter Macduffe, with Macbeths head.*

Macd. Haile King, for so thou art.
Behold where stands
Th'Vsurpers cursed head: the time is free:
I see thee compast with thy Kingdomes Pearle,
That speake my salutation in their minds:
Whose voyces I desire alowd with mine.
Haile King of Scotland.

All. Haile King of Scotland.   *Flourish.*

Mal. We shall not spend a large expence of time,
Before we reckon with your seuerall loues,
And make vs euen with you. My Thanes and Kinsmen
Henceforth be Earles, the first that euer Scotland
In such an Honor nam'd: What's more to do,
Which would be planted newly with the time,
As calling home our exil'd Friends abroad,
That fled the Snares of watchfull Tyranny,
Producing forth the cruell Ministers
Of this dead Butcher, and his Fiend-like Queene;
Who (as 'tis thought) by selfe and violent hands,
Tooke off her life. This, and what needfull else
That call's vpon vs, by the Grace of Grace,
We will performe in measure, time, and place:

So thanks to all at once and to each one,
Whom we invite to see us crown'd at Scone.

Flourish
Exeunt

So thankes to all at once, and to each one,
Whom we inuite, to see vs Crown'd at Scone.
          Flourish.   *Exeunt Omnes.*

FINIS.

Textual Notes

As our Series Introduction explains, our modernized edition remains as faithful as possible to its Folio model. Sometimes, however, it is necessary to intercede on its behalf – where the Folio, in other words, makes little or no sense. These notes are designed to explain these decisions as succinctly as possible, by reference to the play's enormous editorial tradition. It has also sometimes been felt necessary to signal those occasions where the Folio reading we retain has been subject to editorial or scholarly contention. Each numbered note therefore gives the relevant line from the parallel text (with its act and scene, and page-number): '3. **Shipwrecking storms and direful thunders,** (1.2, pp. 4–5)'; and where our modern texts overrule the Folio ('F'), our notes highlight the problem by setting the contested word(s) in square brackets: '15. **Who dares do [F no] more is none.** (1.7, pp. 34–5)'. Our accounts of these intercessions and alternatives range from simple attributions to previous editions, to lengthier discussions of thornier 'cruxes', while seeking always to defend the absolute necessity of such interference. A chronological list of the texts, editions, and scholarship cited there, from the 1623 First Folio to A.R. Brunmuller's 1997 edition, may be found at the end of these notes.

1.   *Second Witch* **Paddock calls.** | *Third Witch* **Anon! [F *All. Paddock* calls anon:]** (1.1, pp. 2–3)
     Alexander Pope (1723–5) first identified the oddity of the Folio distribution of lines here. Witches were superstitiously believed to have their own individual 'familiars' or supernatural companions. The First Witch has just addressed hers, Graymalkin the cat; Pope therefore assigned to the Second Witch this reference to another familiar, the toad (or 'Paddock', as in the modern Swedish *padda*): 'Paddock calls – anon!' Joseph Hunter (1845) finessed the scene's structure by having the Third Witch interject 'Anon!', which, as Nicholas Brooke comments (1990), obeys 'the general rule that they speak in strict rotation'. It is further notable that this arrangement provides three sets of three speeches for the three

witches (before they do indeed '*All*' recite the final couplet) –
'Thrice to thine, and thrice to mine, | And thrice again, to make
up nine' (1.3, pp. 10–11) – and that the Folio's speech-prefix (SP)
remains strictly correct, since all the witches do speak them, but in a
certain sequence.

2.   **Of kerns and galloglasses [F Gallowgrosses] is supplied, |
       And Fortune on his damnèd quarry smiling, | Show'd like a
       rebel's whore.** (1.2, pp. 4–5)
       'Kerns and galloglasses' were kinds of Irish soldiers, the former
       lightly armed, notoriously savage foot-soldiers; the latter élite
       troops, armed with battleaxes or halberds. While 'kern' was in
       common parlance in the period, 'galloglass' was a more specialist
       term, which presumably explains F's mistranscription. Most editors
       since Thomas Hanmer (1743–5) have suspected that F's 'Quarry' in
       the following line should properly read 'quarrel', with the meaning:
       *Thus supplied with reinforcements, Lady Luck seemed to favour rebellious
       Macdonald's devilish dispute* ['quarrel'] *like a fickle whore*. The fact that
       Shakespeare's source, Holinshed's 1587 *Chronicles*, describes how
       'Kernes and Gallowglasses' were among those troops 'offering
       themselves to assist him in that rebellious quarrel [*sic*]', is grounds
       for regarding the emendation as 'certain', according to Kenneth
       Muir (1951). But might Shakespeare have deliberately substituted
       'quarry' for Holinshed's more prosaic 'quarrel'? 'Quarry' (in the
       sense of a *hunter's prey* or the *rack of slaughtered game after a hunt*)
       certainly fits the passage's general context of 'bloody execution':
       'This quarry cries on havoc,' says Fortinbras on entering the corpse-
       strewn stage at the end of *Hamlet*. It is, however, frustratingly
       difficult to establish a precise paraphrase – 'the "damnèd quarry"
       being the doomed army of kerns and gallowglasses, who, although
       Fortune deceitfully smiled on them fled before the sword of
       Macbeth and became his *quarry* – his prey' (Charles Knight,
       1838–43). Modern editors tend to point out that the two words,
       quarry and *quarrel*, were sometimes used interchangeably in the
       period; and that an additional sense of 'quarrel' (spelled as 'quarry'
       in at least one contemporary text) was the viciously headed bolt shot
       by a crossbow – one of the nastiest weapons ever to have been
       invented. The crux perhaps illustrates the maxim that great poetry
       can communicate in advance of being understood.

3. **Ship-wrecking storms and direful thunders,** (1.2, pp. 4–5)
The basic structure of the Captain's simile in this passage is clear: terrible storms can blow up even in the east, where the life-giving sun comes up; and it is from the east, too, that the enemy reinforcements arrived from Norway. The gist is that terrible events can come out of a clear blue sky, though the extraordinary density of its expression allows a variety of preciser interpretation. (The word 'spring', for example, allows both aquatic and seasonal meanings.) The elliptical manner of Shakespeare's mature style may have suffered a further, inadvertent compression in this particular line, however, which the Second Folio (1632) gives as 'Shipwracking storms and direful thunders breaking' – which may suggest that a word has inadvertently dropped out of the Folio text. Alexander Pope (1723–5) certainly thought so, and adapted the F2 reading to fit the metre ('Shipwracking storms and direful thunders break'), and this has become the standard reading. A.R. Braunmuller (1997) resists the temptation to supply the additional word on the grounds that 'The verb "come" is understood here ['. . . and direful thunders *come,*'], though spoken only in [the next line]': 'So from that spring whence comfort seems to *come,* | Discomfort swells.'

4. **[*Exit* CAPTAIN, *attended*]** (1.2, pp. 6–7)
Edmond Malone (1790) was the first editor to specify this stage-direction. Some stage business must surely follow King Duncan's instructions, and it seems more theatrically effective not to have the Captain's 'gashes' distractingly bleeding on-stage during the interview with Ross that follows.

5. **How far is't call'd to Forres [F Soris]?** (1.3, pp. 10–11)
Editors are agreed with Alexander Pope's cross-reference (1723–5) to a map of Scotland, where the coastal town of Forres (Pope spelled it 'Foris') lies twelve or so miles north-east of Cawdor: the manuscript letters *s* and *f* were easily confused in the period. (The phrase itself is apparently a Scottish idiom, meaning 'How far is it to Forres?')

6. **By Finel's [F *Sinells*] death I know I am Thane of Glamis,**
(1.3, pp. 12–13)
Here is a nice problem. Pope's emendation of F's '*Soris*' to 'Forres' has long been accepted as the standard reading (see previous note) because it seems clear that what Shakespeare wrote has been

misunderstood by a scribe or compositor who confused an *f* for an *s*.
An identical mistake has here been made in reverse – not in the
(already complicated) textual transmission of Shakespeare's 1606
manuscript into 1623 print, but via a far longer chain of error.
Macbeth's father (by whose death he inherited the title of Thane of
Glamis) is now known to have been called Finel (or Findlaech, or
Finleg, or Finley). But Shakespeare did not know this: he merely
followed Ralph Holinshed's *Chronicles*, where 'Makbeth, thane of
Glammis' is said to have inherited 'that dignitie and office by the
death of his father Sinell'. Holinshed himself inherited the error
from the sixteenth-century Scottish chronicler Hector Boece.
Similar errors in Holinshed found their way into the Folio texts of
Shakespeare's *Henry V* (where 'King *Lewes* the Tenth' should
properly be 'the Ninth', 1.2) and *Richard III* (where a confusion
between 'mother' and 'brother' leads Shakespeare into a poetically
vivid but historically misconceived sequence, 5.3). Editors generally
correct Shakespeare's history in *Henry V*, but not in *Richard III*,
where to do so would make nonsense of his verse. The present case
lies somewhere in the middle: there was no such person as 'Sinell';
but his sibilant name is arguably what Shakespeare seized upon
('*Stay*, you imperfect *s*peakers . . . By *S*inell'*s* death I know . . .').

7. **Thy personal venture in the rebels' fight,** (1.3, pp. 14–15)
    The Folio praises Macbeth's demeanour in the 'Rebels fight' (= *in
    the battle with the rebels*), but some editors prefer to assume that 'fight'
    might be another example of an *s/f* confusion (see the previous two
    notes) – that Macbeth, in other words, performed his deeds in *sight*
    of the rebels.

8. **Strange images of death. As [F death, as] thick as tale |
    Came [F Can] post with post,** (1.3, pp. 14–15)
    Something has gone badly wrong in the Folio here, and editors
    must decide upon the scale of the problem. All agree with
    Alexander Pope's 1723–5 division of the Folio line into two separate
    sentences: (1) the King has praised the dauntlessness with which
    Macbeth faced those he killed (and their ghastly corpses); (2)
    Macbeth's behaviour is mentioned in a constant series of dispatches
    ('post with post'). Nicholas Rowe's 'Can' for F's 'Came' (1709) is
    likewise generally accepted: messenger after messenger surely *came*
    with reports of Macbeth's deeds, and their accumulated sequence

was *as thick as* . . . well, this is where opinion divides. Rowe proposed 'As thick as *hail*' (1709), and this has become the standard reading, since the simile is both immediately understandable (to hear the many reports of Macbeth's valour was like being pelted in a hail-storm) and a proverbial commonplace of the period. F's 'thick as tale', though, has had its measure of informed proponents, all of whom treat the trite proverbialism of Rowe's alternative as evidence *against* Shakespeare's use of it. F's reading, which we adopt, depends upon 'tale' meaning something closer to our 'tally' (*enumeration, count*) than any idea of a narrative story: *the messengers arrived in such quick succession that it was impossible to count them.* C.J. Sisson paraphrased and unpicked the expression to mean 'The posts came thronging, with tales thronging, to every tale a post, post after post, and tale after tale' (1956).

9. **Is execution done on Cawdor, or not | Those [F *Cawdor?* | Or not those] in commission yet return'd?** (1.4, pp. 18-19)
The Second Folio editors (1632) changed F's 'Or' to 'Are', and it is possible that their emendation in fact corrected an earlier error by the F compositors (the capitals O and A being easily mistaken in contemporary handwriting). It is also possible that neither of these readings is correct, and that Shakespeare intended '. . . *or are* those in commission yet return'd?'. F's construction makes perfectly acceptable sense.

10. **nor keep peace between | Th'effect and it [F hit].**
(1.5, pp. 26-7)
Editors are agreed that F's 'hit' is simply an archaic spelling of 'it': Lady Macbeth invokes the spirits of cruelty to harden her heart against the coming murder, and thwart the workings of remorse, so that her conscience ('compunctious visitings of nature': the phrase may also allude to the menstruation that partly defines the allegedly 'weaker sex') will neither deter her 'purpose' nor intervene between 'it' and its murderous consequence – though Shakespeare reverses the order of this latter clause for effect. (The rhetorical device is rather splendidly known as *'hysteron proteron'* = (Greek) 'latter as former'.)

11. **May read strange matters to beguile the time. | Look like the time:** (1.5, pp. 28-9)
In F, Lady Macbeth rebukes her husband for having a face like an open (and guilty) book *where men may read mysterious matters to while*

away their time, and then instructs him to *behave appropriately to the moment* ('Look like the time . . .'). It is true that in *Twelfth Night* Antonio promises Sebastian to arrange dinner for them, 'Whiles you beguile the time, and feed your knowledge | With viewing of the town' (3.3), but this sense of *idling away* the hours may not in fact be what Shakespeare intended here. For as Lewis Theobald first proposed in 1733, the line might be repunctuated so as to refine the sense of Lady Macbeth's instruction: '. . . may read strange matters. To beguile the time, | Look like the time' (*In order to deceive the present world, behave appropriately to the moment* . . .). This has become the standard reading, though it is perhaps notable that F's version passed unchallenged through four Folio editions and the critical attentions both of Nicholas Rowe (1709) and Alexander Pope (1723–5 and 1728). 'Theobald's repunctuation changes the line's effect,' comments A.R. Braunmuller (1997); our edition tentatively favours the original effect on the simple grounds that it makes good sense – though Shakespeare's punctuation seems to have been both scant and fluid.

12. *Hautboys and torches.* (1.6, pp. 28–9)
     It has been plausibly argued (by John Dover Wilson in 1947) that the Folio's directions here for music and torches, usually indicative of a scene indoors, is incompatible with the scene's implicit setting *outside* Macbeth's castle during daylight hours. Kenneth Muir (1951) comments that 'at sundown, torches would be needed inside the castle, even though it was still light outside' – but what are a consort of hautboys doing outside the castle-gates? Braunmuller (1997) usefully replies that Queen Elizabeth had been welcomed to Kenilworth Castle in 1575 with music (including 'Hautboiz') played *en plein air*, and sees no reason for the scene not to take place after nightfall; Nicholas Brooke (1990) treats F's direction here as an advance cue, 1.6 being so short, for the following scene, which certainly is set indoors, and which likewise calls for 'Hautboys. Torches' (1.7, pp. 32–3).

13. **The temple-haunting martlet [F Barlet], does approve, | By his lov'd masonry [F Mansonry],** (1.6, pp. 28–9)
     As our Introduction explains (above, pp. xliii–xliv), these lines exemplify the problems and opportunities thrown up by *Macbeth*'s

unique textual status. It is quite clear that F's 'Barlet' is a bird, 'this bird' that so auspiciously builds his nest ('his pendant bed and procreant cradle') in the eaves of the Macbeths' castle. But (1) no bird has ever been called a 'Barlet'; and (2) there is no such word as 'Mansonry'. Unlikely as it may seem, the capital letters *M* and *B* were easily confused in seventeenth-century handwriting, and so Nicholas Rowe's 1709 emendation to 'martlet' (the house martin or swallow) continues to be the standard reading – almost certainly correctly, as cross-reference to *The Merchant of Venice* confirms: 'the martlet [F Martlet] | Builds in the weather on the outward wall' (2.9). Editorial consensus divides equally over F's meaningless 'Mansonry': Alexander Pope (1728) assumed that the letter *n* was superfluous, and proposed 'masonry' (*the loving construction of his nest*); Lewis Theobald (1733), probably for the sake of argument, preferred to assume that the letter *i* had been omitted from Shakespeare's 'mansionry' (*the rich buildings he loves to build his nest in*). Either reading is possible (the compositor may have misread an ink-blot as a tilde – 'Māsonry' – or simply interpreted a badly written *i* as a flourish – 'Mansionry'): Pope's is by far the commoner word, but Theobald's may be an example of Shakespeare's habit of coining new words.

Nicholas Rowe (1709) further proposed that Banquo's subsequent observation that the 'air is delicate' where these birds 'must [= *feel the compulsion to*] breed and haunt' might properly and more subtly read 'Where they *most* breed and haunt' (i.e., *the air is sweet where great flocks of these birds build their nests*). Nicholas Brooke (1990) is one of few editors to resist this temptation.

14. **But here, upon this bank and school [F Schoole] of time,** (1.7, pp. 32–3)
Macbeth's soliloquy is so famous that it comes as something of a surprise to discover that its pivotal image ('But here, upon this bank and *shoal* of time') was not given until Lewis Theobald's 1733 edition. Theobald (and most subsequent editors) imagine Macbeth momentarily marooned upon a sand-*bank* in shallow waters ('*shoal*'), surrounded by the endless flow of Time's vastly deep river. (William Warburton (1747) and Arthur Gray (1888) rang the changes by positing 'shelve' (i.e. *shelf*) and 'shore' respectively.) The F-reading has had its defenders, however (which is why we retain it), on the

grounds that the line introduces a stream of imagery comparing
Time to the inevitable process of a didactic legal system: 'bank [=
judicial bench] . . . school . . . cases . . . judgement . . . teach . . .
instructions . . . justice'. (Although the phrase post-dates Macbeth's
hope to 'jump the life to come', his image anticipates our modern
sense of 'jumping bail'.) The truth of the matter is probably that
Shakespeare intended both legal and aquatic senses to play
simultaneously in our minds: the words 'school' and 'shoal' were
spelled and perhaps pronounced interchangeably in the period (as
witness the survival of the collective noun, *a school of whales*). The
full meaning of the passage therefore probably lies midway between
'This *Shallow*, this *narrow Ford* of human life, opposed to the *great
Abyss* of Eternity' (Benjamin Heath, 1765) and 'upon this bench of
instruction, in this school of eternity' (Hastings Elwin, 1853).

15.   **Who dares do [F no] more is none.** (1.7, pp. 34–5)
      All editors are agreed upon the necessity of Nicholas Rowe's 1709
      emendation, George Steevens (1773) first adducing the parallel
      expression in *Measure for Measure* (probably written within two years
      or so of *Macbeth*): 'Be that you are,' says Angelo to Isabel there,
      'That is, a woman. If you be more, you're none' (2.4: *if you behave
      more courageously than a woman should, you're no longer a woman*), where
      the verb 'be' is repeated in just the same way that 'do' is repeated in
      Rowe's emended version of F. Rowe's version of that phrase has
      Macbeth claim that *any man who proves his virility by daring to do more
      than is appropriate to humankind thereby forfeits his claim to humanity, and
      is therefore no man at all*. Joseph Hunter (1845) complained of Rowe's
      'most violent' intercession, instead proposing that the half-line
      should properly be seen as part of Lady Macbeth's reply: 'Who dares
      no more is none. What beast was't then . . . ' The line may work as a
      sarcastic rejoinder (*Whoever dares no more than an ordinary man can rise
      to is not – at least to my way of thinking – a truly virile man at all*) – but it
      is a moot point as to whether Hunter's reassignment of the line
      does any less violence to 'the true text as it flowed from the pen of
      Shakespeare' than Rowe's elegantly minimal adjustment.

16.   **We fail! [F faile?]** (1.7, pp. 36–7)
      Seventeenth-century punctuation rarely distinguished between our
      question mark (?) and exclamation mark (!). The Folio's 'We faile?',

then, may either signal Lady Macbeth's distaste for her husband's even entertaining the idea of failure (*We? Fail?*); or else her stoical acknowledgement that *if we fail, then – dammit! – we fail*. The exclamation mark we adopt carries the original ambiguity. (It should be noted that the 'But' beginning the following sentence is not a qualifying conjunction, but rather carries the sense *If you will only apply courage . . .*)

17. *Enter **BANQUO** and **FLEANCE**, with* [F *Banquo, and Fleance, with*] *a torch before him* (2.1, pp. 38–9)
    The Folio's SD is ambiguous: does Banquo enter preceded by Fleance carrying a torch (a stick wedged with combustible resinous material)? Or are father and son preceded by a torch-bearing servant – the word 'torch' (like 'drum' or 'trumpet') in F's SDs meaning both the required stage-effect *and* the supernumerary carrying the relevant prop? Fleance has to receive Banquo's sword ('Hold, take my sword'), and then some other accoutrement ('Take thee that, too'), which might make for clumsy stage-business; on the other hand, Macbeth subsequently enters preceded by 'a servant with a torch'. Alternatively, Banquo may hand Fleance his sword – and then the torch he himself carries. If F's '*torch*' is in fact (as it were) a spear-carrier, he should exit with Banquo and Fleance (pp. 40–41) before Macbeth dismisses his own servant.

18. **With Tarquin's ravishing strides [F sides], towards his design | Moves like a ghost.** (2.1, pp. 42–3)
    It was Alexander Pope (1723–5) whose emendation made sense of an otherwise baffling sequence. Tarquin was the legendary rapist-tyrant, who 'wickedly . . . stalks' into his victim's chamber in Shakespeare's own 1594 *Rape of Lucrece* (line 365). The corrected line therefore imagines the figure of 'Murder . . . with his stealthy pace' *stalking his victim, as Tarquin did Lucrece*. (The second clause here – 'towards his design | Moves like a ghost' – is a simple inversion: Murder, *like the rapist Tarquin*, moves towards his prey 'like a ghost'.) Though Pope's reading is generally accepted, it would have taken a notably large blunder by the scribe or compositor to misread 'strides' as 'sides', and a series of frankly unconvincing alternatives have been proposed. Zachariah Jackson (1819) provided a near-anagram ('With Tarquin's ravishing <u>ideas</u> [= *corrupt intentions*]'): ingenious, but cloth-eared to the metre. Samuel Johnson (1765)

disliked the idea that a 'stealthy' criminal might so vigorously
'stride', and so envisaged a Murder who, 'With <u>Tarquin</u> ravishing [=
like Tarquin the rapist], <u>slides</u> [= *moves silently*] towards his design' – a
verb appropriate both to ghosts and furtive malefactors: wise, but
optimistic. Charles Knight (1838–43) saw instead a figure who 'with
his stealthy pace | (<u>Which</u> Tarquin's ravishing sides [= *which
movement Tarquin's rape matches in its stealth*]) towards his design |
Moves . . .': diverting, but unlikely. H.B. Sprague (1889) retained
the Folio reading in full, on the grounds that 'Tarquin's ravishing
sides' may mean 'Tarquin's ravishing *party*, the gang of devilish
agencies and auxiliaries . . . that throng around Tarquin. With these,
for the moment, withered Murder joins and moves towards his
bloody deed': wrong, but romantic. The line Shakespeare wrote is
perhaps beyond retrieval, and the spate of tangled obscurities in the
rest of the speech (see Textual Note 19 below) perhaps suggests that
the speech was part of a damaged manuscript page.

19. **Thou sure [F sowre] and firm-set earth, | Hear not my steps,
which way they [F which they may] walk, for fear | Thy very
stones prate of my whereabout,** (2.1, pp. 42–3)
As the previous note details, Macbeth's hallucinogenic soliloquy is
haunted, too, by the spectre of textual corruption. Firstly, F's 'sowre'
must bear some pertinent relationship to its fellow-adjective 'firm-
set': the ground upon which he steps is solid to his tread – indeed,
startlingly so, for the echo they resound might betray his murderous
course. Something therefore seems to be awry with 'sour' (F: 'sowre';
F3: 'sowr'; F4: 'sour'), despite being retained by Nicholas Rowe
(1709). Scholars have flocked to the task: the earth beneath his feet
is variously 'sound' (= *solid*) (Alexander Pope, 1723–5); 'lower'
(= *this sublunary earth*) ('X', 1788); 'sore'; 'stowre' (= *inflexible, sturdy*:
provincial and archaic dialect) (B. Nicholson, 1878); and, finally,
'sure' (conjectured by Alexander Pope, 1723–5, adopted by Edward
Capell, 1767–8, and almost all subsequent editors): Macbeth feels
the earth to be 'sure' (solid, certain) in contrast to the airy echoes
of guilt he fears hearing from his footfalls.

　　Nicholas Rowe's 1709 emendation in the second line has passed
more or less unchallenged, helped on its way by the use of a very
similar phrase in the dedication to King James in the Authorized
Version of the Bible (1611): on Queen Elizabeth's death, 'clouds

of darkness would so have overshadowed this land, that men should have been in doubt which way they were to walk'. Ludwig Herrig's defence of F 'as characteristic of Macbeth's visionary condition' (1853) is another way of saying that the line as it stands makes little sense.

20. *Enter* **MACBETH** [*with two daggers*] (2.2, pp. 42–3)
     Why does Lady Macbeth respond to her husband's entrance by continuing her monologue, and not acknowledge him ('My husband?') until five lines later? It transpires that Macbeth is carrying the daggers ('Why did you bring these daggers from the place?', pp. 46–7), and that his hands are soaked in blood – so his wife's fears here ('I laid their daggers ready; | He could not miss 'em') seem particularly obtuse. Some editors therefore have Macbeth speak his opening lines ('Who's there? What, ho?') '*Within*', and then have him enter after Lady Macbeth has completed her train of thought; others prefer to have him enter here '*Above*' (because he later says he has 'descended'), then exit, and enter '*Below*' after Lady Macbeth's soliloquy. Part of the extraordinary force of the play's second act, however, depends upon the dramatic illusion that it is the middle of a pitch-dark night. (The first line of *Hamlet*, also set at night, and likewise originally played in full daylight at the Globe, is the same as Macbeth's first line here: 'Who's there?')

21. *Knocking* [**F** *Knocke*] *within* (2.2, pp. 46–7)
     It seems sensible to emend F's '*Knocke*' to '*Knocking*' in this and subsequent SDs since people rarely knock at a door with a single rap. Editors, following George Steevens (1773), are generally agreed that the third of these knock-knock-knockings on hell's door – the one that prompts Macbeth's reaction, 'Wake Duncan with thy knocking' (pp. 48–9) – should fall immediately before that response. The relocation is arguably inessential, given the perturbing sense of delay, a sort of underwater ponderousness, with which the scene has opened (see the previous note).

22. **Making the green one red [F Greene one, Red].** (2.2, pp. 46–7)
     This, the culmination of one of the play's most famous passages, has generated a surprising amount of scholarly debate as to its

proper punctuation. Macbeth's ghastly imagination holds that
his bloody hand will stain the vast oceans with its colour ('will
rather | The multitudinous seas incarnadine'). F's punctuation
supplements that idea by repeating it, albeit in a devastatingly
simpler language: . . . *turning that whole green entity red.* The editors
of the Fourth Folio (1685) dropped the comma; and Samuel
Johnson (1765) proposed that it be reinserted after 'green': . . .
turning the green entity one enormous red. (Howard Staunton (1872)
rather missed the point by proposing 'Making the green *zone* red'.)

23. **Come in time!** (2.3, pp. 48–9)
    The sense of this phrase seems to be 'You've come in the nick of
    time!' (i.e. *the fires of hell are all stoked up for you*) – though some
    twentieth-century editors have suspected textual corruption: 'Come
    in, time-server' (John Dover Wilson, 1947); 'Come in, time-pleaser'
    (Kenneth Muir, 1951); 'Come in, farmer' (R.W. Dent, 1969).
    (Farmers *serve* or *please* time by dint of their thrall to the seasons,
    and it has been observed that there were exceptionally bad harvests
    in 1606.)

24. **[*Opens the door*]** (2.3, pp. 50–51)
    Editors since Edward Capell (1767–8) have recognized the need for
    this SD: the Porter – at last – performs his duties. By the same
    token, it seems likely that his final words ('I pray you, remember
    the porter'), despite the resonance of the phrase if addressed to
    the audience, may simply comprise a request for a tip from the
    newcomers for letting them in. (On scholars' belated acceptance
    of the Porter's lines as Shakespeare's, see Introduction above,
    p. xxxvii.)

25. **Our knocking has awak'd him: here he comes.** (2.3, pp. 50–51)
    It is at this point, as the Oxford editors specify (1986), that the
    Porter might conveniently leave. His presence on-stage during the
    horrified reports of Duncan's murder that follow might arguably
    comprise a distraction.

26. **New-hatch'd to th' woeful time. The obscure bird**
    (2.3, pp. 52–3)
    F's punctuation leaves Lennox's observation (that 'The obscure bird |
    Clamour'd the livelong night') dangling as a rather uncharacteristic-
    ally short sentence. Two nineteenth-century editors, H.N. Hudson

(1851–6) and Charles Knight (1838–43), adopted Samuel Johnson's shrewd suspicion (1765) that F's full stop here is misplaced, and instead supposed that it is the 'obscure bird' (the ominous owl) which has been 'prophesying with accents terrible': 'The term *new-hatch'd* is properly applicable to a *bird*,' as Johnson comments.

27. **To countenance this horror. Ring the bell.** *Bell rings*
(2.3, pp. 54–5)
Lewis Theobald (1733) suspected that F's 'Ring the bell', rather than comprising a repetition of Macduff's command ('Ring the alarum bell') six lines before, was in fact originally an imperative stage-direction (like '*Knocke*' in the earlier part of the scene), which simply happened to scan with the rest of his line, and which was then supplemented with another, redundant SD ('*Bell rings*'). If so, Lady Macbeth's next line, 'What's the business?', indeed completes that verse line, in the lineation the Folio provides. Neither arrangement is quite satisfactory, however, and editors continue to divide over the issue: Nicholas Brooke (1990) retains F's reading; A.R. Braunmuller (1997) plumps for Theobald's.

28. *Enter* **MACBETH, LENNOX,** *and* **ROSS** (2.3, pp. 54–5)
Ross's presence in the scene – indeed, in the play as a whole – is subject to a great deal of discussion. The fact that he says nothing in the scene, is not given his own exit, and then enters with the Old Man in the next, suggests that Edward Capell (1767–8) was correct in removing him here.

29. *Lady Macbeth* **Help me hence, ho!** | *Macduff* **Look to the lady.**
(2.3, pp. 56–7)
Why exactly does Lady Macbeth cry for help? Tradition holds that she faints, though whether she is suddenly overcome in earnest or else merely pretending to do so, acting as an innocent woman would ('Not a faint – but a *feint*', as J. Wilson (1849) nicely puts it) has been the subject of endless debate, not least since her husband remains silent throughout the episode. F.T. Vischer (1900) provides one dead end ('this fainting of Lady Macbeth is partly real, partly feigned. She pretends to faint; and this was not difficult, because she was actually on the verge of doing so'); while Nicholas Brooke (1990) usefully points out that, whether real or feigned, her faint will inevitably be ambiguous to audiences of the play. (See also

p. xxxviii above.) Most editors signal her exit ('attended') after
Banquo repeats Macduff's concern for her ('Look to the lady'); A.R.
Braunmuller (1997) positions that SD after Macduff's present line,
on the grounds that Malcolm and Donalbain take the opportunity
of the kerfuffle involved to exchange their brief words in private.

30. **And yet dark night strangles the travailing lamp.**
    (2.4, pp. 60–61)
    In Jacobean English, the verbs 'travel' (journey) and 'travail'
    (labour) were indistinguishable, carrying a simultaneous measure of
    both modern words' sense: the 'lamp' Ross describes is the sun,
    journeying through the sky, *struggling* against the darkness, and
    possibly *labouring* to give birth to the day.

31. **In this day's council; but we'll take tomorrow.** (3.1, pp. 64–5)
    Edmond Malone (1790) corrected F's 'take' to 'talk' (so that
    Macbeth promises to have further discussion with Banquo), but
    most editors retain and accept the Folio reading, a reading that
    William Warburton's 1747 proposal ('take't' = *take your advice*)
    merely spells out.

32. *Murderers* [F *Murth.*] **It was, so please your highness.**
    (3.1, pp. 68–9)
    George Steevens (1793) interpreted F's abbreviated SP as belonging
    to the First Murderer alone; subsequent editors have divided
    between this view and the traditional attribution to both men,
    speaking in unison. The fact that F distinguishes between First and
    Second Murderers in the subsequent dialogue (and bothers to start
    numbering them after this line) may imply that Steevens's
    emendation is unwanted. (The operatic convention of speaking in
    unison, though wrenchingly artificial to modern ears, seems to have
    been acceptable to Shakespeare's original audiences.)

33. **Well then, now have you consider'd of my speeches? [F**
    speeches:] (3.1, pp. 68–9)
    Is Macbeth asking a question or stating a fact? The editors of the
    Third Folio (1663–4) assumed the latter, and emphasized that
    assumption by reversing the word order ('Now you have consider'd
    of my speeches;'); Nicholas Rowe (1709) adopted this word order
    but perversely appended a question mark; and Alexander Pope
    (1723–5) retained both F's wording and Rowe's question mark,

which probably remains the least artificial solution – though
Nicholas Brooke (1990) notes that 'the form *now have you* is fairly
common as a statement'. Both he and A.R. Braunmuller (1997) set
this, and Macbeth's subsequent speech, as prose, which makes good
sense of the dramatic moment – marking the shift from Macbeth's
talk among his peers, and his lofty soliloquy, to a descent into prose
to deal with the 'curs' he commissions to do his dirty work.
Braunmuller comments that 'In these metrically muddled lines
prosaic rhythms occasionally give way to iambic pentameter'; the
same is true of how we normally speak (including the last nine
words). Macbeth bridles from too great a familiarity, however, and
his resumption of blank verse ('Ay, in the catalogue ye go for men')
apparently sponsors an equivalent elevation in his collocutors.

34. *Exeunt* (3.1, pp. 72–3)
Lewis Theobald's 1733 decision to have the Murderers exit before
Macbeth's closing couplet remains tempting.

35. **We have scorch'd the snake, not kill'd it;** (3.2, pp. 74–5)
Lewis Theobald (1733) emended F's 'scorch'd' to 'scotch'd' (= *cut*)
but modern editors tend to trust F, not in the sense of *burned*, but in
the now obsolete sense of *slashed with a knife* or *notched*.

36. **The shard-borne beetle with his drowsy hums** (3.2, pp. 76–7)
Recent editors generally adopt the spelling 'shard-born', first given
in the Third Folio (1663–4), with the sense 'hatched in dung' (as
dung-beetles are) – 'shard' being an old word for a cow-pat. 'What's
he | That was not borne [*sic*] of Woman?' asks Macbeth in F (5.7,
pp. 150–51). The alternative (not a strict one, since Shakespeare was
probably punning) is to treat 'borne' as the past participle of the
verb 'bear' – so the beetle was *held aloft by wings resembling broken
fragments of pottery*. Indeed, 'shard' actually came to mean the wing-
case of an insect – but not until 1811, and directly because of this
passage from *Macbeth*. A similar debate attends Enobarbus's scornful
remark in *Antony and Cleopatra* (1607) – 'They are his shards [*pieces
of shit* or *wings*] and he their beetle' (3.2) – but Belarius's words in
Cymbeline (1610) are surely unambiguous: 'And often . . . shall we
find | The sharded beetle in a safer hold | Than is the full-wing'd
eagle' (3.3). Anyone who has witnessed the strange helicopter-flight
of the stag-beetle on late summer nights will surely find the Folio-

reading altogether more vivid than F3's otherwise irrelevant allusion to the animal's supposed biology.

37.   ***Enter three* MURDERERS** (3.3, pp. 78–9)
Why are there suddenly *three* murderers? 'Who is the third who walks always beside you?' (T.S. Eliot, *The Waste Land*, V. 359). Scholars and directors have variously seized upon this momentary anomaly to audition a range of cunning candidates for the rôle of The Third Man: the Servant who ushers in the other Two Murderers for their interview with Macbeth in 3.1 (pp. 68-9) (Henry Irving, 1877); the shadowy figure of Ross – 'that poltroon Ross, panic-stricken and stabbing in the dark a rival [Banquo] who had recognized him' (M.F. Libby, 1893); a personification of Destiny (cited in Kenneth Muir's 1951 edition); and even – enduringly – Macbeth himself (Allan Park Paton, 1869). Most reasonable people accept, however, that the anomaly is momentary, since the First Murderer immediately asks the same question ('But who did bid thee join us?'), and his colleague's reaction to the answer ('Macbeth') is sufficient to tell us all we need to know: Macbeth mistrusts them, and has, with Stalinist expedience, sent someone else to supervise their work. Samuel Johnson supposed that the Third Murderer is 'the perfect spy o'th' time' with whom Macbeth has promised to 'Acquaint' them in the earlier scene (3.1, pp. 72–3), but this is probably a redundantly literal interpretation of a phrase that simply means *Advise you of the ideal circumstances for your ambush*. Momentary though the sensation is, F's stage-direction nevertheless provokes a frisson in an audience, akin perhaps to the sequence from *The Waste Land* quoted above, which was 'stimulated', as Eliot himself notes there, by Ernest Shackleton's 1916 Antarctic Expedition: 'it was related that the party of explorers, at the extremity of their strength, had the constant delusion that there was *one more member* than could actually be counted.' Much the same delusion visits Macbeth himself in the following scene, where Banquo's ghost prompts him to observe that 'The table's full' (3.4, pp. 84–5).

38.   **To gain the timely inn, and [F end] near approaches**
(3.3, pp. 78–9)
The editors of Second Folio (1632) first corrected this (notably apposite) slip.

39. **Let it come down! [*They attack*]** (3.3, pp. 78–9)
Editors since Nicholas Rowe (1709) have filled in the details
implicit in the sequence's dialogue – the Second Murderer spies
Banquo and Fleance ('A light, a light!'); Banquo comments on the
weather; the First Murderer callously completes his line ('Let it [i.e.
the rain] come down!'), and then extinguishes their torch ('Who did
strike out the light?'), Fleance escaping in the ensuing confusion.

40. *Enter the ghost of* **BANQUO,** *and sits in* **MACBETH**'*s place*
(3.4, pp. 82–3)
The Folio positioning of this extraordinary stage-direction risks
confusing a reader: Macbeth's 'Sweet remembrancer!' is addressed
to Lady Macbeth, who has reminded him – at somewhat anxious
length – to propose a formal welcome (and toast) to his guests, and
is very much *not* addressed to Banquo's ghost, which he only sees
after noticing that 'The table's full' (pp. 84–5; see Textual Note 37
above). The original SD was probably written, divided over a number of lines, in the margin of the manuscript text used to set the
Folio, and so the compositor may simply have associated ghosts with
remembrance (as in *Hamlet*, 1.5: 'Adieu, adieu, Hamlet. Remember
me'), and set the direction where we find it. Our earliest eye-
witness to the play's performance – that of the diarist-cum-charlatan
Simon Forman on 11 April 1611 (see Introduction, pp. xxxi–xxxii) –
records that it was when 'he began to speak of noble Banquo . . .
standing up to drink a carouse to him [that] the ghost of Banquo
came and sat down in his chair behind him; and he, turning about
to sit down again, saw the ghost . . . [whereupon] he fell into a great
passion of fear and fury, uttering many words about his murder'.
Forman's description implies that the ghost should enter during
Macbeth's subsequent speech ('Here had we now our country's
honour roof'd . . .'); on the other hand, Forman describes how
Macbeth and Banquo first encounter the Witches (1.3) while 'riding
through a wood' – a clear example of a suggestive imagination
overriding any accurate account of Jacobean stage-practice.

41. **Shall be the maws of kites. [*Exit* BANQUO's *ghost*]**
(3.4, pp. 84–5)
The editors of the Second Folio (1632) first located the ghost's exit
here, and, as Nicholas Brooke puts it (1990), it 'seems a reasonable
guess'. That it *must* exit is plain from its re-entrance after Macbeth's

call for wine (pp. 86–7); and it seems plain (as Nicholas Rowe first specified in 1709) that it exits for good after Macbeth's 'Unreal mockery, hence!', since he continues: 'Why so, being gone, | I am a man again' (pp. 88–9).

42. **for now I am bent to know, | By the worst means, the worst. For [F worst, for] mine own good, | All causes shall give way.** (3.4, pp. 90–91)
F's 'for mine own good', preceded and followed by non-committal commas, might qualify either of the phrases that surround it: (1) *For I am resolved to employ the worst means to find out the worst, for the sake of my own well-being. All other matters must yield to that.* (2) *For I am resolved to employ the worst means to find out the worst. All other matters must yield to my own well-being.* F's punctuation does not specify which sense is meant, but modern punctuation demands that one or other sense be lent priority. Nicholas Rowe (1709), Alexander Pope (1723–5), and Thomas Hanmer (1743–5) assumed the former; Lewis Theobald (1733), William Warburton (1747), and Samuel Johnson (1765) the latter.

43. *Music, and a song within: '***Come away, come away.***' [F Musicke, and a Song . . . Sing within. Come away, come away, &c.*] (3.5, pp. 92–3)
As our Introduction explains (pp. xxxv–xxxvi), it is now generally agreed that this scene was transplanted into Shakespeare's play. The Folio's two stage-directions at once indicate some sort of confusion in the underlying manuscript (since only one song seems intended) and point the finger of authorship at Thomas Middleton, whose play *The Witch* (*c.* 1615) includes a lengthy song beginning 'Come away, come away, Hecate, come away' – presumably the object of F's shorthand '&c.', which the Oxford editors (1986), followed by Nicholas Brooke (1990), expanded to embrace the entire sequence from Middleton's play. (See also Textual Note 46 below.) The present edition prints a modernized text of these sequences in an Appendix (below, pp. 194–7).

44. **The son [F Sonnes] of Duncan,** (3.6, pp. 94–5)
Lewis Theobald (1733) first corrected this slip: the subject of the verb is singular ('The son of Duncan [i.e. Malcolm] . . . Lives in the English court . . .').

45. **And this report | Hath so exasperate their King, that he | Prepares for some attempt of war.** (3.6, pp. 96–7)
F's little word 'their' exposes a great deal of narrative complication. The clear inference is that 'their King' is the English King, 'pious Edward' (pp. 94–5), who, outraged ('exasperate') by Macduff's reports of Macbeth's regime, is now preparing for war against him. Yet the 'he' of Lennox's next question ('Sent he to Macduff?') must refer to Macbeth. 'He did,' replies the Lord (then convolutedly describes how Macduff refused his summons – 'Sir, not I' – only to suffer the discourtesy of the sullen messenger's implicit threats).

But (and this is the problem) how can Macbeth have sent for Macduff when we have just heard that Macduff is at the English court, recruiting King Edward to his just cause? And, this being so, what on earth is Lennox thinking of when he invokes a 'holy angel' to *precede* Macduff's arrival in England 'and unfold | His message ere he come'? Thomas Hanmer (1743–5) noticed the problem, and changed F's 'their King' (= Edward) to 'the King' (= Macbeth) – so that (a) Macduff has only just set off on his journey to England, but not yet arrived there; and (b) it is 'this report' of Macduff's flight that has outraged Macbeth to prepare for war against England.

This solves the problem – but only temporarily. For when Lennox subsequently tells Macbeth that 'Macduff is fled to England' (4.1, pp. 106–7), Macbeth is obviously taken unawares ('Fled to England?') and immediately retaliates ('The castle of Macduff I will surprise', pp. 108–9), both of which reactions are inapproprate if Macbeth has known of Macduff's treachery since 3.6. Besides, it is indeed King Edward who has mobilized his troops ('Gracious England hath | Lent us good Seyward and ten thousand men', 4.3, pp. 126–7), and not Macbeth, who sits tight in his castle for the rest of the play. And, in any case, Lennox's own rôle seems surprisingly inconsistent, seeking divine vengeance on Macbeth one minute (3.6, pp. 96–7) and calling him 'my good lord' the next (4.1, pp. 106–7).

There seems no obvious way of ironing out these discrepancies – though some editors and directors have attempted to minimize them by cutting 3.6 entirely, reordering the sequence of scenes (3.5– 4.1– 3.6; 4.1– 3.5–3.6), and/or re-assigning Lennox's lines here to an anonymous Second Lord, all of which involve substantial invasive surgery on the Folio text of this sequence. That text seems to have come about from an imperfectly scripted revival (see p. xxx above), and the fact that these two (non-Shakespearean) Hecate scenes surround 3.6 is almost certainly significant. The best that can be said for this sequence as it stands in the Folio is that its many anomalies may arouse a subconscious sense of disorientation in the audience; if so, whether by design or accident, it is not the only such effect the play achieves.

46. *Enter* **HECATE** *and the other three witches . . . Music and a song:* **'Black spirits and white, red spirits and grey.'** [F *Blacke Spirits, &c.*] [*Exeunt* **HECATE** *and the other three witches*] (4.1, pp. 100–101)

The immediate question here is 'Where have these "other three witches" come from?' The answer seems once again to be, 'Middleton's play, *The Witch*' (see Textual Note 43 above). As before, F's abbreviated reference to a song, '*Blacke Spirits, &c.*', evidently alludes to the 'charm-song about a vessel' sung by Hecate and three witches in that play, beginning 'Black spirits and white, red spirits and grey, | Mingle, mingle, mingle, you that mingle may'. Hecate's presence in the scene is generally thought to derive from the mingle-mangle of Middleton's revival of Shakespeare's 'original' play. Editors and directors might either want to excise Hecate's lines here, together with the bothersome extra witches, and so elide (or reassign) the Second Witch's framing speeches: 'Then the charm is fair and good. | By the pricking of my thumbs . . .'); or else expand F's cues to incorporate the relevant eighteen lines from *The Witch*, as the Oxford editors do (1986).

They must also decide whether to specify an exit for Hecate and her arguably superfluous chorus of witches here, or else have them hang about, with nothing much to do or say, until they exit ('*The* WITCHES *dance, and vanish*', 4.1, pp. 106–7). A.R. Braunmuller (1997) follows Alexander Dyce (1857) in preferring the former course; Nicholas Brooke (1990) follows the Oxford editors (1986) in favouring the latter – and in accordingly reallocating the First Witch's final speech ('Ay, sir, all this is so . . . Our duties did his welcome pay', pp. 106–7) to Hecate. The style and manner of that speech in any case suggests that it belongs to Middleton's revising pen.

The punctuation of F's stage-direction, '*The Witches Dance, and vanish*', may either imply a set-routine ('"The Witches' Dance", and

[then they] vanish') – one imported, perhaps, either from
Middleton's play or Jonson's masque (see our Introduction above,
p. xxxi), or else simply be a description ('The witches dance, and
vanish [while dancing]') – though quite *how* they vanished from
the Jacobean stage, both here and earlier, at 1.3 (pp. 12–13), remains
appropriately unclear.

47. **though the treasure | Of nature's germen [F Germaine]
     tumble all together,** (4.1, pp. 100–101)
     F's 'Germaine' (modernized as 'germen') means *seed* (as in our
     modern 'wheatgerm'), but some editors prefer to follow Alexander
     Pope (1723–5) and Lewis Theobald (1733) in making the word
     plural – which is how it appears elsewhere in Shakespeare: 'And
     thou, all-shaking thunder,' cries King Lear, 'Crack nature's moulds,
     all germens [F germaines] spill at once | That make ingrateful
     man!' (3.2). F's singular, however, may here carry a collective sense,
     meaning something like *multifarious essence*.

48. *Enter a show of eight kings in procession, the last with a glass in his
     hand, followed by Banquo's ghost* **[F *A shew of eight Kings, and
     Banquo last, with a glasse in his hand.*]** (4.1, pp. 104–5)
     The wording of F's mention of Banquo here looks like an
     afterthought (or a compositor's muddled conflation of separate
     instructions) and has the consequence of distorting its sense: as
     Macbeth subsequently comments, 'And yet the eighth appears, who
     bears a glass . . .' Editors tend to gloss 'glass' to mean 'magic crystal,
     permitting visions of the future' (A.R. Braunmuller, 1997) rather
     than *mirror* or *looking-glass*, though do not explain what such a prop
     should look like, if not a mirror or looking-glass.

49. **But float upon a wild and violent sea | Each way and move
     [F moue].** (4.2, pp. 110–11)
     F's spelling of the last word here is unambiguous, but the sense
     remains elusive. If 'move' is the correct word, it may be understood
     that Ross abruptly breaks off his train of thought (*We . . . float upon a
     wild and violent sea each way, and move –* [*but I had better not say in what
     direction our movements will lead us, and so*] *I take my leave of you*). This
     punctuation (a dash indicating the interrupted thought) was first
     adopted by Samuel Johnson (1765). It may alternatively – as
     Nicholas Brooke has recently argued (1990) – be intended as a

noun (= 'Each way and *motion*'), in which case F's full stop makes
sense. Neither of these solutions seems ideal, though we adopt the
latter reading in line with our fidelity to the Folio. Other interpreta-
tions of this reading strain the sense of 'move' into somehow
meaning either 'direction' or else a verb meaning 'are tossed about'.
Unsatisfactory as these attempts are, scholars have mined the rich
seam offered by the possible misreadings that might underlie F's
'moue' – 'Each way and *wave*' (Lewis Theobald, 1733); 'Each way
and *none*' (W.G. Clark and W.A. Wright, 1869); 'Each way and *drive*'
(Arthur Gray, 1888); or else have deftly rearranged and tinkered the
line into some approximate sense: 'And move each way' (Edward
Capell, 1767–8); 'Each way we move' (W.J. Rolfe, 1877); 'As each
wave moves' (William Harness, 1838). Perhaps least persuasive of
all is C.M. Ingleby's suggestion (1879), which is as neat a piece of
deduction (chopping up F into the hypothetical *Each way a ndm oue*)
as its result is banal: 'Each day a new one'. (That Ross addresses the
last line of this speech to Macduff's son seems plain from Lady
Macduff's reply, 'Father'd he is, and yet he's fatherless.')

50. **Thou liest, thou shag-ear'd [F shagge-ear'd] villain!**
     (4.2, pp. 114–15)
     Editors since George Steevens (1778) have been dissatisfied with F's
     'shagge-ear'd', on the grounds that ears can scarcely be described as
     'shaggy', whereas hair ('shag-hair'd') can be so described – and,
     indeed, often was in Jacobethan descriptions of villains. The
     evidence against this view – and therefore in favour of F – is
     threefold: (1) The fact that villains were conventionally described as
     'shag-hair'd' is no reason to assume that Shakespeare intended the
     cliché here; (2) corporal punishment in the period included the
     maiming of ears and noses (though vagabonds' ears were, it seems,
     simply cut off rather than slashed); and, (3) as Nicholas Brooke
     points out (1990), Macbeth lengthily equates the Murderers he
     employs with 'curs' (= *dogs*) in 3.1 (pp. 70–70), and Macduff *fils*
     may be making the same association: dogs may certainly be
     described as having shaggy ears.

51. **and like good men | Bestride our downfall birthdom**.
     (4.3, pp. 114–15)
     The sense of F's 'downfall' is clearly 'downfallen', to which ('down-
     fall'n') Samuel Johnson's edition corrected it (1765). Recent editors

have resisted this standard emendation: Nicholas Brooke (1990) suggests that 'downfall' may be a 'noun doubling as an adjective'; A.R. Braunmuller (1997) cites a parallel example in *1 Henry IV* ('But I will lift the downfall [F downfall; Q down-trod] Mortimer', 1.3), which may imply that the F's usage was current in the period – or else, of course, be an identical compositorial mistake.

52. **I am young, but something | You may discern [F discerne] of him through me,** (4.3, pp. 114–15)
    In F, Malcolm worries that there are elements of Macbeth's character that Macduff might come to recognize ('discern') in him, should he replace the tyrant Macbeth on the throne; Macduff might also therefore recognize the advantage to be had from betraying him ('and wisdom | To offer up a . . . lamb') to Macbeth – hence Macduff's angry response: 'I am not treacherous' (pp. 116-17). Lewis Theobald's 1733 emendation ('but something you may *deserve* of him through me') was, until recently, the standard reading (= *but you might earn a tidy sum from Macbeth by betraying me to him*). F's spelling lends a certain credence to Theobald's surmise, but neither alternative is either syntactically impossible or perfectly intelligible.

53. **The title is affeer'd [F affear'd].** (4.3, pp. 116–17)
    Editors since Thomas Hanmer (1743–5) have noticed the technical legal pun operating here: a legal title is 'affeered' when it is ratified or confirmed; F presents the secondary quibble – so that Malcolm is afraid (or 'afeard') of pressing his claim to that title.

54. **By his own interdiction stands accus'd [F accust],** (4.3, pp. 120–21)
    Macduff's rhetorical appeal ('O nation miserable!') forcefully rebukes Malcolm's (tiresome) reticence. Editors must choose between two interpretations of F's 'accust': (1) 'accurs'd' (substituted as early as the Second Folio in 1632, and adopted by most editors since) – so that Malcolm stands accursed by future history for the catalogue he has recited of his own failings ('by his own interdiction'); and (2) 'accus'd' – which feels truer to the play of legal language both in this passage and the scene as a whole (see, for example, Textual Note 53 above).

55. **Whither indeed, before thy here-approach [F they heere approa:h],** (4.3, pp. 122–3)
The editors of the Second Folio (1632) first made good sense out of this otherwise meaningless construction. As subsequent editors have pointed out, the phrase 'thy here-approach' (so finessed in Alexander Pope's 1723–5 edition) anticipates Malcolm's later reference, a few minutes later, to 'my here-remain' (F 'my heere remaine', pp. 124–5).

56. **My countryman; but yet I know him not [F nor].**
(4.3, pp. 124–5)
The Second Folio (1632) first corrected this minor inattention. (Malcolm apparently recognizes Ross as his 'countryman' by the distinctive Scottish costume he wears, perhaps, as A.R. Braunmuller (1997, p. 244) usefully documents from a work of 1618, 'made of a warm stuff of divers colours, which they call Tartan.')

57. **This time goes manly.** (4.3, pp. 130–31)
Editors since Nicholas Rowe (1714) have suspected that F's 'time' represents an easy manuscript confusion of 'tune', either in the sense of *manner* or *mood*, meaning something like 'That's the spirit!', or else as a direct reference to a military march being struck up back-stage (the concomitant SD having for some reason been omitted). But 'time' has had its defenders (which is why we retain it), whether it, too, refers to back-stage music ('time' = *rhythm*), or else obliquely meaning something like *Now's the time for us to show our valour.*

58. **What need we fear? Who knows it, when none can call our power to account?** (5.1, pp. 132–3)
F's punctuation has Lady Macbeth ask two questions – *Why should we be afraid?* and *Who can know [of our crime] when we [as King and Queen] are above the law?* – but many editors, since Nicholas Rowe (1714), have treated the first of F's question marks as misleading, so that she asks just one question: *Why should we be afraid of anyone who knows [of our crime] when we [as King and Queen] are above the law?* Rowe's earlier edition (1709) also (and equally unnecessarily) corrected the Doctor's previous grammar by giving 'Ay, but their sense is [F are] shut': Shakespeare was often playfully and productively surprising about the correspondence between nouns and verbs. (See, perhaps,

Textual Note 47 above, and Sonnet 112: 'my adder's sense
[= *sensitive faculties*] | To critic and to flatterer stoppèd are [*sic*].')

59. **This push | Will cheer me ever, or dis-seat [F dis-eate] me now.** (5.3, pp. 140–41)

F's 'dis-eate' (with its hugely improbable sense of *vomit up*) has generally been rejected ever since the Second Folio (1632), which substitutes 'disease', in its literal, non-medical sense of *render uneasy*. Most editors adopt George Steevens's 1773 reading ('dis-seat' = *unseat*), not least since it activates a quiet pun on 'cheer'/'chair', which Jacobean English seems to have pronounced identically (the chair in question, of course, being the Scottish throne). It is significant that Shakespeare was later to describe how a startled horse 'seeks all foul means . . . to dis-seat | His lord' (*The Two Noble Kinsmen* (1613), 5.4). Peter Daniel proposed the altogether blander 'defeat' (1870); and Samuel Bailey had the grace to admit that he submitted his alternative without himself 'feeling much confidence in it': 'Will *charter* me ever or *disseize* me now' (1862).

William Empson's discussion of this passage includes a brilliant meditation on the principles of Shakespearean textual scholarship. Raising the possibility that 'Shakespeare actually intended, by putting down something a little removed from any appropriate homonyms [i.e. *dis-eate* rather than *dis-seat*, *disease*, etc.], to set the reader groping about their network', he continues: 'One must consider . . . that the Elizabethans minded very little about spelling and punctuation; that this must have given them an attitude to the written page entirely different from ours (the reader must continually have been left to grope for the right word); that from the comparative slowness, of reading as of speaking, that this entailed, he was prepared to assimilate words with a completeness which is now lost; that only our snobbish oddity of spelling imposes on us the notion that one mechanical word, to be snapped up by the eye, must have been intended; and that it is Shakespeare's normal method to use a newish, apparently irrelevant word, which spreads the attention thus attracted over a wide map of the ways in which it may be justified' (1953, pp. 83–4). The parallel texts of our Shakespeare Folio editions seek to provide their readers with just such a network through which to grope, using something of their ancestors' 'comparative slowness'.

60.   **My way of life | Is fallen into the sere, the yellow leaf,**
      (5.3, pp. 140–41)
      Editors have generally resisted Samuel Johnson's emendation of this
      famous line, though his paraphrase is itself an exceptionally fine
      piece of writing: 'I am inclined to think that the *W* is only an *M*
      inverted, and that it was *my May of life;* I am now passed from the
      spring to the autumn of my days; but I am without those comforts
      that should succeed the sprightliness of bloom, and support me in
      this melancholy season' (1765).

61.   **Cure her of [F Cure of] that.** (5.3, pp. 140–41)
      The editors of the Second Folio (1632) first supplied the extra word
      here – necessarily for both sense and metre.

62.   **Cleanse the stuff'd bosom of that perilous stuff**
      (5.3, pp. 140–41)
      Immediate repetition in F often signals the possibility of an error in
      transcription or typesetting – as if Shakespeare's fertile imagination
      could never have countenanced a single word where two might do.
      In this case, editors have crowded to his assistance. The first
      'stuff'd' has been variously altered to 'full', 'foul', 'steep'd', 'fraught',
      'press'd', 'charg'd', and 'clogg'd'; the second 'stuff' to 'load',
      'slough', 'grief', 'freight', and 'matter'. As Nicholas Brooke (1990)
      points out, however, Shakespeare may simply be quibbling on two
      distinct senses of the word (namely the final respective variants
      listed above). Whether the repetition 'insists on the dreadful
      anonymity of morbid oppression', as Brooke asserts, or is simply an
      irremediable mistake, remains open to question.

63.   **What rhubarb, senna [F Cyme], or what purgative drug**
      (5.3, pp. 142–3)
      This line presents a modernizing editor with particular problems –
      problems which editors have struggled with ever since the Second
      Folio of 1632. To modernize to 'senna' (the 'purgative drug' in
      question, given as '*Cæny*' in F2) is to disturb the metre of the line;
      but to retain F's 'Cyme' – or rather 'modernize' it to 'cynne', since
      it is generally agreed that this is how the underlying manuscript
      read – is to obscure the immediate sense. (On the other hand, F's
      'pristiue', for 'pristine', three lines back, is universally agreed to be a
      mistake by the compositor, who may have misread the mansucript
      before him or inadvertently inverted the piece of type he set.)

64. **[*Exeunt all but the* DOCTOR]** (5.3, pp. 142–3)
Since the Doctor's words are openly disloyal, it falls to editors
and directors to decide whether he speaks them as an aside before
a general exit, or hangs back while Macbeth exits with Seyton
(with the piece of armour he has not yet dressed his master in:
'Pull't off . . . Bring it after me'). In theatrical practice, as opposed
to published text, the distinction is a moot one.

65. *Drum and colours. Enter* MALCOLM . . . *and* SOLDIERS
marching (5.4, pp. 142–3)
Many editors swell the allied forces listed here by supplying the
names of Lennox and Ross: Lennox certainly accompanies the army
in 5.2 ('Make we our march towards Birnam', pp. 138–9), while
Ross takes part in the battle itself (entering at 5.7, pp. 154–5, and
describing Young Seyward's death), though this need not prove
their wanted presence here. There is a sudden proliferation of extra
characters in Act Five; Lady Macbeth's Doctor, her Gentlewoman,
and Seyton apart, all of these (Caithness, Menteith, Seyward, Young
Seyward) are generalized military figures, most of whose choric
lines might just as appropriately be spoken by Ross, Lennox – or
Angus, whose speeches in 5.2 (pp. 136–7) are the first (and last)
time he speaks since Act One (pp. 14–17). Samuel Johnson
interestingly bemoaned the play's lack of any 'nice discriminations
of character' (1765), and it is possible that some of this is down to
some sort of textual muddle, somewhere along the way, such that
Lennox's lines 'in one scene or the other originally belonged to
another character' (Muir, 1951, p. xxxi). Whatever the truth, *Macbeth*
has a surprisingly large cast for such a short play, and the King's
Men would have been stretched in their accustomed skills at
'doubling up' the rôles – to breaking point here, perhaps.

66. **For where there is advantage to be given, | Both more and
less have given him the revolt.** (5.4, pp. 144–5)
Another suspicious repetition (see Textual Note 62 above). In this
case, the odder use of the word 'given' is its first. Malcolm's general
point seems to be that Macbeth's subjects, be they of of high or low
status ('Both more and less'), have rebelled against him whenever
'there is advantage to be [*somethinged*]' in doing so. F's 'giuen' does
not at first appear to fit the bill, and a series of alternatives have been
offered: 'got' (George Steevens, 1773), 'gotten' (J.P. Collier, 1858),

and 'ta'en' [= *taken*] (Alexander Dyce, 1864–7) are each at once sensible and lame. W.G. Clark and W.A. Wright (1863–6) rang the changes by retaining the repetition but altering the construction ('advantage to 'em given'). The most persuasively enduring emendation is that of Samuel Johnson (1765), who, recasting the whole sense, gave 'where there is a vantage to be gone' (= *whenever the opportunity arises to flee*). Recent editors have tended to settle for the Folio, though no solid consensus has emerged as to what the line actually means. 'Where they could have given Macbeth the advantage (by staying loyal)' (Nicholas Brooke, 1990); 'wherever opportunity offers itself' (Barbara A. Mowat and Paul Werstine, 1992).

67. **And beat them backward home.** *A cry within of women*
     (5.5, pp. 144–5)
     F sets the stage-direction after Macbeth hears it – though it is just possible that *another* noise prompts his question ('What is that noise?'), and that the '*cry . . . of women*' is a subsequent keening. Malcolm later reports the rumour that Lady Macbeth kills herself ('by self and violent hands', 5.7, pp. 156–7), but the details of her death – as of her possible motherhood – are probably best left occluded, whether or not these mysteries arise from a now irrevocable cutting of Shakespeare's original script. But how does Seyton *know* the significance of the cry ('Wherefore was that cry?' | 'The Queen, my lord, is dead.', pp. 146–7)? Two main options are available: (1) Lady Macbeth is dead *before* the scene begins: Seyton knows it, and the cry is that of her discovery; and (2) Seyton exits after his first lines, and then re-enters, prompting Macbeth's second question. Alan Dessen further comments that such rational analysis risks diminishing the eerie force of the scene (1984, pp. 5–7). *Q*: How does Seyton know? *A*: Well, *exactly* . . .

68. **If thou speak'st false (F fhlse),** (5.5, pp. 146–7)
     The editors of the Second Folio (1632) first corrected this blatant compositorial inattention.

69. **5.7 [F *Scena Septima.*]** (5.7, pp. 150–51)
     This is the last scene-division marked in the Folio. Subsequent editors have further subdivided the remainder of the play on the strict principle that a new scene should begin whenever the stage clears: 5.8 at Macbeth's 'Why should I play the Roman fool, and die'

(pp. 152–3), and 5.9 after Macbeth's death in battle (pp. 154–5). The literalist tradition distinguishes the settings of these scenes as '*Another part of the field*' and '*Within the castle*' (see, for example, Kenneth Muir, 1951); in theatrical practice, of course, the sequence forms a continuous unit – a continuity perhaps emphasized by those editors since Nicholas Rowe (1709) who omit F's scene-division here, and treat all the action from the entrance of Malcolm's army at 5.6 (pp. 148–9) as a single and cohesive battle-scene.

70. **[*Exeunt*] *Retreat and flourish*** (5.7, pp. 154–5)
F leaves the exact details of the climactic stage-business somewhat obscure – so obscure, indeed, that some editors treat the duellists' re-entrance '*and Macbeth slaine*' as a textual confusion. That Macduff must leave the stage (presumably with Macbeth's slain body – or else, as directors sometimes have it, with the two of them fighting again) is proven by the fact that Macduff subsequently enters with Macbeth's head (pp. 156–7). Fs '*Retreat, and Flourish*' refers to the particular tunes played on the contemporary stage by trumpets and drums, and on the contemporary battlefield by drums and fifes.

Authorities Cited

F   *Mr. William Shakespeares Comedies, Histories, & Tragedies* [The First Folio] (1623)

F2   *Mr. William Shakespeares Comedies, Histories, and Tragedies* [The Second Folio] (1632)

F3   *Mr. William Shakespeares Comedies, Histories, and Tragedies* [The Third Folio] (1663–4)

F4   *Mr. William Shakespeares Comedies, Histories, and Tragedies* [The Fourth Folio] (1685)

Rowe (1709)   *The Works of Mr. William Shakespear*, ed. Nicholas Rowe, 6 vols (London, 1709)

Rowe (1714)   *The Works of Mr. William Shakespear*, ed. Nicholas Rowe, second edition, 8 vols (London, 1714)

Pope (1723–5)   *The Works of Shakespear. Collated and corrected by the former editions*, ed. Alexander Pope, 6 vols (London, 1723–5)

Pope (1728)   *The Works of Shakespear . . . The second edition*, ed. Alexander Pope, 10 vols (London, 1728)

Theobald   *The Works of Shakespeare. Collated with the oldest copies and corrected*, ed. Lewis Theobald, 7 vols (London, 1733)

Hanmer   *The Works of Shakespear*, ed. Thomas Hanmer, 6 vols (Oxford, 1743–5)

Warburton   *The Works of Shakespear. The Genuine Text*, ed. William Warburton, 8 vols (London, 1747)

Johnson   *The Plays of William Shakespeare*, ed. Samuel Johnson, 8 vols (London, 1765)

Heath   Benjamin Heath, *A revisal of Shakespear's text, wherein the alterations introduced into it . . . are considered* (London, 1765)

Capell   *Mr William Shakespeare his Comedies, Histories, and Tragedies*, ed. Edward Capell, 10 vols (London, 1767–8)

Steevens (1773)   *The Plays of William Shakespeare . . . with . . . Notes by Samuel Johnson and George Steevens*, 10 vols (London, 1773)

Steevens (1778)   *The Plays of William Shakespeare . . . with . . . Notes by Samuel Johnson and George Steevens*, 2nd edition, 10 vols (London, 1778)

'X'   'X', 'Commentary on a Passage in *Macbeth*', *The Gentleman's Magazine* 58 (1788), 766–7

Malone   *The Plays and Poems of William Shakespeare*, ed. Edmond Malone, 10 vols (London, 1790)

Steevens (1793)   *The Plays of William Shakespeare*, ed. George Steevens and Isaac Reed, 15 vols (London, 1793)

Jackson   Zachariah Jackson, *Shakespeare's Genius Justified: Being restorations and illuminations of seven hundred passages in Shakespeare's Plays* (London, 1819)

Harness   *The Complete Works of William Shakespeare*, ed. William Harness (London, 1838)

Knight   *The Pictorial Edition of the Works and Shakespeare*, ed. Charles Knight, 8 vols (London, 1838–43)

Hunter   Joseph Hunter, *New Illustrations of the Life, Studies, and Writings of Shakespeare*, 2 vols (London, 1845)

Wilson   J. Wilson, 'Dies Boreales', *Blackwood's Magazine*, November, 1849

Hudson   *The Works of Shakespeare. The text carefully restored according to the first editions*, ed. Henry N. Hudson, 11 vols (Boston, 1851–6)

Elwin   Hastings Elwin, *Shakespeare Restored* [*Macbeth*, ed. Hastings Elwin] (Norwich, 1853)

Herrig   Ludwig Herrig, *Macbeth* (Berlin, 1853)

Dyce (1857)   *The Works of William Shakespeare. The text revised*, ed. Alexander Dyce, 6 vols (London, 1857)

Collier   *Shakespeare's Comedies, Histories, Tragedies, and Poems*, ed. John Payne Collier, second edition, 6 vols (London, 1858)

Bailey   Samuel Bailey, *The Received Text of Shakespeare's Dramatic
                       Writings, and its Improvement*, 2 vols (London, 1862–66)

Clark and Wright
                       The Works of William Shakespeare, ed. William George
                       Clark, John Glover, and William Aldis Knight, 9 vols
                       (Cambridge and London, 1863–6)

Dyce (1864–7)   *The Works of William Shakespeare. The text revised*, ed.
                       Alexander Dyce, second edition, 9 vols (London,
                       1864–7)

Paton   Allan Park Paton, *Notes and Queries*, 11 September and
                       13 November 1869

Daniel   Peter Augustin Daniel, *Notes and Conjectural Emendations
                       of Certain Doubtful Passages in Shakespeare's Plays* (London,
                       1870)

Staunton   Howard Staunton, *The Athenæum*, 19 October 1872

Irving   Sir Henry Irving, *Nineteenth Century*, April 1877

Rolfe   *Macbeth*, ed. William James Rolfe (New York, 1877)

Nicholson   B. Nicholson, 'Shakespeariana', *Notes and Queries*,
                       25 May 1878

Ingleby   C.M. Ingleby, *Robinson's Epitome*, 15 May 1879

Gray   Arthur Gray, 'Shakespeariana', *Notes and Queries*, 28 April
                       and 7 July 1888

Libby   M.F. Libby, *Some New Notes on 'Macbeth'* (Toronto, 1893)

Vischer   Friedrich Theodor Vischer, *Shakespeare-Vorträge*
                       (Stuttgart, 1900)

Sprague   *Shakespeare's Tragedy of Macbeth*, ed. H.B. Sprague
                       (Chicago, 1889)

Furness   *Macbeth: A New Variorum Edition*, ed. H.H. Furness, rev.
                       ed. H.H. Furness junior (Philadelphia, 1915)

Dover Wilson   *Macbeth*, ed. John Dover Wilson (Cambridge, 1947; rev.
                       ed., 1950)

Muir   *Macbeth*, ed. Kenneth Muir (Arden, 1951; 9th edition,
                       1962)

Empson   William Empson, *Seven Types of Ambiguity*, 3rd edition (Chatto & Windus, 1953)

Sisson   C.J. Sisson, *New Readings in Shakespeare*, 2 vols (Cambridge, 1956)

Dent   *Macbeth*, ed. R.W. Dent (Blackfriars, 1969)

Dessen   *Elizabethan Stage Conventions and Modern Interpreters* (Cambridge, 1984)

Oxford   *William Shakespeare: The Complete Works*, gen. ed. Stanley Wells and Gary Taylor (Oxford, 1986)

Brooke   *The Tragedy of Macbeth*, ed. Nicholas Brooke (Oxford, 1990)

Mowat and Werstine
      The Tragedy of Macbeth, ed. Barbara A. Mowat and Paul Werstine (New Folger Library, 1992)

Braunmuller   *Macbeth*, ed. A.R. Braunmuller (Cambridge, 1997)

Additional Passages

from Middleton's *The Witch*

As we explain in our Introduction, scholars are generally agreed that Shakespeare did not originally intend to include Hecate (the Queen of the Witches) in the cast-list of *Macbeth*. Her appearances (in 3.5 and 4.1) seem to have been part of a wholesale revision of the play, some years after its 1606 première, designed to introduce an element of spectacle to the play facilitated by the later vogue for elaborate stage-machinery and effects – such as those Shakespeare himself deployed in *The Tempest* (1612). The style and form of these sequences, however, appear quite distinct from Shakespeare's, and it is thought that the versatile and prolific dramatist Thomas Middleton was responsible for them. The key evidence for this attribution lies in two Folio stage-directions calling for songs in the relevant scenes, namely '*Come away, come away, &c.*' (3.5, pp. 92–3) and '*Blacke Spirits, &c.*' (4.1, pp. 100–101). These puzzlingly casual abbreviations (unlike any other in the 1623 Folio) were ostensibly explained by the rediscovery, in the eighteenth century, of an unpublished play of Middleton's called *The Witch*, which includes the full text of both songs. (Isaac Reed edited the manuscript for publication in 1778.)

Editors of *Macbeth* are faced with a series of difficult decisions. (1) They may cut all the play's extraneous 'non-Shakespearean' material: all of 3.5, and the two speeches by Hecate and the First Witch in 4.1 (pp. 100–101 and 106–7) – but then, where should this process end? For, as our Introduction details, scholars have, at one time or another, rejected Shakespeare's authorship of whole swathes of the play, already one of the shortest in the canon. (2) They may expand F's cues ('&c.') into a reconstructed version of the sequences drawn from Middleton's *The Witch*, as William Davenant was the first to do in his 1672–4 adaptation – but then, which version of the songs should editors follow? (Nicholas Brooke's 1990 edition provides a full collation of the six immediately relevant texts.) (3) They may – as most have done – simply retain the Folio text *in extenso*, while acknowledging the variously insoluble problems outlined above.

This edition prefers not to interfere with its Folio model, and instead provides a working text of these sequences, modernized from the original transcript, via the excellent *Three Jacobean Witchcraft Plays*, ed. Peter Corbin and Douglas Sedge (Revels, 1986). The majority of relevant textual variants concerns the lines' distribution among Hecate, Spirits, and Witches, and the following versions deliberately incorporate a degree of latitude. The departure from, and return to, the Folio text of *Macbeth* is signalled by a set of closed and open angle brackets (> <).

3.5, pp. 92–3 (*The Witch*, 3.3)

Hecate	And you all know, security Is mortals' chiefest enemy.
	Music, and a song within >
Spirits	(*In the air*) Come away, come away, Hecate, Hecate, come away!
< *Hecate*	Hark, I am call'd. My little spirit, see, Sits in a foggy cloud, and stays for me. >
Spirits	(*In the air*) Come away, come away, Hecate, Hecate, come away!
Hecate	I come, I come, I come, I come, With all the speed I may, With all the speed I may. Where's Stadlin?
Spirit	(*In the air*) Here.
Hecate	Where's Puckle?
Spirits	(*In the air*) Here. And Hoppo too, and Hellwain too, We lack but you, we lack but you. Come away, make up the count.
Hecate	I will but 'noint, and then I mount.
Spirit	(*Above*) There's one comes down to fetch his dues: A kiss, a coll, a sip of blood;
	A spirit like a cat descends
	And why thou stay'st so long I muse, I muse, Since the air's so sweet and good.
Hecate	O, art thou come? What news, what news?
Spirit	All goes still to our delight, Either come or else refuse, refuse.
Hecate	Now am I furnish'd for the flight.

(*Going up*) Now I go, now I fly,
Malkin, my sweet spirit, and I.
O, what a dainty pleasure 'tis
To ride in the air
When the moon shines fair,
And sing and dance and toy and kiss.
Over woods, high rocks, and mountains,
Over seas, our mistress' fountains,
Over steeples, towers, and turrets
We fly by night, 'mongst troops of spirits;
No ring of bells to our ears sounds,
No howls of wolves, no yelps of hounds,
No, not the noise of water's breach
Or cannon's throat our height can reach.   *Exit*

Spirits   No ring of bells to our ears sounds,
                 No howls of wolves, no yelps of hounds,
                 No, not the noise of water's breach
                 Or cannon's throat our height can reach.   *Exeunt*

< 1 Witch   Come, let's make haste, she'll soon be back again.
                                                                        Exeunt

4.1, pp. 100–101 (*The Witch*, 5.3)

Hecate   And now about the cauldron sing
                 Like elves and fairies in a ring,
                 Enchanting all that you put in.

                                                      Music and a song >
                         A charm-song about a vessel
Witches   Black spirits and white, red spirits and grey,
                 Mingle, mingle, mingle, you that mingle may.
                 Titty, Tiffin, keep it stiff in.
                 Firedrake, Pucky, make it lucky.
                 Liard, Robin, you must bob in.
                 Round, around, around, about, about,
                 All ill come running in, all good keep out!
4 Witch   Here's the blood of a bat.
5 Witch   Put in that, O put in that!
6 Witch   Here's leopard's bane.

5 Witch	Put in a grain!
4 Witch	The juice of toad, the oil of adder.
5 Witch	That will make the yonker madder!
Witches	Round, around, around, about, about,
	All ill come running in, all good keep out!
< 2 Witch	By the pricking of my thumbs,
	Something wicked this way comes.

And I the Miſtris of your Charmes,
The cloſe contriuer of all harmes,
Was neuer call'd to beare my part,
Or ſhew the glory of our Art ?
And which is worſe, all you haue done
Hath bene but for a wayward Sonne,
Spightfull, and wrathfull, who (as others do)
Loues for his owne ends, not for you.
But make amends now : Get you gon,
Aud at the pit of Acheron
Meete me i'th'Morning : thither he
Will come, to know his Deſtinie.
Your Veſſels, and your Spels prouide,
Your Charmes, and euery thing beſide ;
I am for th'Ayre : This night Ile ſpend
Vnto a diſmall, and a Fatall end.
Great buſineſſe muſt be wrought ere Noone.
Vpon the Corner of the Moone
There hangs a vap'rous drop, profound,
Ile catch it ere it come to ground ;
And that diſtill'd by Magicke ſlights,
Shall raiſe ſuch Artificiall Sprights,
As by the ſtrength of their illuſion,
Shall draw him on to his Confuſion.
He ſhall ſpurne Fate, ſcorne Death, and beare
His hopes 'boue Wiſedome, Grace, and Feare :
And you all know, Security
Is Mortals cheefeſt Enemie.
Muſicke, and a Song.
Hearke, I am call'd : my little Spirit ſee
Sits in a Foggy cloud, and ſtayes for me.
Sing within. Come away, come away, &c.
1 Come, let's make haſt, ſhee'l ſoone be
Backe againe. *Exeunt.*

Scæna Sexta.

Enter Lenox, and another Lord.

Lenox. My former Speeches,
Haue but hit your Thoughts
Which can interpret farther : Onely I ſay
Things haue bin ſtrangely borne. The gracious *Duncan*
Was pittied of *Macbeth* : marry he was dead :
And the right valiant *Banquo* walk'd too late,
Whom you may ſay (if't pleaſe you) *Fleans* kill'd,
For *Fleans* fled : Men muſt not walke too late.
Who cannot want the thought, how monſtrous
It was for *Malcolme*, and for *Donalbane*
To kill their gracious Father ? Damned Faƈt,
How it did greeue *Macbeth* ? Did he not ſtraight
In pious rage, the two delinquents teare,
That were the Slaues of drinke, and thralles of ſleepe ?
Was not that Nobly done ? I, and wiſely too :
For 'twould haue anger'd any heart aliue
To heare the men deny't. So that I ſay,
He ha's borne all things well, and I do thinke,
That had he *Duncans* Sonnes vnder his Key,
(As, and't pleaſe Heauen he ſhall not) they ſhould finde
What 'twere to kill a Father : So ſhould *Fleans.*
But peace ; for from broad words, and cauſe he fayl'd
His preſence at the Tyrants Feaſt, I heare
Macduffe liues in diſgrace. Sir, can you tell

Where he beſtowes himſelfe ?
Lord. The Sonnes of *Duncane*
(From whom this Tyrant holds the due of Birth)
Liues in the Engliſh Court, and is receyu'd
Of the moſt Pious *Edward,* with ſuch grace,
That the maleuolence of Fortune, nothing
Takes from his high reſpeƈt. Thither *Macduffe*
Is gone, to pray the Holy King. vpon his ayd
To wake Northumberland, and warlike *Seyward,*
That by the helpe of theſe (with him aboue)
To ratifie the Worke) we may againe
Giue to our Tables meate, ſleepe to our Nights :
Free from our Feaſts, and Banquets bloody kniues ;
Do faithfull Homage, and receiue free Honors,
All which we pine for now. And this report
Hath ſo exaſperate their King, that hee
Prepares for ſome attempt of Warre.
Len. Sent he to *Macduffe* ?
Lord. He did : and with an abſolute Sir, not I
The clowdy Meſſenger turnes me his backe,
And hums ; as who ſhould ſay, you'l rue the time
That clogges me with this Anſwer.
Lenox. And that well might
Aduiſe him to a Caution, t hold what diſtance
His wiſedome can prouide. Some holy Angell
Flye to the Court of England, and vnfold
His Meſſage ere he come, that a ſwift bleſſing
May ſoone returne to this our ſuffering Country,
Vnder a hand accurs'd.
Lord. Ile ſend my Prayers with him. *Exeunt*

Aƈtus Quartus. Scena Prima.

Thunder.   Enter the three Witches.

1 Thrice the brinded Cat hath mew'd.
2 Thrice, and once the Hedge-Pigge whin'd.
3 Harpier cries, 'tis time, 'tis time.
1 Round about the Caldron go :
In the poyſond Entrailes throw
Toad, that vnder cold ſtone,
Dayes and Nights, ha's thirty one :
Sweltred Venom ſleeping got,
Boyle thou firſt i'th'charmed pot.
All. Double, double, toile and trouble ;
Fire burne, and Cauldron bubble.
2 Fillet of a Fenny Snake,
In the Cauldron boyle and bake :
Eye of Newt, and Toe of Frogge,
Wooll of Bat, and Tongue of Dogge :
Adders Forke, and Blinde-wormes Sting,
Lizards legge, and Howlets wing :
For a Charme of powrefull trouble,
Like a Hell-broth, boyle and bubble.
All. Double, double, toyle and trouble,
Fire burne, and Cauldron bubble.
3 Scale of Dragon, Tooth of Wolfe,
Witches Mummey, Maw, and Gulfe
Of the rauin'd ſalt Sea ſharke :
Roote of Hemlocke, digg'd i'th'darke :
Liuer of Blaſpheming Iew,
Gall of Goate, and Slippes of Yew,
Sliuer'd in the Moones Ecclipſe :

Noſe